THE LIMITS
OF
MULTICULTURALISM

THE LIMITS
OF
MULTICULTURALISM

INTERROGATING THE ORIGINS
OF AMERICAN ANTHROPOLOGY

SCOTT MICHAELSEN

UNIVERSITY OF MINNESOTA PRESS
MINNEAPOLIS
LONDON

A version of chapter 1 was published as "Re-Sketching Anglo-AmerIndian Identity Politics," in *Border Theory: The Limits of Cultural Politics*, ed. Scott Michaelsen and David E. Johnson (Minneapolis: University of Minnesota Press, 1997), 221–52; reprinted by permission. A version of chapter 3 was published as "Ely S. Parker and AmerIndian Voices in Ethnography," *American Literary History* 8, no. 4 (winter 1996): 615–38; reprinted by permission of Oxford University Press. A much shorter version of the prolegomenon was published as "The Grounds and Limits of Multiculturalism," *The Centennial Review* 42, no. 3 (fall 1998): 649–66; reprinted by permission of *The Centennial Review*.

Excerpts from the Ely S. Parker Papers appear courtesy of the American Philosophical Society. Excerpts from the Lewis Henry Morgan Papers appear courtesy of the Department of Rare Books and Special Collections, Rush Rhees Library, University of Rochester, Rochester, New York.

Published by the University of Minnesota Press
111 Third Avenue South, Suite 290
Minneapolis, MN 55401-2520
http://www.upress.umn.edu

A Cataloging-in-Publication record for this book is available from the Library of Congress.

Printed in the United States of America on acid-free paper

The University of Minnesota is an equal-opportunity educator and employer.

11 10 09 08 07 06 05 04 03 02 01 00 99   10 9 8 7 6 5 4 3 2 1

CONTENTS

This book could not have been completed without the generous assistance of a year-long fellowship from the American Council of Learned Societies (1995–96), a summer award from the National Endowment for the Humanities (1994), two faculty development grants from the University of Texas at El Paso (1993–95), and an award from the UTEP University Research Institute for travel to archives (1992–93). I wish to single out UTEP's Dean of Liberal Arts, Carl Jackson, for his constant support of my work.

Permission to quote from Ely S. Parker's papers was granted by the University of Rochester Library and the American Philosophical Society Library in Philadelphia. I am especially indebted to help from Karl Kabelac, manuscript librarian for special collections at University of Rochester Library, during my visit to the Lewis Henry Morgan Papers.

My greatest help as I began this project came from Neil Schmitz. Without his encouragement, enthusiasm, and advice these last several years, this book would not have been written. Over the years, other important friends of the project include, alphabetically, Chuck Ambler, Alan Axelrad, Alejandro Lugo, Peter Messent, Barry O'Connell, Ileana Rodríguez, Frank Rothschild, Benjamin Alire Sáenz, Pat Seed, Scott Shershow, Elisabeth Tooker, and John McWilliams. I thank each of them for different kinds of support and help at crucial moments. My long, weekly conversations with Scott, in particular, have been of enormous importance to the development of this project's argument. Also, Kenneth Haltman and Steve Rachman lent emergency aid toward researching the cover image.

My editor at the University of Minnesota Press, William Murphy, has been as helpful and useful as anyone might dare hope. William has made smooth the complex path to publication, and the book owes him much thanks. And Kathy Delfosse's superb editing of the manuscript has produced a fundamentally better book.

I want to single out David E. Johnson, my coeditor and collaborator on *Border Theory,* for special mention. David read the entire manuscript and improved it enormously, and my collaborations with him have resulted in a book manuscript in which elements of his thought and influence are stitched throughout.

Finally, my gratitude to my partner and general co-conspirator, Theresa Meléndez; "always" knows no bounds.

No, it [anthropology] is not surrealism. It is the realism of the commonsense world.

— STEPHEN A. TYLER, *THE UNSPEAKABLE* (1987)

If *The Limits of Multiculturalism* begins anywhere, it begins with the commonplace in cultural studies that "we" are still too much like ourselves, that "we" have a need or a duty to hear the voices of those "other" than ourselves who share this world with "us." The presumption is that the West's white male has played out his chances, reached his disastrous-to-dull limit, whether conceptualized as modernity or rationality in general, or, in somewhat more petite formulations, as instrumental reason or agglomerating capitalism. Attempts to cross this limit, for some time now, have been made in an array of disciplines: postmodern anthropologists construct new methodologies and technologies in order to represent the word of the other and in order to engage in full dialogue with the other. Historians write from the "bottom up" in order to give voice to those typically excluded from master narratives. Literature scholars are expanding the canon so that the works of others share space with the "classics" in a multicultural classroom. In the process, broad claims are frequently made about culture — about the nature of culture, about what makes cultures different from one another, about the alternative-to-resistant-to-liberating contents of those differences.

The Limits of Multiculturalism is a general attempt to take up these burdens once again, beginning from a recognition that the attempt to locate, define, and preserve things different from "ourselves" has led to a terrible impasse. This impasse, described in great detail in the prolegomenon that follows this introduction, is of such a magnitude that the entire epistemological and political project of cultural studies is collapsing. Briefly, everything presumably wrong about "us" has been redeployed in modern cultural analysis of the "other" with precisely its traditional contents and contours. Multiculturalism, for example, in whatever its formulation, has proved to be as coercive and exclusionary as everything it supposedly surpassed. This is so because the essential framework and tools of multiculturalism are necessarily borrowed from cultural analysis in general—that is, from the history of anthropology. To the extent that such a borrowing is acknowledged, multiculturalism aligns itself with strategies derived from modern and postmodern anthropology, which presumably have exceeded the problems of anthropological knowledge formation in general and its colonial, panoptic, disciplinary project.

The Limits of Multiculturalism therefore begins by sketching the limits of one crucial field within modern cultural analysis, multiculturalism, and then returns to one of several possible locations for the beginnings of such systematic analysis—the U.S. nineteenth century—in order to complicate anthropology's original vision: to "pluralize" it at its foundations, for example, to search out its "original" "multicultural" ground(s), to take seriously, perhaps for the first time, the urgency of the search for an alternative to a monadistic, ethnochauvinist account of culture—in the present example, in Amerindian auto-anthropology of the early to midnineteenth century.

Among this book's presuppositions is that the critics of the West's white male are right, but only in a certain way:

> We know indeed that it is *the end of the world,* and there is nothing illusory (nor "fin de siècle" nor "millenarian") about this knowledge.... One must attempt to envisage in all of its scope—which may well be infinite, namely, infinite in finitude—this *end of the sense of the world,* which is the *end of the world of sense* in which we had—and still have, day by day—all the points of reference we need in order to continue to manage our significations. (Nancy, *Sense* 4, 5)

The end or limit of this world will not, however, lead to a recognition of entirely other lifeworlds around us, lifeworlds that might save us or support us in a time of crisis. Indeed, it is the premise of *The Limits of Multiculturalism* that every commonsense attempt to determine and demarcate such a world ends precisely in the same position as anthropology, which must be judged as a total system of possibilities elaborated over the last 175 years. That is, multiculturalism is merely one of the inner possibilities of anthropology and its practices of diminution and exclusion; it is yet another signal of the end of the world of sense and commonsense.

The bulk of this book is a demonstration of precisely this, and it focuses on a nexus of issues related to the professionalization of U.S. anthropological discourse — specifically, that concerning the Amerindian — in the early to mid-nineteenth century. During the period between the mid-1820s and the mid-1860s the field of anthropology as such emerged. European Americans began to make all or almost all their living by studying the "Indian" — most spectacularly, James Fenimore Cooper, with the success of his Indian novels, but also, to a lesser degree, other white figures addressed in this book, including Henry Rowe Schoolcraft, Lewis Henry Morgan, John Lloyd Stephens, and William Hickling Prescott. Prominent publishers learned that there was money to be made by the right book: Cooper, Stephens, and Prescott enjoyed the rewards of having written best-sellers, for example, and at least one major publisher, Putnam's, began an anthropological series, entitled American Archaeological Researches. The Smithsonian Institution and the American Ethnological Society were organized, which meant that scientific standards for the field began to come into play. And within this milieu, the publication of anthropological work began to be juried (especially in the case of the Smithsonian's massive publications), and nonmilitary monies became available for seemingly disinterested inquiry into the status of various Indian populations. Indeed, it is in this period that anthropology *as such* emerged as something that "anthropologists" do, rather than missionaries, Indian affairs agents, or state-financed "frontier" explorers. As a result, unprecedented debates over method began to take place — debates in which expertise and prestige were at stake — and anthropological "theory" began to emerge.[1]

And, of equal importance for the present study, a small but significant number of persons who understood their identity as fundamentally Amerindian began to write and publish auto-ethnographic accounts of their own peoples: texts that contributed to or quarreled with mainstream anthropological knowledge claims. Only one emerged as a professional (that is, full-time and self-sustaining) anthropological writer and editor during this era: George Copway, who, during the time he published his New York–based newspaper, *Copway's American Indian,* corresponded with all of the major white anthropologists.

But other such writers included Jane Johnston, David Cusick, William Apess, Ely S. Parker, Peter Jones, Maungwudaus (George Henry), and John Rollin Ridge. Their writings, in general, have gone unacknowledged during the last 150 years. That their work appeared only in local or specialized books and periodicals or as part of white anthropologists' projects, or even went unpublished, has meant that this aspect of anthropological history is virtually unknown, even among those who teach the history of anthropology.[2] And, indeed, no existing history of nineteenth-century anthropology mentions any of these figures.

These texts are equally unknown in ethnic literature studies, primarily because the reconfiguration of the nineteenth-century canon to include Amerindian literatures has focused upon poetry, fiction, autobiography, sermons, and white anthropology's reconstruction of folklore.[3] One might go on at some length about the confusions created by existing attempts to incorporate midnineteenth century Amerindian literatures into a multicultural canon, but two examples, perhaps, will suffice. Paul Lauter's *The Heath Anthology of American Literature,* volume 1 (1990), which fundamentally altered the terms for nineteenth-century textual studies and which has been imitated by most anthologies produced by the major publishing houses since, includes portions of the work of Cusick, Ridge, Parker, Apess, and Johnston—five of the seven authors considered in *The Limits of Multiculturalism.* At first glance, this appears to be a surprisingly high level of "inclusion." But Ridge's anthropology goes unmentioned, and he appears in the *Heath* primarily as a poet. Johnston appears as an author in her own right of some of the Schoolcraft Indian fables, although a reading of the texts should at least suggest the involvement of her husband, Henry Rowe Schoolcraft, in the crafting of the texts, given that the reprinted tales' moralisms are entirely consonant with Schoolcraft's interpretations of similar material. Parker appears in the pre-European, "Native American Traditions" portion of the volume, rather than in the nineteenth-century section, with attribution to Parker only by footnote, thereby completely obfuscating the text's origin in and relationship to nineteenth-century anthropological speculation and masking Parker's shaping hand in Amerindian materials he committed to paper. Finally, Cusick and Apess are well served through carefully chosen excerpts in the anthology's first edition, but the Cusick text was eliminated from the second edition in 1994.

Thus, in the most recent version of the *Heath,* only Apess is usefully presented. The point is simply to suggest that the *Heath Anthology* is an example of where things stand: A surprisingly large and distinctive body of nineteenth-century Amerindian writing on anthropological matters, running parallel to the development of "white" anthropology, is not yet within our sights; and it is not clear, yet, that anthropology was always already a "plural" or "multi-" discourse — in fact, "more plural"[4] in its points of departure and conclusions than present-day multiculturalism.

A second example: Bernd C. Peyer's book *The Tutor'd Mind: Indian Missionary-Writers in Antebellum America* (1997) takes up many of the same figures as *The Limits of Multiculturalism* and addresses Apess and Copway in particular in lengthy chapters. Peyer's framework is implicitly one of strong multiculturalism, with its focus on the presumed loss, but then retention and recovery, of important and morally and cognitively superior alternatives to the West. But Peyer, for all the considerable interest that his book commands, ultimately does not read these auto-anthropologists as anthropologists; instead, he *anthropologizes them.* Broadly following Victor Turner on questions of liminality and community, Peyer defines these writers as "transcultural" "mediators" who work, in a dubious biological analogy, to protect the survival of a culture in the midst of colonization: "It [the role of Apess and Copway] can be likened to the semipermeable membrane of one-cell marine organisms, which permits the life-sustaining exchange between the inner cell and the surrounding ocean environment without direct contact" (Peyer 17). A certain kind of multicultural frame is in operation here, with whites or the West as the ocean and Native American groups as amoebas. The story-frame here reiterates the enabling narrative of multiculturalism, with which this preface began. The story-frame is of the total versus the singular, and the battle of the singular for its maintenance in all of its smallness and fragility in the process of its engulfment. The singular, curiously, is preserved precisely through selective contact with the total, which, on one level, is to completely misunderstand the philosophical problem of the singular — that is, the problem of alterity in general — from Immanuel Kant's aesthetics through Jean-Luc Nancy's elaborations of the minimal conditions for a community of singularities.[5] One might say that the singular disappears at the moment Peyer determines "who" Indians are with respect to "us" and that it is precisely the decision to determine the difference in contents between the single-cell creature and the ocean that prevents the singular from ever appearing. Suffice it to say that the singular could not make its appearance in the guise of an "amoeba," for to so formulate it is to already determine the singular in terms of its shape and workings and purposes — in other words, to already determine it as mere difference rather than singularity.[6]

The Amerindian auto-anthropologists are so fully determined anthropologically by Peyer that their existence on the liminal border and their labor serve as the very possibility of demarcating the difference between "red" and "white" and determine the ability to assess their borrowings from and resistance to the white West. Their texts, then, disappear under the shellac of anthropology, and it is impossible to determine, in the first place, whether anything of these texts poses an alternative to white anthropology because the reading of these texts has been, in a very real sense, predetermined and preconditioned by the overarching anthropological framework.

The details of Peyer's largest analysis of the contents of Amerindian culture are of some significance for the problems presented in *The Limits of Multiculturalism*. Briefly, Peyer argues that the Western impositions and borrowings (the latter made possible by the liminal figures) are simply "compartmentalized" by an "oral society" (Peyer 13), so that "retention of diverging older ideals" is retained and preserved (12), including less "abstract," "impersonal," and obfuscatory methods of negotiation and interaction (10), a less-alienated "language of daily interaction" that opposes, at least metaphorically, Western mind/body dualism, and the like (6).

But what would be urgent and necessary, however, in the present anthropological context, is to determine whether Amerindians held or hold alternatives to "the fabrication of racial stereotypes to set the proper mood for conquest" (Peyer 13). On this ground, Peyer is less clear, although he notes that it "seems very unlikely that the various native groups dealing with the colonists did not soon come to recognize certain sociocultural and biological characteristics which set them apart from the latter collectively, such as material culture, religious beliefs, social structure, military practices, uses of land, physical features, and so on" (14). All of which at least implies that Amerindians, as anthropologists, necessarily determined anthropological differences, but Peyer is silent as to whether such differences would also constitute "racial stereo-types." In other words, does an oral culture establish a less ethnocentric, more truthful, account of difference, akin to more truthful practices of dialogue and negotiation? Such, at least, might be a logical conclusion. It is a conclusion taken to its limit by anthropologist Keith Basso in his study of the western Apache, *Portraits of "the Whiteman"* (1979), in which jokes about white people are not said to be " 'acting out' a set of prefigured ethnic stereotypes"; rather, they are said to be "contemporary," "experimental," and creative in content, and they are also credited with performing important communal functions for their tellers' Indian audiences. Basso's passage hints, at least, that such jokes are based on recent experiential interaction and are thus more truthful than nineteenth-century anthropology's stereotypes (Basso 80). This is wishful (al-beit typical) thinking in the extreme, and its privileging of something called "experience" will be taken up below. The important point, here, is that Peyer grasps many things in his analysis, but one might say that he grasps every-thing *but* the problem *that is anthropology*.

On the other hand, the white anthropology that *The Limits of Multicultur-alism* explores has many times been carefully examined. Indeed, there is a long and honorable list of works devoted to reading the midnineteenth-century United States on matters of race, and the short list of significant titles includes Roy Harvey Pearce's *Savagism and Civilization* (1953; orig. ed.), William Stan-ton's *The Leopard's Spots* (1960), Thomas F. Gossett's *Race* (1963; orig. ed.), Richard Slotkin's *Regeneration through Violence* (1973) and *The Fatal Envi-ronment* (1985), Richard Drinnon's *Facing West: The Metaphysics of Indian Hating and Empire Building* (1980), Stephen Jay Gould's *The Mismeasure of Man* (1981), Reginald Horsman's *Race and Manifest Destiny* (1981), and Robert E. Bieder's *Science Encounters the Indian* (1986), in addition to the important, related work done on the history of British anthropology in this pe-riod, most notably George W. Stocking's several books.

One might summarize the rhetorical strategies available to these writers in the following way: nineteenth-century anthropologies and proto-anthropologies either (1) never encounter their objects and are therefore nothing but a series of myths, episodes of racial hatreds, or (2) relate a progressive tale of mis-takes gradually moving toward scientific truth. Both strategies, perhaps, have missed something along the way. The latter strategy — one might use Gossett and Gould as examples — typically too easily assumes that later, professionalized anthropology resolves the problems of an earlier generation; good intentions here count for much: "Schoolcraft was never wholly able to free himself from the notion of savagery as ineluctably connected with the Indians, but Morgan left such ideas behind" (Gossett 251). Gossett goes on to say that Morgan's methodologies produced real "discoveries" about Amerindian life because "he strove to see the Indians in terms of their own societies and not in terms of his own." Such a progressive narrative concerning anthropology is highly persuasive, and highly flattering to present-day anthropologists of all sorts, but this introduction and the prolegomenon that immediately follows will argue against it at some length.

The former strategy — and here one might highlight Drinnon and Slotkin — errs in two directions at once. First, despite a general commitment to critique rather than prescription, unspoken commitments to a notion of "Indianness" produce deformed readings of texts, as when Drinnon suggests that James Fenimore Cooper's *The Oak Openings* is his most racist novel because of its investment in Christian conversion.[7] The implication is progressivist: some anthropological approaches involve a greater respect for the other than do others. Second, and relatedly, scholars' lack of information concerning Amerindian self-definition in the nineteenth century results in reading texts only for the ways in which they shore up definitions of whiteness. Amerindians as such play no part in the tale (there are only "Indians" here), and therefore they can safely be presumed to be living in cultures that, even if not safe from white imposition, are beyond the world of white words.

But *The Limits of Multiculturalism* begins from the fundamentally different, but absolutely irrefutable, premise that the discipline of anthropology is invented across the "red"/"white" color line, and not simply through the mechanism of Amerindian informants (although this, of course, is true too) but in the writings of Amerindian anthropologists. Perhaps the single most intriguing recent book for purposes of comparison to *The Limits of Multiculturalism* is Eric Lott's *Love and Theft* (1995), with its commitment to unearthing the hidden linkages that made midnineteenth-century blackface minstrelsy something more than stereotype, a something that Lott demonstrates as crossing the color line in ways once thought unimaginable. The comparison works on many levels: Scholarly works on minstrelsy and nineteenth-century anthropology share, for example, the presumption of ministrelsy's and anthropology's nonrelation to an object of study. Lott, in fact, refers at a strategic moment to Schoolcraft's folklore collecting, arguing that "cultures of the dispossessed usually, for better or worse, come to us mediated through dominant-culture filters" (103). But Schoolcraft and the school of "*scientific* anthropology," Lott notes with ironic emphasis, did little more than "soothe" rather than "disturb" racial/cultural boundaries, unlike minstrelsy, a "nonscientific anthropology" that "brought to the surface . . . the culture of black people" (103).

The Limits of Multiculturalism sets out to "disturb" this formulation in more than one way, first by producing the documentary record whereby the lie will be put to the notion that anthropologies involve less transgression of the color line than other forms of expression. Indeed, materially, the reverse may well be true: Unlike early minstrel T. D. Rice, whose meeting with the African American performer "Cuff" was brief and probably invented, Schoolcraft *married* his informant, Jane Johnston, and published the work of another, David Cusick. And Morgan's ongoing relationship with Parker dwarfs anything Lott can document concerning minstrelsy. Finally, Apess, Parker, Copway, and Ridge are all, among other things, close readers of anthropological literature, and Copway's network of white anthropological contacts was astonishingly complete. Anthropology emerges, then, out of a process in which many hands on both sides of the color line are writing simultaneously, though admittedly within asymmetrical, power-laden contexts — whose impact is felt most at the level of the invisibility of the auto-anthropologists' texts then and now.

And the anthropologies under consideration here disturb secure racial and cultural representational boundaries far more than do the anthropologisms of minstrelsy.[8] These texts demonstrate that culture, rather than mixed, "miscegenated," or "appropriated" in this period, as Lott would have it, is born anew — that anthropology, like minstrelsy, invents culture in such a way that the color line is reimagined on all sides, re-embodied, and interlinked in such a way that there are no separate, secured "cultures" to which one might have recourse or to which one might nostalgically return.

Such is anthropology's "nature," one might argue. The concept of culture, in the first place, is always a matter of *total significance*. E. B. Tylor established the master definition in 1871: "Culture, or civilization, . . . is that complex whole which includes knowledge, belief, art, laws, morals, custom, and any other capabilities and habits acquired by man as a member of society" (quoted in Kroeber and Kluckhohn 81). Culture is "complex whole," then, or, as the anthropology of the twentieth century reiterated, "the sum," "that totality," "that complex whole," "the accumulated treasury."[9] Culture is neither an individual practice, nor is it a group of such practices — or, rather, it is never *merely* this. Rather, it is a practice or group of practices or a totality of practices enlarged into a meaning or significance — typically an account of the ordering of "mind" (whatever terminology is used) — and at the moment of that enlargement, at the moment of the decision that makes practices count for something, "culture" is produced, made visible.[10]

It is the concept of culture's necessary *significance,* though, that prevents culture from appearing in the abstract, by itself, as such. Meaning or significance, as structuralism taught, is a matter of relations, and as soon as one constitutes "culture," culture can only appear in relation to another "culture." A relationship is established between the "one" or the "self" and the "other" such that an endless play of differences and similarities is inaugurated. The game of anthropology in general is to stabilize the differences, although this can be brought about only through the crudest of formulations. A "serious" anthropologist continues to sift the data and determine the limits, and inevitably and ultimately, such study destabilizes the categorizations and significances achieved as the "one" and the "other" simultaneously oppose and duplicate each other. This same serious anthropologist registers alarm at the mirror effects that "culture" produces and begins to complicate the account through narratives of diffusion or the universally human, or through seemingly less totalized, more nuanced, accounts of individual cultures (culture as a struggle of tendencies rather than as control). Alejandro Lugo's research demonstrates how the last century of anthropology and sociology negotiates the binary of culture understood as monolith and conflict (or as structure and agency, dominating and enabling, and so on), in such a way that, however far anthropology moves away from "total" narratives, it nevertheless is bound up with them in the last instance, and in such a way as to mark the closure of the field of culture studies — the "the erosion of the monopoly of culture theory as 'cultural patterns'" (Lugo, "Reflections" 61).

Anthropological "culture" finds itself not "crossed" in the time of fieldwork and at the moment of experience but, rather, double-crossed in a loop that re-

turns to its origins. One might draw it as a version of the symbol for infinity—
"∞"—with the horizontal limits understood as "cultures." In this sense, anthropology's twisted, roundabout shape suggests the possibility of its being
crossed out from the research agenda. One cannot but agree with Lott that, after minstrelsy, "there could be no simple restoration of black authenticity" or
black culture as such (Lott 103). There is, in this world, no culture as such at
all, but *only anthropology. The Limits of Multiculturalism* maps this *mutual encirclement* and highlights attempts to evade, withdraw from, and destroy the
anthropological circle as pressure is applied from within anthropology to its
knotted crossroads.

Lott's book is mistaken, finally, although useful for providing a clear concept of anthropology that must be overcome. Lott's definition of midcentury
nonscientific anthropology—"love and theft"—implies that anthropology actually touches its objects, draws something from them, appropriates elements
of them. In short, it defines anthropology as *experience,* and Lott goes to great
pains to document different sorts and levels of white and black interaction in
the midnineteenth century. Indeed, *Love and Theft* finally stabilizes its narrative in numerous places—locates original African American culture, for instance—by suggesting those cultural artifacts that minstrelsy precisely appropriates: the slave tale trickster figure, southwestern humor—"itself often
an interracial creation" (23, 94)—the instruments of the banjo and jawbone,
"black banjo techniques and rhythms" (94) and "vigorous earth-slapping foot-
work of black dances" (94), and, perhaps, "linguistic patterns, naming practices, hairstyles, and physical demeanor" (40).[11]

This is a list of five or six characteristics in search of an anthropology[12]—
an anthropology that Lott is reticent to suggest. Indeed, those matters of *significance* that greatly interest Lott, such as the forms of white-masculine affect
produced in minstrelsy, do not seem in his narrative to be derived from African
Americans at all. Rather, they seem to derive from "white ideologies of black
manhood" (52). Therefore, according to Lott's definition, some of minstrelsy's
crucial matter amounts to ideological invention rather than anthropological appropriation or rather than experience. And yet, to redouble the problem, Lott
refers to such "masculinity" as "appropriated" (52). Lott's contradiction is un-
derstandable: Given his desire to show minstrelsy's connection to African Americans, he is reluctant to part from a formula of "appropriation." Yet given min-

strelsy's wildly racist and hopelessly clichéd representations of African Americans, he cannot bring himself to determine such representations as related to an actual African American "culture." Lott's crisis, finally, is entirely bound up with his affirmation of anthropology and the culture concept. The minstrels, in generating significances, were doing anthropology, and it is precisely my point that anthropology is "ideology," in the loose sense, rather than appropriation. Anthropology does not touch its object in developing significances, no matter how many potsherds it unearths, rituals it witnesses according to a logic of participant-observer, or interviews it conducts. Material contact and even appropriation are precisely *not yet* anthropological. And "experience," rather than being a category that guarantees to anthropology an unmediated form of information or knowledge, is riven by the problematics of space and reflection; anthropological "experience" can only be experienced through concept and method. Anthropology, at its moment of establishing meaning, experiences nothing, or at least nothing that might be understood according to a commonsense notion of experience. As David E. Johnson wrote, with respect to border studies, anthropology "situates the subject at the edge of experience," yet "the border (experience) remains unapproachable" (Johnson, "Time" 135). Anthropology must content itself, then, with an encirclement of its object, without ever touching it, even though it thereby invents it.

Because of this, no claim will be made in the pages that follow regarding the culture of Amerindia or regarding the culture of the Amerindian auto-anthropologists of the nineteenth century, and one might imagine two obvious "cultural" objections in this regard. The first objection: the Amerindian writers taken up in *The Limits of Multiculturalism* might be said to be something less or something more than Indian with regard to religious affiliation, English-language literacy, occupation, adult residence, and the like. An acknowledged dean of Native American studies, Arnold Krupat, for example, distinguishes Indian and Western autobiographical forms by tropes of collectivity and individuality, respectively.[13] Of the eight Amerindian writers taken up at length in *The Limits of Multiculturalism*, the one most likely to meet some standard of "purity" is David Cusick: he is not explicitly a Christian convert, unlike several of the others; he is the least literate in English of the group (Krupat finds "questionable...grammar" to be a sign of continued participation within oral and therefore collective traditions [Krupat 221]); and his book is clearly the most "local," as opposed to white-market mediated, publication originating from Amerindia in this period. And yet his text may be the most aberrant, the most difficult to comprehend, in terms of any of our current, commonplace notions of Amerindian identity. Indeed, if one begins from the modern, critical stereotype or network of characteristics said to constitute an Amerindian identity (such as collectivity), the writer among these eight whose work most embodies the stereotype would perhaps be Ely Parker[14]—and yet Parker, as has already been suggested, so modified and worked over his field transcriptions that the most crucial sections for anthropology can be shown to be pure invention on his part. And he is also the Indian writer most clearly colluding with white anthropology, to the extent that, as the *Heath Anthology* makes clear, he has nearly no identity today as a writer in his own right. Setting a standard of representativeness, therefore, is merely to play another "culture" game, another game of truth, and one in which every expectation will be turned upside down.

One needs to press an elaboration of these problems in Krupat, because the type of work he undertakes is so common in studies of Amerindian writing. Indeed, Krupat recognizes that his cultural division is imperiled from the start: in order to claim texts written by converted Indians as "Native American," he argues that "nonracist" Christianity is a fundamentally communal identity or affiliation (229). White women's autobiographical writings, too, are said to be organized around communal tropes (217, n. 18). Thus the prime marker of Amerindian identity or personhood is located in the West as well, and in multiple places and spaces, which forces his conception of "Indianness" to tremble. Shoring up his claims, however, Krupat writes, with respect to women, "It remains to add what recent feminist criticism has solidly established, that orality—speech, the voice, and the *mother* tongue—and textuality—writing and the *father's* pen(is)—are, indeed, perceived as gender-related in the West" (217, n. 18). Here is Krupat's fundamental misprision: "are, indeed, perceived" is elided into an account of cultures. In short, he turns a reflection on the anthropology of men and women into a cultural truth, and the same reflection might be made with respect to the West and its others. Anthropology establishes relations that, once imposed, can be lived and enacted. But this is not the same thing as *culture as such*. There well may be a *denominated "Indianness"* that is understood as oral and/or collective and that may even be understood by those so denominated as such, but this belongs to the history of hierarchies and exclusions that Jacques Derrida famously deconstructs in his *Grammatology*. Culture is not a condition but, rather, a relation of power. And it is a political act of exclusion, part of the history of colonial relations, for Krupat or anyone else to pass judgment on the "Indianness" of texts.

A second objection concerns the relationship of two identity issues addressed throughout *The Limits of Multiculturalism,* and not always held separate in the analysis. The first involves what appears to be a strictly anthropological-epistemological issue: the establishment of parameters of difference and sameness — in other words, the production of an anthropological analytic — in order to manifest race, color, culture, and the like. The second involves seemingly nonprofessional matters: the everyday experience of culture, the constant assertion in the world that one belongs to or partakes of a single (or multiple) culture. It is important to address this here because it is the most common critique of the sort of work attempted in *The Limits of Multiculturalism* — that is, the critique and de-structuration of anthropological knowledges — to suggest that the defamiliarizing of social scientific truth is both an affront to ethnic minorities invested in such identities and of no value to them, as well, in an everyday world in which whiteness, for example, constantly reasserts its prerogatives. Another way to say this would be to suggest that the nineteenth-century Amerindian auto-anthropologists are co-opted elites, cut off from the realm of everyday culture or experience.

The pages that follow, and particularly the prolegomenon, address such matters, such a call for instrumental reason, and clarify the problems associated with minority cultural membership *and* a predominantly white social scientific cultural analysis. But there is, finally, no difference between these two objects of analysis because when a person asserts an allegiance to culture or is subjected to the problem of color on the street corner, anthropology is enacted. Anthropology is not just something that people perform in anthropology departments; its generalized dissemination means that it *always already* is that which constitutes the everyday experience of persons.

Thus, to utilize or affirm or embody in any way concepts of culture, race, or color is to be doing anthropology. Anthropology's practices and decisions are lived out and reiterated every day of modern life. Many of the anthropologists considered in the pages that follow had to make a relatively complicated decision in this regard or had such complex decisions made for them, which brings us to a final turn on the question of purity and representativeness. Some of the writers, such as Cusick and Jones, were "biracial" by birth; Morgan, among the "white" writers, was granted an Indian identity by the Iroquois; several of the Indian auto-anthropologists used both red and white names to signify dual identity; and several of the anthropologists — both Anglo and Indian — married "across" race (Schoolcraft, Copway, and Jones, for example) and lived for extended periods in their spouse's world.

The most dramatic thing that can be said of the Amerindian auto-anthropologists as a group is that their work does not cohere around the most crucial of anthropological decisions, such as the origin of the "Indian" or the matter of precontact personhood. Indeed, these nineteenth-century texts also fail to clear the way for an understanding of Amerindian personhood that has endured for even two hundred years, much less five hundred or a thousand years. Current commonplaces about Amerindians as long-standing keepers of the earth, as constitutional democrats, as pacific communitarians, and the like are not supported by a close reading of these texts (which is, perhaps, one reason why such materials have consistently *not* been read as anthropological exercises). One can identify certain figures, certain moments in the nineteenth-century materials, that are more in keeping with our current conceptions than others. But here one will have to circulate over the red/white color line and assemble a canon that includes not only Ely S. Parker and George Copway but also Lewis Henry Morgan and James Fenimore Cooper's *Mohicans*; and one will necessarily cut across the bow of Amerindian experts such as Peter Jones and David Cusick and formulate some way to exclude their ethnographic "experience." It may be precisely the right time to ponder this problem — the sheer diversity of Amerindian auto-anthropology in the midnineteenth century, as anthropology "proper" is institutionalized — given that an increasing number of theoretical texts in anthropological, historical, and literary studies have argued for the epistemological significance of auto-knowledges read either in relation to mainstream white writing or as a better alternative to it. In fact, calls have been made in recent years for inaugurating the production of such knowledges — calls that are significantly belated in the context of the works read in this study.[15]

But the Amerindian auto-anthropologies, whatever their divergences from one another in terms of contents, are coherent *as anthropology* — coherent within the context of anthropological thought in general — although use of the term "anthropology" to describe these texts needs some explanation given that *The Limits of Multiculturalism* examines white and red novels, histories, folklore collections, travel narratives, and ethnographies. Anthropology is not a genre, unlike ethnography, and in its largest sense it is simply the "study of man." This book is interested in the variety of antebellum genres and strategies, often overlapping, that attempt to address anthropology's large question, the "who" question: "Who is an Indian?" "Anthropology," more particularly, will be any discourse that grounds the truth of its answer to this question on the basis of lived experience and experience with the living, just as Lott implicitly suggests: folklore, ethnography, history (Prescott's works, which were informed by the Spanish conqueror's accounts of Amerindian identity; the Amerindian historians' North American versions of same, as well as gathered oral testimony and their own experiences), and even novels (Cooper's stories based on his anthropological reading and field trips), poems (Henry Wadsworth Longfellow's work, colored by Schoolcraft, for one), and archaeology (Stephens's work, for example, which depends heavily for its conclusions on contact with and observations of contemporaneous Central American indigenous peoples). The limit case for experience-based accounts of the other might be Samuel Morton's work, for though he studied, behind laboratory doors, the size and shape of skulls, his *Crania Americana* is as fundamentally grounded on experience, on ethnography, as any of the other texts, as Morton's long introductory pages make clear.[16] In this manner, "anthropology" will be used throughout as the master term that encompasses history, science, and literature. Whatever is wrong with anthropology — and this book advocates, strongly, an end to all of its practices — will not be solved by a firmer grasp of scientific truth, as Gould or Kwame Appiah might suggest,[17] or by a return to the writing of history, as happened in anthropology in the 1980s in the work of Renato Rosaldo, Eric Wolfe, and Marshall Sahlins, among others.[18]

Nineteenth-century anthropological texts, as this book demonstrates, are extremely difficult to classify according to our most recent understandings. Before professionalization, works of anthropology assumed many overlapping forms. In terms of content, they are not of a piece in terms of their investment in "race"-based thinking, for example, much less in terms of their understanding of the term "race," which will surprise those who have argued that the nineteenth century's practices of othering are dominated by the discourses of scientific racism, evolution, or both. Questions of what one can only identify as "cultural" concern constantly emerge, even though the rise of cultural anthropology is generally understood as taking place two or three decades after the period under discussion. And the "older" versions of othering — by color, by religion, by gradations of civilization — are alive and well in these texts and are not necessarily related to strictly racial matters. Finally, some of these texts present contact-based arguments in order to explain group identities. One might call the results "colonial culture," or, using a more recent terminology, "hybridity."

This book's interest, finally, is in the problems that the production of anthropological knowledge of any sort inevitably raises, and the particular patterns assembled are merely examples of a more general problem that might be endlessly multiplied in terms of its particularities. This is only occasionally, then, a work that seeks to tell a story of direct influence and effect. Rather than narrate anthropology's antebellum years, *The Limits of Multiculturalism* isolates, or better yet, *constructs hypothetical moments* of nineteenth-century representational conflict and crisis and analyzes them in terms of debates taking place at the end of the twentieth century concerning the status of alterity; the texture of the text of the other; and the value and epistemological status of concepts of race, color, ethnicity, and culture.

The procedure at the heart of *The Limits of Multiculturalism* involves situating nineteenth-century works written from white and red subject positions in relation to one another, on the basis of method, object of study, geography, or all three. Briefly, in chapter 1 Schoolcraft, his coworker and wife Johnston, and Cusick are brought together, the last because Cusick's text was Schoolcraft's folkloric bête noire, as evidenced by two decades of reference in Schoolcraft to Cusick's inadequacies. This chapter elaborates general problems involved in attempting to "locate" culture and isolates moments in Johnston's and Cusick's work that speak to the strictly unresolvable problem of anthropology's calculation of the significance of difference. Chapter 2 is organized around questions of color and animality, thematics explored in Cooper's *Last of the Mohicans,* Morgan's study of the beavers, and Apess's meditation on the light and the dark. Here, in the context of modern "whiteness studies," attempts to complicate the portrait of the "white man" in Cooper and Apess are analyzed in terms of their potential for forecasting the limit of white identity. In chapter 3 Ely S. Parker's thinking is linked to the work of Lewis Henry Morgan because Parker was Morgan's chief informant for his first book, his ethnography of the Iroquois, and because Parker, in many cases, is speaking directly to Morgan and to Morganesque anthropological concerns, such as field experience and evolutionary schema. In this chapter the differences in identity politics between ethnographer and informant—readable on the page in Morgan's *League of the Iroquois*—are contextualized as the poles or limits of the anthropological project in general, while other Parker fragments can more productively be read into the long tradition of what one might call auto-anthropological anti-anthropology.

Chapter 4 is thematically *and* geographically organized, examining the anthropological writings of converted Ojibwa Indians—Copway, Jones, and Maungwudaus—and Cooper's novel about same, *The Oak Openings*. Here, the drive to determine authentic Indian personhood or belief is counterposed to strategies that, in general, seek to minimize the question of identity. In chapter 5, Prescott and Ridge make perfect partners because both are concerned with triangulating "red," "white," and "brown" identities in the Americas, and both do so by presenting the cultural biography of an-other, a Spaniard. Both, too, situate their work as historical and in relation to an emerging scientific racism, typified by and analyzed with reference to Morton's work. This chapter demonstrates that early attempts to turn anthropology to history (and in particular, to colonial interrelationships) are at least as problematic as the work that these attempts implicitly oppose.

These are, in the main, strategic encounters: the book might be organized differently, with the texts shuffled so as to produce other but not necessarily or fundamentally different patterns. The book ends with a coda on social scientific method in which the archaeological work of John Lloyd Stephens and Benjamin Moore Norman is taken up because of the large claims made in the twentieth century regarding Stephens's exemplary working methods and because Stephens and Norman devote tremendous attention to questions of empirical analysis. The coda demonstrates that the foundations for determining the identity of the alterior in anthropology are entirely insufficient—that anthropological empiricism is wholly imaginary, that the house of anthropology is built on sheer belief.

Thus whatever the differences, whatever the heterogeneous elements that make up these texts and ground their arguments, the emphasis in the title, *The Limits of Multiculturalism,* is on the closure or bounded limit of the total discourse of cultural analysis — that is, anthropology — rather than on its progressive development. The ground of anthropology, understood in its largest sense, is the establishment of the limits and contours of group identities rather than, more narrowly, the discovery of kinship or the establishment of the methodological conventions of fieldwork. And this process of identification — the crucial component of or strategy for what Michel Foucault calls the "will to knowledge" — is always founded upon an exclusion of the other as such. The exclusion is anthropology's very possibility, even though anthropology's project, its goal, is to attend to the other according to its own terms — that is, to make a space for the other in the world, to record and account for its differences.[19] And yet anthropology inevitably domesticates alterity, conceptualizes it in relation to its-self, establishes the ground for comparison and hierarchy. This is why Derrida was able in the late 1960s to argue with some confidence that "the ethnologist," or cultural comparatist, "accepts into his discourse the premises of ethnocentrism at the very moment when he denounces them" (283).

Testing this thesis involves attending to the Amerindian auto-anthropologists — determining whether the discourse of the other can be situated as a successfully alternative anthropology or as *other than anthropology.* And, if this sounds too easy, given a social scientific perspective that might readily dismiss nineteenth-century anthropological writing — even the writings of those denominated as Amerindians — as hopelessly muddled and compromised, the task of the prolegomenon that precedes the five chapters proper is to examine these same matters on recent ground, in terms of the strategies of multicultural writing "across" the color line. In the prolegomenon a multiplicity of "postmodern" voices from around the globe — all adopting a broadly "culturalist" anthropological perspective — will be shown to be complicit with nineteenth-century anthropology and will emerge as a collective and equally corrupt remnant of that anthropology. I begin the prolegomenon from the perspective of what I term "anti-anthropology," a seemingly recent development associated with figures such as Vine Deloria Jr. and V. Y. Mudimbe but that emerged, obliquely, at the very beginnings of professional anthropology. Anti-anthropology's sketching of the closure of anthropology involves measuring critical rigor, reflexivities, or markings of the limit of the discourse. Certain texts discussed in the five main chapters figure, finally, as more prescient than others in terms of their recognition and their partial-to-full enactment of these problematics: among the Indian writers, David Cusick and portions of Ely S. Parker's unpublished writings; among the whites, Cooper above all, and Norman, who served as Stephens's shadow nemesis in the mid- to late 1840s. But it may go without saying that it is impossible to write anthropology without foregrounding, in some manner or other, the problem that is anthropology, and even the most explicitly racist or ethnocentric texts can be read against the grain in order to understand the problematic foundations that undergird anthropology's project. The readings of Morgan, Stephens, Morton, and Prescott within these pages highlight such possible interpretive strategies.[20]

Each of the writers, though, on either or both sides of the color line, will be examined for strategies either complicit with or positioned against identity politics' exclusions. And *The Limits of Multiculturalism* forecasts not simply the end of professional anthropology and all it has produced in a scholarly way, but the end of all commonsense versions of it—that is, "our" "own" identities. Such, at least, is this book's invitation.

For American Indians, the struggle of this century has been to emerge
from the heavy burden of anthropological definitions.

—VINE DELORIA JR., *RED EARTH, WHITE LIES* (1995)

MODERN ANTI-ANTHROPOLOGIES AND
AUTO-ANTHROPOLOGIES

Long before multiculturalism and before the thought that is modern diversity
theory, before anthropology's time of crisis, and, indeed, even during the years
of its professionalization in the midnineteenth century, auto-anthropology, or
anthropology written by the discipline's ostensible "subjects," mounted a series
of challenges to anthropology. Occasionally, and even increasingly, such a challenge took the form of "anti-anthropology," or a call for anthropologists to
cease and desist. One of the earliest of these calls came from James Africanus
Horton, a staff assistant surgeon at Netley, in Sierra Leone, where Horton was
born. Horton published *West African Countries and Peoples* in 1868, and in a
chapter therein entitled "False Theories of Modern Anthropologists" he asked,
"When will that happy time come when modern anthropological philosophers,
who at present are one-eyed, and totally ignorant of the capacity of the African
race, will desist from fabricating in their studies the most egregious calumnies
on the race already sufficiently downtrodden?" (37). What Horton calls anthropology, or anthropological philosophy, specifically is scientific racialism,
but Horton argues that such work hardly merits the name "science" because it
has yet to find an object; one prominent figure, Carl Vogt, Horton says, has
"never seen a negro in his life" (Horton 38). Yet another "knows nothing of
the negro race," and his work is composed simply of "descriptions . . . borrowed
from the writings of men who are particularly prejudiced against the race"
(33). Horton does not recognize the African as constituted by anthropological

1

discourse: "Where are to be found negroes with pendulous bellies as the anthropoid apes?" (39).

Horton, it should be noted, relies on a countertradition within anthropology of monogenism, or racial unity, in order to critique anthropology's "base prostitution of scientific truth" (39), but later writers would go further in their claims. Américo Paredes, the dean of Chicano folklore studies, notes the history of rejection by Chicano writers (including, prominently, Octavio Romano) of anthropology in toto as "a field of inquiry... that is racist to the core" (Paredes, *Folklore* 73). V. Y. Mudimbe's *The Invention of Africa* (1988) attempts much the same, using a Foucauldian notion of discourse as a conceptual frame; anthropology, writes Mudimbe, is founded on "ethnocentrism":

> It is not, as some scholars thought, an unfortunate mishap, nor a stupid accident, but one of the major signs of the possibility of anthropology.... It is surely possible, as structuralism and functionalism have proved, to have [anthropological] works that seem to respect indigenous traditions. And one could hope for even more profound changes in anthropology.... But so far it seems impossible to imagine any anthropology without a Western epistemological link. (19)

Foundationally racist and ethnocentrist: These are the crucial charges leveled at anthropology in general, made in differing ways and with different prescriptions. Professional anthropologists — those trained in fieldwork and ethnographic representation — have joined the argument in the last three decades. Ruth Behar reminds her readers of anthropology's prolonged reflexive crises, to which anti-anthropological writing has greatly contributed: "anthropology's complicity with conquest, with colonialism, with functionalism, with realist forms of representation, with racism, with male domination" (162). The major anthology statements in this regard loom large within the field: Dell Hymes's *Reinventing Anthropology* (1972), Talal Asad's *Anthropology and the Colonial Encounter* (1973), James Clifford's and George Marcus's *Writing Culture* (1986), and Richard G. Fox's *Recapturing Anthropology* (1991), to cite just four. Behar, for her part, affirms anthropology's ability to "weather the storm and come out stronger, more inclusive, at once more vexed and more sure of itself" (163). And it is the rare ethnographer who can admit to the depth and permanence of the crisis.[1]

Perhaps the most all-encompassing anti-anthropological statement from auto-anthropology during this same time is Vine Deloria Jr.'s "Anthropologists and Other Friends" (1969); it also may be the most famous, since it was widely disseminated in *Playboy* and also appeared as a chapter in *Custer Died for Your Sins,* a book eventually published as a mass-market paperback. And Deloria's writings in general have played prominent roles — at times determinative, at other times simply exemplary — in the separate but absolutely linked "worlds" of reflexive anthropology and multiculturalism. As a 1997 volume of essays devoted to Deloria's contribution to anthropology makes clear, the reverberations from Deloria's *Custer* are still being felt. Deloria's position in this essay, in which his work is read as representative of the far ends of possible positions within recent anthropological and multicultural thought, can easily be validated through reference to prominent "white" anthropologists of the Amerindian. Far from staking out strange or eccentric positions, Deloria's work identifies the "centers" of present cultural concerns.[2]

For "Anthropologists and Other Friends," Deloria's first and most sustained shot across anthropology's bow, there can be no progressive anthropology — no answer to anthropology's relentless "who?" that might serve the interests of Amerindians. Unlike Mudimbe, who at least always holds open the possibility of an indigenous, non-Western perspective on identity (a nonanthropology, thus, that, ironically, might be able to answer anthropology's questions); unlike Paredes, who seeks to inaugurate a more subtle and nuanced field methodology of "gesture"; and unlike Horton, who might best be understood in the end as a cultural evolutionist, Deloria is strictly and fully anti-anthropological.

Multiple rationales lead him to such a conclusion. In the first place, anthropology is, necessarily, genocide's discursive counterpart: "Indians are certain that all societies of the Near East had anthropologists at one time because all those societies are now defunct" (Deloria, *Custer* 83). This is so not simply because proto-anthropologies so frequently served as ex post facto justification for colonial and state Indian policy but, more importantly, because anthropology is an antihuman discourse: "The fundamental thesis of the anthropologist is that people are objects for observation, people are then considered objects for experimentation, for manipulation, and for eventual extinction" (86).

Anthropology, in short, is a necessarily dominating instrumental reason. "An anthropologist comes out to Indian reservations to make OBSERVATIONS" (84).

This may seem innocent enough, but the very possibility of its truth claims — that is, its constitution in the first place of an object of analysis — assures its link to the manipulation of persons, the constitution of Indian reservations, and murder.

How can this be, given that anthropologists so often consider themselves "friends of the Indian"? The very representation of groups, whether done as friend or foe, comes with devastating consequences, opens up space for social engineering; it justifies projects designed either to shore up traditional Amerindian culture or to tear it down. All types of anthropology necessarily fabricate an ideal Amerindian against which "Indian people begin to feel that they are merely shadows of a mythical super-Indian" (86). The power of anthropological representations is such that they become imposed on Amerindians over time; they bear, as Deloria argues, no relation whatsoever to Indian life as it is lived in the late twentieth century (or ever, for that matter). Instead, they generate depression, guilt, longing, and reactionary identity politics (Indian resistance, for example, premised on the image of the warrior). And Deloria says that anthropology bears no relationship to the issues upon which an improved Amerindian quality of life depends: land and resource questions, not identity questions (90–91).

Anthropology, in any case, is a hermetically sealed discipline that never interrogates or communicates with an object of study. In fact, it never looks for one: "You may be curious as to why the anthropologist never carries a writing instrument. He never makes a mark because he ALREADY KNOWS what he is going to find" (85). Deloria argues that methodological niceties such as the thematization of objectivity, fieldwork, friendship, canons of evidence, criteria for proof, and truth reflect nothing but relationships *among* anthropologists; they are, therefore, matters of funding, prestige, promotion, and the like (84–85; 98–89).

Deloria's point, finally, is that Amerindians cannot and should not be represented. *Cannot* because Amerindians, left to themselves, are a multiplicity: "There is little sense of a 'lost identity,' " and they "choose from a wide variety of paths of progress," many of which are newly invented by Amerindians (89). An Indian is potentially anything, then, and not a something — or, perhaps, only a "something" without determination. And this, finally, is not an anthropological problem of outsider versus insider or of observing versus experiencing. Amerindians themselves take no position on the "who" question: "None of us would stand up and say, 'This is what really is' " (Deloria, "Criticisms" 97). Deloria understands Amerindians, then, as particularities or as endlessly complex bricolages that cannot be disentangled either practically or intellectually. To be human, he seems to argue, is to be, in the end, nonidentifiable at the level of group identity. The group or the tribe or whatever aggregate is always what is on the verge of coming to be; or, then again, maybe not. But to name it is to kill.[3]

A shift in Deloria's thinking, however, has taken place over the course of the last third of the twentieth century, as his work entered into conversation over the terms and conditions of multiculturalism.[4] In Deloria's next books, particularly *God Is Red* (1973) and *The Metaphysics of Modern Existence* (1979), he elaborates the epistemological divide separating white and red cosmologies. The full implications for anthropology, however, only became clear with the publication of *Red Earth, White Lies* (1995). In this text, in which Deloria confronts in great detail the findings of one of anthropology's four subspecialties, archaeology, he elaborates the need for an Amerindian auto-anthropology that would *replace* mainstream traditions. The attack on anthropology is again at full force, but this time in the name of a cultural truth that is close at hand if only one attends to Indian accounts of the real:

> The institutionalization of knowledge in the academic setting has made status more important than accomplishments or ideas when determining the canon of truth that will give the best explanation of our planet. We are living in a strange kind of dark ages where we have immense capability to bring together information but when we gather this data, we pigeonhole it in the old familiar framework of interpretation, sometimes even torturing the data to make it fit. (*Red Earth* 231)[5]

In *Red Earth,* then, Deloria condemns the practice of anthropology as being circular, much as he did in *Custer:* it begins with racist, received ideas and never exceeds this threshold.

The reconstruction of anthropology depends upon a linked set of presuppositions, some of which Deloria makes explicit and some of which come into view only by reference to his earlier critiques of the field. First, there are

Amerindian knowledges that cross all national and tribal affiliations; that is, there is a cultural tradition that unites Amerindian identities. These are old knowledges — oral traditions and stories — that record the truth of the world under the terms of an explicitly Indian epistemology (*Red Earth* 51; 251). They are a secret for the most part, preserved by elders, and passed on to outsiders only under special circumstances ("if the elders think you are serious") (251).[6] Second, Indian knowledge and the Indian worldview are untranslatably different from white knowledge: "The premise accepted by Indians and rejected by scientists" is that "the world in which we live is alive" (55). Thus, "Indians came to understand that all things were related" (57). All of this is embedded within the oral tradition, which is, in turn, expressed in Indian language, a "completely accurate rendering of a specific experience *which Western languages could not possibly duplicate*" (emphasis added; 53). Third, the import of this is that there are multiple epistemologies available to the social scientist: that is, "more than one explanation" for the same data (251).

Deloria's argument in *Red Earth* is of a piece with larger trends in anthropological circles and, finally, in the humanities and social sciences in general. And its logic is reproduced in texts written by any number of scholars, including Amerindian writers such as Georges Sioui, Ward Churchill, and M. Annette Jaimes Guerrero. Sioui's *For an Amerindian Autohistory* (1992), for example, argues that Amerindians are a completely "homogeneous" people of one blood, one culture, and one language family (11) and that Indian cosmology is completely opposed to that of Europeans (it is based on the "sacred circle of life," which acknowledges the "universal interdependence of all beings" and therefore "guarantee[s] . . . abundance, equality, and, therefore, peace" [xxi]).[7]

All of these works are, generally and specifically, related to one another. For one thing, these texts agree, in broad terms, about the status of Amerindian difference (the ideas of "relation" and the "circle" and "holism" are each attempting to grasp the same fundamental point for Amerindian epistemology), as well as about its critical value for rethinking the Western mind. In terms of anthropological theorizing in this century, these texts occupy a space that Louise Newman, in reference to Margaret Mead's work, calls "cultural comparativism." One might call this a "soft" version of cultural relativism, in which cultures are seen "as developing along different, incommensurable lines" — not judged according to "western practices" understood "as the only morally legitimate forms of cultural arrangements" — but in which the anthropologist still attempts "to determine which arrangements represent... better ways of living" (Newman 237).

Anti-anthropology has been brought to a critical juncture by arguments such as these, which purport to treat the other from the space of the other, which claim to have crossed Mudimbe's epistemological divide, and which are voiced with all of the special authority and experience of the insider who holds authentic and even secret knowledge. These arguments, in turn, bear a relationship not only to the strategies of cultural relativism but to modern multiculturalism because they come with calls for a refiguration of political relationships among the cultures of the Americas. And these arguments, finally, raise the problem of whether a certain sort of multicultural thinking can truly account for and do justice to the other and constitute an anthropology that has "weathered the storm" of political/representational crisis.

Have a certain multiculturalism's definitions of culture exceeded Deloria's original determination of anthropology's thresholds or limits? Has multiculturalism, indeed, found a legitimate object, adequately described it, purged anthropology's racism and ethnochauvinism, and become, in short, a foundation for cultural truth and cultural justice? Answers to these questions revolve around the anthropological concept of "culture," an idea that historically belongs to anthropology. The word has been deployed for more than a century. Used for the first time in a technical sense by Tylor in the 1870s in his evolutionist schema, as a measure of "civilization," and then, after a break of some forty years, by the Boasian generation of anthropologists in order to begin to replace the concept of "race,"[8] "culture" is the single most important modern anthropological term. Its importance is underscored by its rapid journey across the disciplines and its use today in a manner that makes it seem an entirely natural and commonsense existent for specialists in many fields, as well as for everyday sociopolitical conversation.

The double question for culture involves, precisely, the twin thresholds of evolutionary and racial anthropologies, both of which are easily dismissed in the present moment. Can "culture" outlive evolutionism, its home ground, and racialism, its counterformulation? Can "culture," born in evolutionism, ever truly be redeveloped and deployed in a nonhierarchical, nonjudgmental manner? And can "culture," as the replacement concept for "race," evade the problems of racial theorizing by emphasizing history over nature? Some, along with Deloria in his early work, believe that it cannot: Sneja Gunew, for example, notes that "the very concept of culture" is "imperialist and centrist," and Bernard McGrane calls it "a great trivialization of the encounter with the Other" (Gunew 24; McGrane 129).[9] "Culture," then, might be every bit as problematic a category for analysis — subject to the same concerns and difficulties — as "race," and the invention of "culture" may solve none of the difficulties that "evolution" and "race" clearly raise.

THE GROUNDS AND LIMITS OF NEGOTIATION

A large literature today surrounds multiculturalism, not the least of which concerns definitions of the concept itself. One might argue that multiculturalism begins with the conversation about American pluralism that took place in the second decade of this century — the same moment as the rise of "culture" studies proper in anthropology. Randolph S. Bourne produced one of the most often cited treatments of the theme in 1916, in which he argued:

> America is coming to be, not a nationality but a trans-nationality, a weaving back and forth, with the other lands, of many threads of all sizes and colors.... How are we likely to get the more creative America — by confining our imaginations to the ideal of the melting-pot, or broadening them to some such cosmopolitan conception... ? (Bourne 106)

Pluralism, as both undeniable fact and future project, is an attempt to think the thought of the "many" and the thought of national "integration" at the same time (Bourne 108), holding both in play, valuing both at once. Pluralism's poles set the terms and conditions of modern multiculturalism, versions of which tend to emphasize the differences, the resulting unity, or both at once, but all with respect to an answer to the question of how what is different *from* "America" yet also *within* the borders of "America" might be conserved, recognized, and granted the right to be itself. Jürgen Habermas summarizes a possible working definition of multiculturalism as a set of "claims to the recognition of collective identities and to equal rights for cultural forms of life" (Taylor and Gutman 109).

David Theo Goldberg has usefully attempted to distinguish various multi-culturalisms from one another, and his distinctions are helpful for identifying the intellectual tendencies within the late work of Deloria, as well as that of Sioui, Churchill, and Jaimes Guerrero.[10] Broadly, these works are part of what Goldberg describes as "antiassimilationist and anti-integrationist" multicul-turalism ("Introduction" 9). What others have described as "separatist" — because of their emphasis on the nontranslatability, the absolute alterity, of cultural others — Goldberg characterizes as a strategy of *"incorporation"* which "does not involve extension of established values and protections over the formerly excluded group"; rather, it "seeks to undermine and alter from within the dominant, controlling, confining, and periphractic values of the cultural dominant" ("Introduction" 9).

This takes place at every level of the modern Amerindian auto-anthropologists' texts: Amerindian thinking and even Amerindian feeling begin from values and presuppositions entirely different from white ones. Sioui's text, for example, elaborates not only the terms of an-other social scientific epistemology — "autohistory" — but of an-other emotional structure that both brings it into being and produces its possibility for reaching the ear of the other.[11] The crucial contours of the Amerindian mind, then, cannot be evaluated from a white perspective. Instead, its radical alterity must be recognized, and this in turn, necessitates a willingness to question all of the infrastructures of white being.

What Goldberg and others have described as a "critical multiculturalism" turns on a set of appealing propositions: (1) the recognition of the existence of cultural alterity (culture's "undeniable variety" at every level, including the epistemological, the political, and the economic); (2) the philosophical necessity and political will to suspend judgment of alterity in order to begin a process of cultural negotiations; (3) the recognition and affirmation of "hybridity" as "the central value" of the "incorporative principle" (in other words, acceptance of cultural crossing and the resultant transformations of cultures in contact).[12]

These elements of a "strong" multiculturalism are each more or less present in the texts of Deloria and the others. Deloria, Sioui, Churchill, and Jaimes Guerrero all heavily emphasize the first point. The second is taken up in Deloria ("Criticisms"), as well as in Sioui's preparation of the emotional ground of communication. The third is underscored by the sense of audience for all of these texts: the Amerindian auto-anthropologists are addressing white readers and suggesting the value of incorporating Amerindian perspectives in the so-cial sciences. Sioui, for example, goes so far as to argue that Amerindians, for all of five hundred years, have valued and undertaken the task of " 'American-izing the White Man,' that is, doing everything possible to help this new child discover the essential, primordial wisdom of the new Earth-Mother he had just found" (13). And here, once more, one might want to underscore the typi-cality of such a position within mainstream, "white" anthropological discourse.[13]

Finally, however, there is a fourth component to critical multiculturalism: the understanding that meeting each of the other three terms will not a priori guarantee harmonious interaction among cultural participants.[14] As Christopher Newfield and Avery F. Gordon argue, "the strong version of pluralism . . . de-nies that the many are finally united by the one" (81). Again, this is a tempting formulation, but one that is beyond the edge of the envelope of the Amerindian auto-anthropologists' multicultural schema. Deloria argues that a new anthro-pological methodology should supplant the old one, and this new methodol-ogy's procedure involves using the Indian oral tradition as a constant touchstone. He describes Immanuel Velikovsky's methodology approvingly: Velikovsky, according to Deloria, noted great changes in a local environment, posited dra-matic or even cataclysmic reasons for such change, and then corroborated his speculations by searching the "traditions of tribal peoples" (Deloria, *Red Earth* 47). The most striking feature of each of the Amerindian auto-anthro-pologist's arguments is that the rationale for the preservation of Amerindian "culture" (which is seen as a historically deep, all-encompassing procedure for ascertaining one's relationship to the world and its others) depends on just this sort of already existing judgment of its relative value. The circle, vitalism, relatedness, interdependence, holism, totalism: none of these mental maps have meaning in and of themselves; they have meaning only because such world-views are inherently more attentive to history, more truthful with regard to the reality of the world, and more just with reference to an ultimate politics of harmony and cooperation. Each text gestures toward inclusivity with regard to differences, but each, in turn, results in hierarchical judgments and exclusions.

Nowhere in this auto-anthropology, for example, can one find a justification for any version, or even any part, of white thinking. As a first example, Jaimes Guerrero implies that white knowledge "perpetrate[s] political factionalism and divisiveness," whereas Indian knowledge is "grounded in the principles of intellectual decolonization" (60). Indian thinking, finally, is universal—a "more enlightened comprehension of the affairs of humankind" (59). And in Deloria's *Red Earth* Indian methodology is held to be inherently superior to white for many reasons: white archaeology is almost never correct, particularly concerning original Amerindian occupation or possession of the Americas; Indian knowledges about the deep past are almost always verifiably true. And Deloria's main point is to demonstrate not only that the standpoint and procedure of white science gets everything wrong but also that the gestalt of white science is destructive: Upon arrival, whites unwittingly destroyed American "megafauna" (wooly mammoths, giant bears, giant beavers, and so on)—sacred creatures to the original inhabitants. A science of man that relies in the last instance upon the oral tradition will not only reveal the truth about the deep past but will, in its very essence, promote a nondestructive relationship to the environment. Sioui too says that Indian epistemologies should be assimilated by whites, because the Indian perspective on the world is inherently superior to diseased and destructive white knowledges. For each of these thinkers, auto-anthropology repudiates and supplants the white mind on the basis of its epistemological and political limitations.

There is, finally, no room for negotiation in the writings of the most recent generation of critical multiculturalists. One might suggest that this is not some oversight on their part—some failure to embrace one of the terms, or the final term, of critical multiculturalism—but rather that the thinking of multiculturalism in even its most advanced, progressive formulations is inherently shot through with hierarchies and exclusions. It is theoretically impossible to imagine any version of multiculturalism that would not depend on teleological—or, more insidiously, presuppositional—exclusions in order to ground the possibility of multiculturalism, which is always, and in the last instance, the possibility of a "something in common."

To return to Goldberg for a moment, because his work is careful enough to address this problem: he writes that "the admission of more or less prevalent heterogeneity places a very narrow limit on the desirability of fixity and closure, of the totalized boundedness and inward posture of the homogeneous and common" ("Introduction" 25). And yet he recognizes the need for such a "limit" in principle, and argues that "a renewably critical multicultural commitment would be underpinned by a thin set of common rules of logic and basic inference" (17). The point worth noting here is that Goldberg, along with other theorists of critical multiculturalism, tries to distinguish between exclusions at the level of the *ends* of multiculturalism (multiculturalisms that forecast, in advance, a negotiation that concludes with a just, peaceable, and harmonious world), and a "thin set" of common commitments in order to make communication between different cultural entities possible *in the first place.* All critical multiculturalisms—including those of the Amerindian auto-anthropologists—produce some version of this distinction.

If Goldberg is right, then the problem with recent Amerindian auto-anthropological texts is that they prescribe an end to whiteness before whites reach the bargaining table. The auto-anthropological texts would be fixable: Keeping to a "thin set" of original, common commitments would open them to the possibility of true negotiation of the differences they sketch.

But there can *never,* in principle, be a "narrow limit" to the something-in-common, if one takes arguments about difference seriously—that is, if one accepts that some of the most fundamental differences between cultures are best understood by attention to questions of logic, as Deloria and the others would argue. Any "common rules of logic and basic inference" would render moot the arguments made by the new auto-anthropologists: in each case, that which is said to make auto-anthropology interesting and worthy of study is dependent upon the recognition that Indian epistemology is absolutely alterior to white epistemology because of the very way that it thinks—because of its fundamental logics. If there were *already* a something in common at the level of, say, "logic," there would be no "anti-integrationist" claim worth making. Amerindian auto-anthropology would simply be a *version* of a larger whole: Anthropology in general. It would be a position *within* a field of endeavor rather than a true alternative to it. In other words: Goldberg's minimal foundation for multiculturalism ends up silencing the voices of Deloria and the others.[15]

Or, in reverse, these foundations silence white anthropology, if one adopts the "logic" of antiassimilationist multiculturalism. Perhaps not surprisingly, the very foundations for communication in the Amerindian auto-anthropologists' texts work in precisely this manner. As noted, the ground for Sioui's argument is at least in part an emotional politics: multicultural cross-fertilization begins with the "release of previously stifled emotions that keep people of all

cultures from expressing compassion and respect, producing only guilt and ha-
tred and preventing individuals from seeing their responsibility" (7). In Sioui's
formulation, whites must learn to feel the way that Indians do; they must adopt
Indian patterns of affect. The *condition* for multiculturalism, then, is that all
people feel in precisely the same way. This is an exclusion at the level of emotional life, and one that comes with great consequence if one believes, as many
recent feminists and anthropologists do, that the study of affect is crucial to
the recognition of and respect for differences of all sorts.[16]

In Deloria's auto-anthropological texts, minimal "common rules" are also
in effect. His account of Velikovsky's methodology is one such example. Another concerns Western science's "fragmentation of human knowledge," to the
detriment of holistic thinking and living (*Red Earth* 52). A commitment to
"fram[ing] coherent explanations of the whole," to "surveying the totality of
knowledge" and "bringing it into a coherent and simple explanation which
can be made available to the rest of society," is one of the crucial terms under
which multicultural participants can negotiate (52). This means, quite simply,
that many postmodern or poststructuralist accounts of knowledge formation — any accounts that begin with the questioning of universality, totality,
theory, and even the possibility of truth claims — must be excluded from multicultural community *from the beginning* in order to produce a something-in-
common.[17] In sum, what seem like minimal commitments to some — rules of
inference, healthy emotional responses to pain and tragedy, a desire to draw
together the implications of knowledge formations — are necessarily, to others, invitations to abandon oneself (one's logics and feelings, one's organizing
preconceptions of the world) as one enters the multicultural arena.

Put another way, the minimal conditions under which the bargaining table
and chairs can be assembled are always and necessarily maximally significant
demands concerning the *outcome* of multiculturalism. Thus, despite the fact
that the texts of the modern auto-anthropologists bear all the marks of inclusivity, it is no surprise to find that the contours of whiteness will be purged
from the hybrid identities that make up a more just and inclusive world. There
is no difference, finally, between defining a minimal something-in-common
and a prescriptive, silencing determination of the shape of the world to come.

If the condition of the planet is "strong" cultural difference — understood
in the Amerindian auto-anthropologies as well as in the work of many white

multiculturalists as manifesting itself at all levels of personhood and thought, in terms of affect, logical principles, values, and the like—then incommensurability is "our" terminal condition. Difference *as such* is necessarily nontranslatable, as Deloria argues with respect to Amerindian difference, and he should not, as an Indian, be able in principle to thematize white difference—how it works, thinks, or feels. Given such difference, the possibility of conversation, or, beyond that, negotiation, would depend upon the "death" of that which is other. It could not be hybridized or modified or placed in any relation at all to an-other. The condition of difference necessitates, at the level of social relations, a world premised on *nothing-in-common:* impermeable borders across which nothing, in principle, can pass. Deloria's *Red Earth,* then, must be understood as absolutely *unreadable* to a non-Indian, to the extent that it represents Indianness at all (or, perhaps, unreadable from an Indian subject position, given that the text is written in English and is therefore already what Deloria would demarcate as a necessarily failed translation of Indian matters). Unless, of course, one becomes Indian. (Deloria and Sioui leave the possibility of becoming Indian open, given their multiple references to nonmainstream white scholarship that bolsters their historical claims.)[18] Because the condition that would make possible the reading of the other is the death of one's cultural self. To the extent that the recent Indian auto-anthropological texts seek white readers (and they do), they are requesting cultural dissolution, cultural suicide. *Any politics that begins with difference and ends with multicultural communication and negotiation must necessarily involve the death of all others save one.* Which is to say, that to recognize "strong" difference is already to end the mutuality of communication: Difference is out there somewhere, but it can be neither hailed nor heard. To begin with difference is already to suggest that *each culture is occult and therefore dead to all others.* Ernesto Laclau describes this as the logic of apartheid asserted from the reverse direction (89). Going further, genocide (whether cultural or involving the obliteration of bodies) and cultural incommensurability are two sides of the same coin: a logic in which an-other cannot be valued and cannot even be thematized as different. The world will end as a monoculture, or multiple monocultures. And it makes no difference—not for thinking.

As a further, related point, it has to be assumed for purposes of taking Deloria and the others seriously that they understand themselves as having become fully "white" in their thinking, at least for the purposes of producing their evaluations of white social science. If not, "strong" cultural relativism—or alterity—would prevent such an evaluation. But beyond that, even if one grants the possibility that Deloria, for example, can occupy both white and Indian subjectivities—evaluate both white and Indian epistemologies—the problem of alterity returns when it comes to judging cultures' relative epistemological and political values. Mead's "cultural comparativism" is an impossible creation: One could understand whiteness when one is thinking white and Indianness when one is thinking Indian, but nontranslatability demands that even so ambidextrous a scholar could never bring the two together for the purposes of judgment. One could still never know two cultures within one subjectivity; one literally would be two persons. And each culture would still be dead to all others.

THEMATIZING ORIGINAL RELATIONS

Inescapably, then, antiassimilationist multiculturalism is an anthropological remnant, a project defined and shaped by ethnochauvinism. Deloria's latter-day concept of "culture" suffers precisely from the conditions explored in *Custer Died for Your Sins:* such an anthropology cannot have an object, cannot conceptualize its other, cannot accommodate an-other, can only ask the other to become the same or disappear. This is, for some multicultural theorists, an unacceptable condition, and the exhaustion of the very possibility of inclusiveness in a world of cultures theorized as absolutely different has produced the two most frequently proposed alternatives to such thinking. One argues that cultures are different only in relation to a common humanity. Cultures can successfully be thematized as different because there has always already been a something-in-common: all cultures perform similar tasks (they are "functionalist"), responding to basic human needs and desires. Even nineteenth-century evolutionary anthropology operates in this fashion: Amerindians may be "different," but "they" are really an earlier version of "us," solving problems at a "primitive" rather than "civilized" level. "We" may not like "them" or want to share the world with "them" but "we" can understand "them" because we are them, and they us. This very large something-in-common—our humanity—enables us to negotiate with our relative-others, and mutually to judge what should and should not be part of a shared world. This axis of argument can be identified as *humanist/idealist,* with different theorists tending to emphasize one or the other pole.

Another option involves historicizing or systematizing difference. William Roseberry argues that multiculturalism that relies upon cultural relativism is "conceptually and historically weak and leave[s] us in poor position to understand the central importance of intercultural relations . . . in the making of the modern world" (847). From this perspective, though cultures may look very different, these differences are in reality the products of long interactions among peoples. Roseberry urges multiculturalists to search for "systematic connections, for hierarchy and differentiation" in order to conceptualize diversity and relation at the same time (850). In the strongest formulation of such a position, some scholars argue that culture can only be produced in relation to an other. Something-in-common, then, is guaranteed as soon as there is culture. To put it another way: consciousness of culture is proof of relationship to an other; without an other, one simply could not imagine that one has a culture. Some Marxist frames of reference say the same thing but emphasize that differences are products of class relations within modes of production. To put one version of it crudely: Indians become Indians only in relation to emergent American capitalism. Culture is the product of such power relationships. Cultural identities, therefore, correspond to emplacements/coercions and responses/ resistances within a political-economic totality. One might call this axis of argument *historicist/structuralist.*

Critiques of "difference," "separatist," or "antiassimilationist" multiculturalism are often of one of these two arguments. The humanist/idealist critique, broadly the position sketched out by Tzvetan Todorov in *On Human Diversity,* which he calls "critical humanism" or "well-tempered humanism": we all belong to the "same species"; universal goals such as morality, equity, and justice can be affirmed by all, and the world's diverse cultures can be judged accordingly.[19] Goldberg, who, as has been noted, considers hybridity crucial to the formulation of a strong multiculturalism, is quite sympathetic to the second critique, phrased liberally and historically rather than structurally or from a left viewpoint: "Movement and migration . . . are the defining sociohistorical conditions of humanity," he suggests, and "historically, the human condition is the condition of going and resting" ("Introduction" 22).[20] He posits, then, a world of original differences, quickly usurped by migration-driven hybridity, but he imagines that this process has not gone far enough: "we" are still too much like ourselves — we need more relation with others — and a critical multiculturalism will massively expand the heterogeneous effects of migration. In essence, communication will be the modern (and far more effective) form of migration and transformation. It will forge identity links, in every conceivable direction, that enable the possibility and process of cultural comparison and judgment.

As accounts of difference, both versions of critique seek to overcome the problems of "difference multiculturalism" — what Peter Connor calls "ethnocentrism ... of a more subtly reactionary kind" (240).[21] But where do such critiques come to rest in terms of valuing culture for purposes of producing multicultural community? In Todorov's version of the humanist/idealist argument, which is related to famous multiculturalist formulations by Habermas and Taylor, the emphasis is upon communication, negotiation, and eventual consensus rather than difference. Even though Todorov nods toward valuing difference (culture is essential to "the full development of each individual," and he urges each person to love his or her own culture [*Diversity* 387]), his argument is primarily directed at the problem of cultural relativism: "The relativist inevitably ends up contradicting himself, since he presents his doctrine as absolute truth. ... What is more, a relativist, even a moderate one, cannot denounce any injustice, any violence" (389). Cultural relativism, then, is both illogical and politically dangerous — limit relativism would have to affirm, in principle, clitoridectomies, human sacrifice, and the Nazi holocaust.[22] On the other hand, ideas such as "justice" and "equity" take the entire human race into account: "Universality is an instrument of analysis; a regulatory principle allowing the fruitful confrontation of differences" (390). Ethics demands a "hierarchy of values" about which all can agree and through which cultures can cohabit the world, interact, and alter one another to approach ideals.

As a first point, the notion of cultural relativism that Todorov condemns is simply unthinkable. The very term "relativism" implies a *relationship*; in order for cultures to be "relative," they must be relative to a something that permits them to be seen as equally valid rather than as better and worse, more developed and less developed. That something is the very idea of culture and its absent, codeterminant term, "nature." Thus the foundational assumption of cultural relativism must be that everyone has a culture that operates equivalently to every other culture in relation to human being. McGrane calls this a "paradox" because "if all cultures are democratically relative, then in this respect, in this deep respect, none are different" (118). To put this another way, the work of *comparison* has already begun with the introduction of the term "cultural relativism," which is to say, finally, that all cultural relativisms end up — indeed, begin — as "cultural comparativisms."

But to focus on what Todorov forecasts, at least two further problems can be raised. Todorov himself presents both of these in a modest way. First, his argument depends upon ideals having particular and unchanging contents, at least to the extent that one can judge between more just and less just social formations, more equitable and less equitable resource distributions, and so on. This is a fallacy as old as Platonism, frequently remarked upon in postmetaphysical philosophy. Todorov admits something of this when he says that a universal principle's content "cannot be fixed: it is always subject to revision" (*Diversity* 390). But, for Todorov it appears that even though universality is not achievable in principle (it is an absent totality), it can be endlessly approximated: The world can become increasingly more just without ever entirely reaching "justice" as such. There is, then, only one "justice" in the world. This argument refuses to acknowledge that patriarchy appears "just" to some, holocausts to others, capitalism to still others. One might argue, in fact, that no concept of justice could ever exist without a competing version of it. Todorov's formulation depends upon the ideal in which justice has the same meaning for all. But justice inevitably involves censure (as Todorov acknowledges), and this means, in addition, the censure of alternative conceptions of justice. There will be one "justice" in Todorov's multicultural world only because all other versions of justice have been suppressed. This is not an approximation of justice as such but, at best, a hegemonic justice. Laclau has written persuasively that the problem that is universalism is always, necessarily, linked to arguments concerning particularity, and vice versa. Neither can be thought without the other (87). In Laclau's formulation, universalism is nothing more than "democratic interaction" of particularities, which is to say that universality may be an ideal but it is also the same thing as *struggle* (90). It is a paradoxical formulation that cannot be distinguished from, in the most generous terms, consent through persuasion.[23] Again, most generously, the price of universalism is democratic suppression of politically minoritarian conceptions of uni-versals.[24] There would be no guarantee — and, in principle, it would be impos-sible to imagine — that struggle would "disappear" or be "suspended" because "social forces which lose out in any particular historical period" remain part of the field of cultural relations (Hall 14). And there would be no guarantee that a particular hegemonic conception of "justice" would not emerge in the shape of holocausts of one sort or another.

A second, related point: Todorov's teleological horizon is, inevitably, mono-cultural. Space is left in his formulation for differences about which no one cares — differences that are ethically indifferent to everyone — but it is diffi-cult to understand what such differences might be. Culture understood as ten-dencies with respect to food or clothing, for example, might easily be sub-jected to censure on the basis of an expanding, universalist ethics — think of vegetarianism or environmentalism as portions of an expanding conception of world justice. There is no domain into which such an ethics will not trespass. But monoculture, like a singular notion of justice, is an impossibility, and for precisely the same reasons. A "strong" culture can only be formed in the pres-ence of other such cultures, and Chantal Mouffe, among others, has argued that the rise of identity politics (what she calls the "new social movements") are in fact a structural response to the increasing imposition of unification and uniformity at the level of social life — itself a product of global capitalist-media monoculture (Mouffe 93). In other words, the stronger Todorov's cultural center becomes, the stronger the cultural periphery. The more definition his universalist culture achieves, the more dramatic will be oppositional cultures founded upon other versions of his universal values or other relative weight-ings of his network of values. The more a "well-tempered humanism" achieves, the larger the implications for increasingly diversifying cultural spaces. In general, that is, "ideals" are the same thing as "values" and affirmation of val-ues — which is the minimal condition for culture — always produces and mul-tiplies competing cultures rather than mediates them.

The historicist/structuralist accounts of relational difference tend to err on the other side of the cultural values problem — making the most of difference rather than attempting difference's reduction — but such historicist/structuralist approaches get no further than Todorov, for example, toward negotiating uni-versals and particulars with equal care. Indeed, despite strong claims to the contrary, historicist/structuralist accounts of difference tend to reinforce the most common commonplaces from anthropological narratives of modernity. Again using Roseberry and Goldberg as examples, both texts emphasize in the strongest possible terms *the limits of difference:* Roseberry goes so far as to suggest that "the [cultural] traditions themselves have been forged in unequal and power-laden contexts" (849). But both suggest that the solution to the problem that is difference depends upon recrossing the boundaries of distinction in order to mix and multiply identity formations. The explicit values set forth are "creativity and inventiveness," the "new," and "variety" (Roseberry 858) and "irrepressible" heterogeneity and animation, novel expression, and "vigor" (Goldberg, "Introduction" 28, 33). Goldberg explains in greatest detail why such values matter: They are human essences, affirmations of life (which links his argument to humanist strains of multicultural thought), and they "multipl[y] in number and quality the available nature and range of knowledge and practical wisdom" (32).[25] In both Goldberg and Roseberry, too, it is implicit that this hybridity overcomplicates traditional cultural categories, making them unusable for racist and ethnocentrist programs. The more cultures that exist, and the more entangled they become, the less likely it is that one can be set against another.

Granting the logic of the concept of hybridity (whose history is enmeshed in a very old project of colonial biology, as Robert J. C. Young has mapped in *Colonial Desire*), one might wonder whether hybrid multiplicities result not in fusion or confusion (tolerance by means of the difficulty of locating cultures) but, rather, in a simple expansion of the field of difference. That is, the so-called inter- or bicultural phenomenon is immediately and always already formed into yet *another culture* situated within the field of original relations. And such multiplication of cultures results not in less purchase or hold for inflection, hierarchization, and chauvinism but, following a Foucauldian analysis of dominance through self-identification, more.

Furthermore, at the moment that multiculturalist argumentation brings forth *examples* of successful and interesting hybridization, the full implications of hybridity analysis become apparent: the thought of the hybrid, rather than confounding essentialisms, promotes them through an inner logic that presumes that there were (and are) cultural essences from which to begin. That is, hybridity utterly recapitulates anthropology. Hybridity analysis, in short, may multiply cultures, may multiply heterogeneity, but only within a larger and very traditional anthropological frame. For instance, hybrid multiculturalist emphasis on "vigor" and "variety" locates such work within a nineteenth-century biological framework.

In a first example, Peter McLaren's lead piece in Goldberg's *Multiculturalism* collection, the critique of "essentialist" multiculturalism is expressed in postmodern, relational terms (that is, he is broadly "structuralist" in his approach to the problem of sameness and difference), and he argues for the value of hybrid identities, which, along with many other theorists, he finds forming in the U.S. cultural "borderlands": the U.S. Southwest/Mexican border region. Like border studies theorists Renato Rosaldo, D. Emily Hicks, or Gloria Anzaldúa (he cites the last two), he suggests that borderlands identities are inherently "critically utopian": he describes them as "anti-capitalist" and "counter-hegemonic" (66).[26] But his description of the force of hybridization, in his final paragraph, is indistinguishable from romantic-racist discourse:

> The sounds produced in the borderlands are quite different from the schizophrenic boundaries of Weber's iron cage. Here it is in the *hybrid polyrhythms of the drum* that the new pulse of freedom can be felt. Within such borderlands our pedagogies of liberation can be invested once again with the *passion of mystery* and the reason of commitment. This is neither a Dionysian rejection of rationality nor a blind, prerational plunge into myth but rather an attempt to embrace and reclaim the memories of *those pulsating, sinewed bodies* that have been forgotten in our modernist assault on difference and uncertainty. (Emphasis added; 69)

This is a passage shot through with descriptions straight from *National Geographic:* McLaren's description of the borderland's rhythms, passions, and pulsations belongs, in fact, to a tradition of anthropological and proto-anthropological longing for the "primitive" that is as old as the European migrations and voyages beyond its understood boundaries. And the predetermined, anthropological character of the other in his description is only magnified by McLaren's placing of "Africanist" "jungle-isms" at the U.S.-Mexican border. McLaren's text, furthermore, is nothing if not ambivalent in terms of its identity politics: praising the other-of-the-other (borderlands personhood) even as it diminutes it. McLaren's main point is that whites, or moderns, need an application of color, a dose of premodern "rhythm" or vitality, just as a plant specialist might argue that a weak species needs to be grafted to a strong stock or an animal specialist might claim that an inbred species needs fresh genes.

James Clifford's prominent work operates in reverse, but the point is much the same: he celebrates "hybrid and subversive forms" and an "inventive future" for the world's other cultures, understood as originally alterior but increasingly "lost" and "literally murdered" (Clifford, *Predicament* 17, 16). As an example of creative survival, he quotes Ulf Hannerz on Africans:

> The people in my favorite Nigerian town drink Coca Cola, but they drink *burukutu* too; and they can watch *Charlie's Angels* as well as Hausa drummers on the television sets which spread rapidly as soon as electricity has arrived. (17, n. 6)

Clifford notes that his book's "utopian, persistent hope for the re-invention of difference risks downplaying the destructive, homogenizing effects of global economic and cultural centralization," but such is the risk if one's project and "primary goal is to open space for cultural futures" (15). Clifford affirms, then, the penetration of the Third World by the Coca Cola Company and Hollywood because the result is "difference"—because "pollination" and "transplanting" are taking place—even as "futures" markets reorder the world. Clifford's "risk," then, his bet or investment, is that capitalism's hybridizing essence—that is, its multiplication of consumptions premised on multiple identities—is better than the world's "traditional orders" (15). His version of multiculturalism involves saving space on television for drums at seven in the evening, but only if *Charlie's Angels* comes on at eight. And the very appearance, here, of jungle "drums" yet again should produce reason for caution: Clifford's example temporalizes colonial relations in highly familiar ways, plays on established stereotypes (drums versus television, primitive versus modern), in order to specify the results of hybridization.

In such ways, the recent emphasis on hybridity in multiculturalist theory and cultural theory in general, as Young has argued, amounts to "repeating the past"—reiterating a colonial discourse that relied on "hybridity" for purposes of distinguishing, separating, and dominating "races" (Young 27–28). It is the very thought of the hybrid, finally, that grounds the possibility of demarcating new and old, modernity and its others. Rather than dislocating colonial representations and producing multicultural justice, the work of the hybrid conditions and determines hierarchical identities in precisely the same fashion as did nineteenth-century anthropology. Renato Rosaldo, in criticizing García Canclini's call for hybridization of "modern" and "traditional" cultures in Latin America (and, it should be remarked, García Canclini's examples suffer from precisely the same problems as McLaren's and Clifford's), notes its dependance on conceptualizations of "zones of purity": "Hybridity [is] all the way down," Rosaldo counterargues, but such a view would logically make the culture concept impossible, would force upon anthropology a project of entirely negative reflection concerning "how ideological zones of cultural purity . . . have been constructed" (Rosaldo, "Foreword" xv).

MARXISMS

Marxisms may not be the most obvious place to search for an alternative to multiculturalism's exclusions. Indeed, and at the risk of simplification, one might suggest that there are two Marxist accounts of anthropology: one that accepts anthropology's insights, from the nineteenth century onward, and enfolds them within an account of historical modes of production, and a second that dismisses anthropological knowledges about enduring races and cultures as a misunderstanding of what are, in actuality, effects of world capitalism.[27] The first, in which Marx and Engels dabbled in their later work,[28] is easily subjected to the same critiques as anthropology in general. The second, however, comes with its own set of complications, because the codetermining of capitalism and anthropology, or late capitalism and multiculturalism, implies that the "ends" of capitalism — its beginning or its conclusion — would necessarily resolve or limit the problem that is anthropology.[29]

The examples of Fredric Jameson and Immanuel Wallerstein are instructive: There is broad agreement between the two on the question of why multiculturalism or "antisystemic movements" (Wallerstein 11) or the "micropolitics" of "small-group nonclass political practices" (Jameson, *Postmodernism* 318) have emerged in recent years. They both date such movements to the 1960s and argue that "the new social movements and the newly emergent global proletariat both result from the prodigious expansion of capitalism in its third (or 'multinational') stage" (Jameson, *Postmodernism* 319). Wallerstein and Jameson thus both read the assertion of cultural "traditions" as historically shallow, historically specific reactions to political-economic developments that are generally contemporaneous with such assertions. (This, perhaps, is not a problem in and of itself, but it becomes one once one recognizes that the "new social movements" are anthropological through and through and thus owe their concepts and trajectories to far longer histories of colonialism and anthropology.) Wallerstein additionally emphasizes that recent assertions of culture and their use as political weapons are "expressions of the structural constraints" of global capital accumulation: "In particular, they derive from the antinomy that is constituted by the existence of multiple states within the bounds of a single social division of labor, the capitalist world-economy" (Wallerstein 139). The word choices are worth elaborating: "result," "expressions," and "derive from." Modern "cultures" are produced on the periphery of and in response to and in relation to a "center" culture (what Wallerstein calls "geoculture"), which is itself the manifestation of and the undergirding for global capitalism (11). The mode of production determines, or at least sets in motion, the production of oppositional cultures.[30]

These are totalizing accounts of the problem of culture — accounts that resolve the culture crisis by subordinating culture to socialist "History." That is: Jameson and Wallerstein broadly accept a structural account of identity but resolve the tensions found in multicultural hybrid theory by subsuming them in a larger totality that organizes and "relates the relations." If Jameson and Wallerstein are correct as to the relationship between culture and political economy, it would logically follow that socialism would make identity politics (and, therefore, multiculturalism) obsolete. But Wallerstein and Jameson in addition have taken up a seemingly more complex problem, which is the potential for something like multiculturalism to contribute to the foundation for socialism.

On this ground both thinkers waver, and an exploration in some detail of Jameson's multiple readings of this problem will prove instructive for re/deconceptualizing the limits of multiculturalism.[31] Jameson has written at great length on ethnocultural matters: briefly but importantly in *The Political Unconscious* (1981), much more broadly in *Postmodernism* (1991), and rather infamously in a related text, "Third-World Literature in the Era of Multinational Capitalism" (1986). Significant transformations in his thought took place in the ten years between *The Political Unconscious* and *Postmodernism.* In the former, Jameson writes approvingly of the study of "folk" culture:

> Since by definition the cultural monuments and masterworks that have survived tend necessarily to perpetuate only a single voice in this class dialogue, the voice of a hegemonic class, they cannot be properly assigned their relational place in a dialogical system with the restoration or artificial construction of the voice to which they were initially opposed, a voice for the most part stifled and reduced to silence, marginalized, its own utterances scattered to the winds, or reappropriated in their turn by the hegemonic culture.
>
> This is the framework in which the reconstruction of so-called popular cultures must properly take place — most notably from the fragments of essentially peasant cultures: folk songs, fairy tales, popular festivals, occult or oppositional systems of belief such as magic and witchcraft.... But ... only an ultimate rewriting of these utterances in terms of their essentially polemic and subversive strategies restores them to their proper place in the dialogical system of the social classes. (*Unconscious* 85–86)

And he goes on:

> Popular narrative from time immemorial — romance, adventure story, melodrama, and the like — is ceaselessly drawn on to restore vitality to an enfeebled and asphyxiating "high culture." Just so, in our own time, the vernacular and its still vital sources of production (as in black language) are reappropriated by the exhausted and media-standardized speech of a hegemonic middle class. (*Unconscious* 86–87)

In part, these remarks are reminiscent of nineteenth-century theoretical statements about the value of folklore studies. His choice of the word "folk," for example, is interesting in itself, and his concern with the "vitality" of the objects of analysis places him perilously close to antimodern romancing of peasant knowledges and utterances. It marks him as a liberal, "hybridizing" anthropologist.[32] The axes of distinction between literary classics and the texts of cultural anthropologists are those of death versus life and modern versus folk.

Later, in "Third-World Literature," Jameson's affirmation is far more qualified. Colonial and postcolonial texts are here described as related to First World literature by "inversion": the former is allegorical and presents questions of "psychology" in "primarily political and social terms," whereas in Marcel Proust or James Joyce, for example, "political commitment is recontained and psychologized or subjectivized by way of the public-private split" (72, 71). The result is that Western representational practices are "epistemologically crippling," whereas Third World texts take up the burden of "the whole laborious telling of the experience of the collectivity itself" (86). Here, the axes of distinction are private versus public and allegory versus psychology.

Finally, in *Postmodernism*, Jameson argues that the rise of ethnicity as politics is nothing more than yuppies' nostalgia for real people and that ethnicity is not nostalgia for class politics but " 'nostalgia' for politics *tout court*" (*Postmodernism* 342, 331). It is "offensive," he argues, and politically visionless: "There are no levers for them to control and not much in the way of production for them to manage. Only the media and the market are visible as autonomous entities" (349). This is the same point that Wallerstein makes: the "culture" of the "antisystemic movements" is "the capitalist world-economy" (180). And here the axis of distinction is elided: the new social movements, according to Jameson, are liberal capitalist through and through—they are virtually one with the system—and cultural difference is nothing but a category of consumption.[33] "It is felt that something precious and existential, something fragile and unique about our own singularity, will be lost irretrievably when we find out that we are just like everybody else. In that case, so be it: we might as well know the worst" (*Postmodernism* 343).

A possible rebuttal to this analysis would argue that Jameson, in these three texts, is writing about quite different things: in order, folk or popular culture, colonial culture, and mass culture. One might also argue that Jameson is talking about the different sorts of cultures that emerge out of different political economies, as well: the first and second being at least partially the products of "primitive, or tribal society," "the Asiatic mode of production, or the great bureaucratic imperial systems," and the third clearly a product of late capitalism and the culture of postmodernism ("Third-World Literature" 68). To some degree, Jameson does draw these distinctions, but any distinction he might draw between these categories will be difficult to sustain: "Third-World Literature," for example, implicitly draws analogies between Third World texts and the mass cultural productions of Dashiell Hammett, as Clint Burnham notes (Burnham 154). And, with regard to *The Political Unconscious,* it would be impossible to uphold a distinction between the "folk" and the production of the "folk" through the thoroughly modern discipline of folklore studies. Folklorism is nothing if not part of the consumption of difference that Jameson decries in *Postmodernism.*

A more plausible reading of Jameson's writings on culture is that the status of "other" cultures gradually shifts along the arc of the 1980s and early 1990s, with the concept of "culture" beginning its journey as the lifeblood of vitalist folk who inhabit a different time in history and, relatively, a different mode of production from "ours"[34] and reaching its dead end in *Postmodernism* when understood as presentist. A crucial aspect of Aijaz Ahmad's critique of Jameson's "Third-World Literature" hinged on this issue, denying Jameson's argument that there *is* a "Third World" that can be separated from the First on the basis of a different weighting of imbricated modes of production (Ahmad 103). Capitalism dominates the globe, then, and to argue otherwise is to indulge in yet another version of imperialist nostalgia.

As Jameson's perspective — his reading of the timing of "culture" — shifts, his understanding of its political significance does as well, as the passages cited above implicitly reveal. In *The Political Unconscious* "folk" texts are "polemic and subversive," seemingly inherently so by virtue of their positioning opposite "hegemonic" texts, and the "vernacular" are "still vital sources of production," even "in our own time." Even within capitalism, the "folk" bear something that is useful, even "vital," in the war of position. *"Still vital sources of production"*: The use of the term "production" highlights the importance of this formulation, and it contrasts sharply with Jameson's later figuring of ethnicity as "consumption." In "Third-World Literatures," by contrast, Jameson figures ethnic/cultural identification ambiguously. He argues that such identification is a version of the problem of nationalism and that sometimes " 'cultural identity' has powerful and revolutionary consequences," "which may not obtain" once the revolution has come to be ("Third-World Literature" 78). A commitment to the study of "concrete historical situation[s]" means that "culture" has no necessarily positive or negative consequences for purposes of equalitarian struggle. But in this text, as well, Jameson explicitly commits himself to the demarcation of "difference," disagreeing with Edward Said that "differentiation" is the "mechanism" of colonial othering ("Third-World Literature" 77).

Once Jameson wrote *Postmodernism,* however, it might be argued that he had dismantled his own desire to establish differences. At one point, for example, he seems to be arguing that there is no legitimate difference between understanding culture as part of capitalism's *system* or as the *agency* that opposes it. Both statements are equally true (*Postmodernism* 326). And this results in a pronounced pessimism in his text. For example, he writes that in the face of the new micropolitics, "the only 'genuine politics' is to watch closely the withering of totalizing politics" (*Postmodernism* 330). Here Jameson represents himself as some gloomy owl of Minerva, keeping watch over a very dark moment when the political field could not be more differentiated and scattered in terms of the identity positions within the field (that is, capitalism) and when the positions themselves hold little promise for revolutionary change.

But perhaps it is useful to go back to the last text in *The Political Unconscious* — "The Dialectic of Utopia and Ideology" — in order to think about culture in another way (and, perhaps, not the way Jameson intends in this essay). Jameson here argues that, on the one hand, "cultural production" is always bound up with "class dynamics" — it participates, inevitably, in the formation of class differences, in the structuration of the parts of the social totality (*Unconscious* 292). On the other, he suggests that all cultural productions necessarily express a "collective" or "Utopian" longing that prefigures, allegorically, "a classless society" (293). Jameson says that in a truly utopian world, such a distinction between "ideological" and "Utopian" readings of culture (or "functional-instrumental" and "collective" readings) "will have become a false one" (293). That is, "collective" culture is not imaginable according to the terms by which culture is described in a class society. What might culture look like, then, in a world without a class structure? Even the "Durkheimian or Lukácsean vocabulary of collective consciousness," whose importance Jameson affirms, are nothing but "imperfect allusion . . . to the as yet untheorized object — the collective" (294). And such vocabularies are necessarily ideological; as Jameson claims in *Postmodernism,* even the most "purely critical operation . . . can nonetheless generate the ideological illusion or mirage of a position, a system, a set of positive values in its own right" (*Postmodernism* 393).

The point—which Jameson made several times in writing about science fiction's utopian literatures prior to *The Political Unconscious*[35]—is that the condition of classlessness is unrepresentable: no cultural production can do more than incompletely allegorize it while at the same time constructing and representing class difference (that is: all cultural productions contribute to a social system of differential relations). In other words, though allegories of utopia can be read as approximately classless (as Jameson does), they can equally well be read as hopelessly partial and ideological—prescriptive and dominating—and they can be examined for all of the sorts of exclusions that multicultural theory necessarily produces (again as Jameson does). One possible reading, then, of the implication of Jameson's text is that in a classless society representation of community would cease, cultural production of community would cease. The condition of classlessness—of absolute equality— could not sustain culture, given culture's limit condition of relating to an-other.

And one could only imagine this under the more general condition of the end or the death of the subject. Jameson, as noted briefly above, has been critical of Marxist theory's too easy "assimilation of the consciousness of the individual subject to the dynamic of groups" (*Unconscious* 294). Put another way, a key problem for socialist theory is the "Hegelian move" by which such theory "claim[s] to retain the new richness of individual subjectivity developed under the market system" on behalf of the collective subject (*Postmodernism* 380). To the extent that Jameson has affirmed the "death of the subject," the death of "inner-directed individualism,"[36] any account of collectivity that affirms the collective's (and the collective's members') development of human potentialities—the completion of such, their richness, or even their expression—must also be deconstructed if one seeks to think Jameson through to his logical conclusion. In other words, retaining an individual or collective subject's *identity* within a theory of the condition or consciousness of classlessness marks the theory as epistemologically naive, as politically an expression of the present mode of production, and, of course, as *productive of difference itself*. To break with the "subject," or the culture of the subject, is crucial to Jameson's strategy for overcoming or destabilizing the culture that is capitalism, and this necessarily means breaking with the "group" or "community" *as such* (and, of course, their cultures) because, as Foucault argued, the group is nothing but the individual subject writ large. To rethink the problem of community, then, and particularly of a classless one, is to rethink subjectivity. Subjects and their identities — including their group or cultural identities — must wither in order to conceptualize radical equality.

Given that in *Postmodernism* Jameson eliminates the possibility that "culture," expressed through micropolitics, might serve some useful purpose on the way to classlessness, it appears that the politics of culture has little to no revolutionary value in a Jamesonian frame. And even if one could imagine that culture does have some useful, agential force — if one could read it in liberal-functional terms as a series of "responses to infrastructural realities" and "attempts to resolve . . . fundamental contradictions," as Jameson strives to in "Third-World Literature" — it manages to "outlive" these "situations" and become "part of the new problem" ("Third-World Literature" 78).[37] A cultural revolution, then, will only lead to the need to revolt against culture.

"Custer" Dies, and "Indians," Too

Brought to such a powerful impasse, it is Marxism's — and, indeed, any thought system's — frequent recourse to totalization that must be rethought. Socialism as the *sum* of human history, as the achievement of the ends of man; and multiculturalism, as the sum of our differences, as the positive account of all of our values, *necessarily must be reconceptualized as the condition of classnessness irreconcilable with such counting.* If socialism is nothing but a totality of beings, its project with respect to beings can never amount to anything more inclusive than multiculturalist difference (which is nothing but totality under a different guise). Political projects of difference and of sameness and of sameness in difference and of difference in sameness all run up against the same limit, which exposes their inherent violence. *Indeed, the possibility of community without exclusion cannot be founded on the positive contents of persons; it can only be founded on the un(ac)countable exteriority of singular beings,* as Jean-Luc Nancy has argued (*Inoperative,* chap. 1). Classlessness begins necessarily without presuppositions or determinations of persons, "without human beings *defined* at all," and this prescription includes even the most sophisticated versions of intersubjective accounts of being, as Nancy argues, and as the preceding analysis demonstrates with respect to a multiculturalism founded on original relations (Nancy, *Inoperative* 2). The possibility of a something-in-common without exclusion depends entirely on a sharing or "compearing" of singular beings' finitude(s). In other words, all that is shared is each being's singular relationship to "my existence outside myself" (26). Analogously, as Giorgio Agamben has written with respect to the problem of nations, the condition of a community without exclusion is something akin to "reciprocal extraterritoriality" (164).

This is decidedly a thought on an entirely different terrain from anthropology, from multiculturalism, for which culture is always an object thematized in relation to *the different and the same,* rather than to *the exterior and the singular.* The former are nothing but projects of expulsion and domination, and the latter, thought together, amount to sharing without positive similitude. In order to imagine radical equalitarianism, the production of culture—which is anthropology—must find a stop. "Custer" must die, and therefore so must "Indians."

For example, with regard to the recent tradition of auto-anthropology, it is tempting to critique the type of argument made in Deloria's *Red Earth* from the perspective of his earlier book, *Custer.* It is often the case that foundational documents that inaugurate a strong line of thinking are more internally reflexive and rigorously unforgiving than those that come after. Deloria, in his later work, appears to have distanced himself from nearly all of his most crucial insights regarding the practices of anthropology. For example, his grounding of Indian identity on an enduring "oral tradition" has been a crucial prop in anthropology's attempt to "folk" the Indian, and his homogenization and totalization of Amerindian identity creates an "ideal Indian" every bit as much as does mainstream anthropology. It is an act of exclusion or representational violence directed at any Indian who might not accept an epistemology grounded in "life" and "relation."[38] Deloria's identity politics in *Red Earth* has merged with long-standing romantic traditions of representation, traditions that Renato Rosaldo and George Collier, among others, refer to as "imperial nostalgia" and whose racist potentialities Deloria had underlined in *Custer.*[39]

At the level of identity formation, then, Deloria denies what he claims all Indians have always understood: that "all things" are "related." If true, Indian epistemology and therefore Indian identity would have to be related to its other—to Western scientific orthodoxy and white identity. That is: red and white (read as color, race, culture, or even class-based differences), structural (relation-oriented) and nonstructural (object- or agency-oriented) knowledges, and so on. One might argue, for example, that the sort of relational knowledge claimed for Indians by the Indian auto-anthropologists is nothing but the *same* insight produced by strong white anthropology and sociology in its Marxist and structuralist traditions. And, further, the ever turning and returning "circle" is a version of the Western, pre-Christian philosophy of time, reinvigorated in modern times by Nietzsche and others. Recent accounts of Indian epistemology and cosmology, then, are reminiscent of both old and new Western traditions of thinking—sometimes discredited, marginal, or nearly forgotten traditions, admittedly, but never alterior to the West, never not already internal to the traditions of the West. But in *Red Earth* Deloria disarticulates the representation of Indianness from whiteness, resulting in just another form of "Indianism."

All of which is a negative way to indicate the power of Deloria's original line of questioning, in *Custer,* which denied both the intellectual possibility and the political utility of demarcating the "Indian." *The Limits of Multiculturalism* returns, then, to such questions, in order to reinvestigate and reinvigorate this critique. As soon as whites begin to conceptualize Indians (and themselves), and as soon as Indians begin to conceptualize whites (and themselves), it is already too late to imagine a real difference. For thinking, it was always "too late." And as multiculturalism's promise recedes—as its hope for the resolution of difference through increasing assertion or hybridization or communication of culture or some combination is recognized, even in its strongest and most progressive formulations, as just another liberal politics of exclusion— "another" approach becomes possible. Without anthropology, the world would indeed be a "poorer" place, at least in terms of identity. And that may be precisely its promise.

But what has been fancied as life in the forest, has had no little resemblance to those Utopian schemes of government and happiness
which rather denote the human mind run mad.

— HENRY ROWE SCHOOLCRAFT,

THE MYTH OF HIAWATHA (1856)

How do "we" get to Amerindia, as such, to Amerindia without "whites," to a
space or time of Amerindian voices separate and distinct from colonialism?
There is, finally, *only one way:* Daniel K. Richter's magisterial history of early
Iroquois politics and identity, *The Ordeal of the Longhouse* (1992), moves
from the deep past (approximately A.D. 1000) forward: "The story perhaps
best begins in the beginning," reads the first line of the text (8). Richter is able
to accomplish this feat through the process that historians call " 'upstreaming,' that is, the interpretation of historical sources in light of ethnological and
folkloric materials collected in later periods; one moves 'up' the historical
stream from a better to a less well documented era" (5).

Richter's work in this regard discovers Amerindians of "sublimely" "spiritual
unity" (7) — "busy," "calm," "warm," "peaceful" (18). This is a world of "nu-
clear families" linked by an "ethic of sharing and reciprocity" (19), an "upside-
down capitalism" in which leaders competed to "give the most away" (22). To
give this its proper name, Richter's Iroquois society is "liberal communitarian," a kind of cross between Andrew Carnegie's "Gospel of Wealth" and the
sense of American lower-middle-class values expressed by Christopher Lasch
in *The True and Only Heaven.* And this is, above all, an Amerindian society of
"consensus," a "noncompetitive" and "noncoercive society" that, in Richter's
most remarkable claim, engaged in a series of terrible wars against neighbors
only because their neighbors failed to live up to Iroquois values of reciprocity or
gift giving (22, 45, 40, 49). Algonquian peoples, then, from an Iroquois perspective, simply were not generous enough to justify their continued existence.

Richter's book absolutely *belongs* to the anthropological tradition of read-ing the "West" and its "others" in terms of the opposition of a restricted to a general economy—a tradition over which the work of Marcel Mauss, more than anyone, presides, a tradition that still exerts a hold over anthropology in both its most sophisticated and its popular guises, and a tradition that has come un-der increasing scrutiny as a colonial invention and a postcolonial moraliza-tion.[1] This might be enough to give one pause. But if one looks at the previous generation's major statement on Iroquois identity, Anthony F. C. Wallace's *The Death and Rebirth of the Seneca* (1969), a far stranger problem becomes apparent: Wallace imagines Iroquois men to have been maximally competitive individualists, in need of psychic healing—the very opposite of the Iroquois in Richter's account. Wallace produced, for the 1960s, the Iroquois as the straw men of the New Left men's movement; Richter's Iroquois, on the other hand, would be perfectly comfortable in a New Age spirituality group. The very fact that Richter and Wallace are *both* moralizing about community and acquisi-tiveness, with the Iroquois positioned in polar opposite ways, should make one suspicious of the production of cultural history. Each generation, one might conclude, gets the "Indians" it needs or wants.[2] The Mayans, at the hands of archaeologists, have traversed a reverse path since the 1960s, with a pacific narrative of the Maya gradually displaced by the now dominant view of Linda Schele and others (see Schele and Freidel, for example) of Mayans locked into cycles of dynastic war. The possibility and, indeed, the frequency of such shifts of position along a political continuum ought to convince one, at the very least, that anthropology is neither progressive nor even epistemic in the Kuhnian sense of unrelated, shifting paradigms; rather, it exists in a more radi-cal space, without an object through which it can ground its claims, with its representations "up for grabs" in a larger political war of position. The varied and conflicting positions that "Indians" have held in anthropological narratives, even in the last generation or two, necessitate an absolute vigilance to the matter of renewed attempts to reposition "Indians" properly.

Not surprisingly, Richter's account depends upon an Iroquois identity that perseveres over time; all upstreamed anthropology operates in this manner and presumes, for instance, a stable oral tradition.[3] Iroquois identity is "flexi-ble," Richter concedes, but "perdurable" (3). He says that "core traditional values" "survived" the whole of colonization—that the Iroquois of A.D. 1000 are the *same* people who were Iroquois in the middle sixteenth century and the late twentieth (4). There is a "rock of traditional rituals," a "spiritual... unity," that transcends history, even hundreds of years of encounter history. And Iroquois identity, focused on the spiritual, manages to exclude everything else as secondary or even utterly marginal to itself, such as the colonial, the diplomatic, the economic, the political, the juridical, the sexual.[4]

As anthropology, this gesture—the centering of the identity of the other around the spirit world and religion in general—is very old and has been questioned by anthropologists. Talal Asad, as one example, has recently attempted to "problematize the idea of an anthropological definition of religion by assigning that endeavor to a particular history of knowledge and power (including a particular understanding of our legitimate past and future)" (*Genealogies* 54). As a colonial morality tale, it is ambivalent: the other is either more elevated (less debasedly secular) or more primitive (more superstitious), depending upon whether the anthropology in question is romantic or evolutionary. Either way, such a presentation radically simplifies and types the anthropological object, othering and simultaneously disciplining in the strictest manner.

But the stakes of such narratives, which are already high, are raised to another level when one moves onto the terrain of anthropological dialogue across the red/white color line. Here, two recent texts, read in conjunction, prove instructive: Oren Lyons and John Mohawk's collection, *Exiled in the Land of the Free* (1992), and Sam D. Gill's *Mother Earth* (1987). Both texts rely more subtly on upstreaming; in both cases, the scholars primarily attempt to read an existing documentary record of red/white relations. Yet the problem of upstreaming remains impossible to avoid, given the ambition of the arguments.

Both Lyons and Mohawk claim Iroquois identity as well as identity as American Studies scholars at SUNY-Buffalo. They contend that the framers of the Articles of Confederation and the U.S. Constitution sought "to take the applicable principles of the visible Indian democracy" in constructing the polity of the United States (Lyons 33). In order to make this contention stick, Mohawk argues that *no* intellectual traditions of the European Enlightenment harbored ideas of equality: "No important political thinker of the seventeenth century proposed a government representative of the population to be governed" (Mohawk, "Democracy" 68). And all ideas of equality, of radical democracy, emanated then from "the Indian camp fire" (69). As one example, "the origin" of the natural rights ideas in the Declaration of Independence, says Mohawk, "is clearly rooted in exchanges with the Indians" (71). And though Mohawk concludes that Amerindian politics is merely "one of the streams" of the Constitution and the Bill of Rights, this argument is of a piece with that of Lyons, who concludes that everything in the Constitution that is *not* Iroquois amounts to a compromising of (Iroquois) League principles, mortgaging them to "private property interest" (Lyons 33).

The language Lyons uses to suggest an Iroquois League origin for all major U.S. political ideals is indeed striking: Iroquois polity is organized around "freedom from coercion," "free speech" and the "individual . . . right to voice an opinion," freedom of dissent ("free to disagree"), "participatory democracy," concepts of "peace" and the "just," states' rights, and in general a deep "tradition of democratic thought." Iroquois democracy was a "revolution" similar to the American Revolution. It was designed to promote such bourgeois ideas as "healthy minds and bodies" and rational "clear thinking" as opposed to "confuse[d]" emotionality.[5] At the limit of this sort of rhetoric, Lyons argues that the Iroquois conceptualized a version of multiculturalism, "the Haudenosaunee principle of respect for the laws and customs of different cultures," which amounts to a politics of "the right of peoples and their societies to be different" (42).

The implication of Lyons's and Mohawk's collection in terms of a politics of identity is clear: Amerindia literally *invented* the humanistic, bourgeois, democratic individual. Everything most crucial for modern U.S. self-identity and self-ideality is, in fact, an Iroquois cultural construction, and U.S. personhood, then, is Iroquois through and through.

Sam Gill's *Mother Earth* makes the grand counterclaim, contending that everything most central to a pan-Indian spiritual identity—that is, the very idea of the earth as a mother, and therefore the whole of the modern Amerindian sense of religion, of nature worship, of the stewardship of the environment, and of a kind of deep ecologism—is in fact part of the cultural baggage of Europe. Gill reads John Smith's story of Pocahontas, for example, as the invention of the first Amerindian "earth mother." Once Smith publishes his tale, "the seeds are thus sown. The conception of Mother Earth in North America has taken place" (Gill 39). And though Gill will go on to argue that Amerindians have altered the Mother Earth concept in creative, "reasoned," and even "sophisticated" ways (64), the bulk of his story concerns the constant imposition of the idea upon Amerindians, even as late as the end of the nineteenth century by anthropologists such as James Mooney and A. S. Gatschet. After three hundred years of prodding and cajoling, then, Amerindians finally "appropriated" the spiritual and ecological idea of Mother Earth (Gill 66).

In both cases, the claims made rely primarily upon the reading of a benevolently inflected, white colonial record that depicts, for Lyons and Mohawk, Amerindians as democrats and, for Gill, Amerindians as ecologists. The difference between the claims is that Lyons and Mohawk read documents about Amerindians as speaking the truth about Amerindian identity, whereas Gill reads the same record as a history of white stereotyping that eventually appealed to Amerindians and became part of Amerindian identity claims. In both cases, the authors upstream by implication: one implicitly claims that before contact Amerindians really were progressive political philosophers, and the other that before contact Amerindians really were not progressive nature philosophers. Not surprisingly, both of these dramatic positions have come under methodological attack from significant sources: by Elisabeth Tooker ("United States Constitution"), for example, with respect to the contours of the Lyons-Mohawk argument, and by Ward Churchill, an Amerindian cultural studies scholar, who has issued a stinging critique of the Gill volume, quoting Martin Sheen's character in *Apocalypse Now* for his final verdict on the book: " 'Frankly, sir, I can't find any valid method at all' " (Churchill, *Fantasies* 206).

But it is better to suggest, as another way of thinking, that these two narratives are in some sense inevitable. Rather than reading the history of anthropological verdicts on identity as progressive, with a true picture of Amerindians gradually appearing through increasing discovery and detail, one might choose a short film from 1898, G. A. Smith's *The Miller and the Sweep,* as an emblem for the anthropological enterprise. Smith's film, essentially a joke frequently told and retold in popular materials at the turn of the century, concerns the miller, a man caked white and carrying a bag of flour, and the chimney sweep, blackened and carrying a sack of ashes. The two fight, pummeling each other with their sacks, and the miller quickly becomes black, and the sweep white.

This is a fundamentally agonistic anthropology's principle of reversibility, and such are the tricks and traps of the five-hundred-year-long attempt to discover the essential "differences" between Anglo and Amerindian cultures. The two narratives are locked into abyssal relation, each one ceaselessly trying to empty out the other. And if one were to accept both of these narratives, it would be Amerindians who are bourgeois subjects, protective of their individual rights and liberties and concerned with their physical and mental health,[6] and it would be Anglos who have spent the last five centuries worshipping at altars of earth. At the maximum expansion of the anthropological thinking of the other, one may no longer know who "we" and "they" are, and identity comes to seem extremely precarious, contingent, and without a center.

THE EXCLUDED INFORMANT

Contact changes everything. The very possibility, for example, of sites of translation and communication *between* cultures implies that the cultural situation is *always already* shaped in such a way that something more than cultural translation or cultural crossing takes place. And the academy's (in some disciplines, fast fading) metaphors of cultural travel and assimilation — the "cross-cultural," the "transcultural," the "intercultural," and the "bicultural" — do not begin to grasp how fundamental is the ground rending and ground mending that take place in such contact situations between incommensurables at the level of identity or personhood.

The historian Richard White has argued, for example, that a "middle ground," or "elaborate network of economic, political, cultural, and social ties," opened up between French and Amerindian peoples in the Great Lakes region in the seventeenth and eighteenth centuries (33). White focuses on "basic issues of sex, violence, and material exchange" to make his point that such and other matters needed joint juridico-economic resolution through "cultural fiction" and improvisation, thereby producing a new culture, new identities (56, 80–81). "Such changes, worked out on the middle ground, could be remarkably influential, bringing important modifications in each society and blurring the boundaries between them" (93). But to White's account one must add that cultural *difference* is a product, too, of the same encounter and that cultural difference is produced at the very same moment as the most minimal "middle ground." A middle ground, in fact, is culture's very condition of possibility, of visibility. Culture quite literally cannot appear until such a space is opened.

And today Anglo and Amerindian identities remain wedded within a contentious shared space, even though White's particular middle ground "withered and died" in the early nineteenth century (White, *Middle Ground* 523).

This can be explored further with reference to two proto-anthropologies, in both cases in the form of folklores, written during the Jacksonian era, just after White's "middle ground" period: David Cusick's *Sketches of the Ancient History of the Six Nations* (1827) and Henry Rowe Schoolcraft's *Algic Researches, Comprising Inquiries Respecting the Mental Characteristics of the North American Indians* (1839), which he was drafting, and parts of which he was publishing, with the assistance of his wife, Jane Johnston Schoolcraft, and other members of her family as early as 1826. These are, then, precisely contemporaneous texts in similar formats, and yet there are no end of differences between them.

Cusick is not very well known today, but Henry Schoolcraft may be *the* crucial proto-anthropologist, bent on establishing a *method* (however vague, in the final analysis) for collection of, digestion of, and historical reflection on Amerindian oral knowledge and stories. During the middle third of the nineteenth century it was nearly impossible to avoid his work on the Amerindian mind. Avid readers of Schoolcraft included prominent midcentury litterateurs (most dramatically, Henry Wadsworth Longfellow), historians (Francis Parkman), and anthropologists (Lewis H. Morgan) as well as Amerindian auto-anthropologists (Ely S. Parker and George Copway).

The difference in subject position of the authors of *Algic Researches* and the *Sketches* is both dramatic and not. Cusick represents himself as Iroquois (specifically Tuscarora) and explains that he is researching his own culture's beliefs and stories, while Schoolcraft clearly represents himself as Anglo, intent on studying the ancient Amerindian other. And yet Jane Johnston, whose contribution to the final text can hardly be overestimated, was the child of an Irish fur trader, John Johnston, and a Chippewa woman, Neengay (later Susan Johnston), and "Jane and the other children were educated in Ojibwa lore by their mother" (Parins, "Johnston" 1216).

Cusick, in turn, was the son of Nicholas Cusick, who, far from living the life of imaginary Amerindians, had served as Lafayette's bodyguard during the Revolutionary War (Parins, "Cusick" 1225). Nicholas Cusick's time on the Tuscarora reservation followed a life lived primarily within the so-called Anglo world. David Cusick lived across the divide, as well. He had a "fair education," according to William Beauchamp, and he "was thought of as a good doctor by both whites and Indians" (Beauchamp 41). So even if one accepts, on some level, narratives about the cultural difference of Amerindians and Anglos (and if one could be quite particular about the status of that difference — understanding it as radical or relational or utterly trivial, to give just three possible choices), what can be said with any conviction about culture and text in these particular cases?[7]

Henry Schoolcraft, for his part, is rarely unsure about the unique status of Amerindian culture, even though at first there are indications that *Algic Researches* accepts the idea of a universal human subject. The "Indians" or "aborigines," as Schoolcraft says, share a "desire" "implanted in the minds of all men, to convey to their contemporaries and transmit to posterity the prominent facts of their history and attainments" (*Indian Legends* 5).[8] So Amerindians desire to speak history, just as Anglos do, although Schoolcraft's remark is more a reflection of nineteenth-century historical consciousness than of some timeless drive or desire.[9]

But once past a certain minimal humanistic intelligibility, everything else about the Amerindian is differently constructed — distinctly non-European. Just as does Columbus, or the contemporaneous novelist James Fenimore Cooper or Catharine Maria Sedgwick, Schoolcraft divides Amerindians into two groups and presents a "fierce and dominating" Ostic, or Iroquois, and a nearly idyllic Algic, or Algonquian who is "mild and conciliating," full of the dreams of "independence" at the level of "personal or tribal freedom" (*Indian Legends* 7). (One might note that the Lyons-Mohawk Iroquois are here turned upside down, with the Algonquians made the northeast's liberal individuals.) Schoolcraft argues, "One is descended from . . . shepherds or pastoral nomads, and the other from a line of adventurers and warlike plunderers" (7). Reading Schoolcraft, it seems at times as if anthropology has traveled no distance at all from Columbus's imagined Taino and Caribs.[10] Henry Schoolcraft is at no remove from this hoary "split image" of Amerindia, a split that, as John McWilliams has argued, "allows the white reader to mourn for the loss of the heroic red man without having to protest against it" (McWilliams, "Historical" 360).

Schoolcraft's occasional discussion of the Amerindian in terms of the savage/civilized opposition is of no more recent vintage,[11] but what makes his text a bit more "modern" is, first, his inchoate notion of "race," which, as Winthrop Jordan has shown, is a concept that was not explicitly and fully thematized until the late 1700s and was not fully applied to the Amerindians until the 1770s.[12] The shepherds and the plunderers are "races," says Schoolcraft, and he argues that Amerindians can be divided into four different races: the Algic, Ostic, Abanic, and Muskogee (*Indian Legends* 5). This "quadrat" shares certain features as part of a larger Amerindian race. They have "distinctive opinions," for instance, as a result of a unique "mental constitution" (4).[13]

Also more "modern" is Schoolcraft's implicit evolutionary scheme. Though Schoolcraft is vague on this point (the details are hardly worked out at all), *Algic Researches* is partly an attempt to explain the origin and transformation of human beings. Tracing this out, Amerindians can be shown to be in various "states." The Algic, upon encounter, were in "the hunter state," for example, and lagged behind those quasi-capitalist Iroquois/Ostics.[14] The Algic race did not yet know "the value of time" and "could not endure the tension, mental and physical, of long-continued exertions" (8). In short, the Algic race had not yet learned the work ethic, a seemingly central step in the evolution of a higher order of "man."[15]

None of this is particularly novel for 1839, but what is interesting is that Schoolcraft's views of Amerindia encapsulate all of the several hundred years' worth of framing mechanisms within proto-anthropologies described in Bernard McGrane's work.[16] Schoolcraft is a grand imbricator and proof that exclusionary practices never die in the Colonial Era — they are simply absorbed and redeployed by each seemingly new paradigm for understanding. As close as Schoolcraft gets to doubting such metanarratives of identity or the aboriginal tales that bolster or support the metanarratives is a diary entry of 26 January 1838, in which he wonders about the future reception of *Algic Researches:* "There are so many Indian tales, fancied, by writers, that it will hardly be admitted that there exist any *real* legends" (*Indian Legends* 310). But Schoolcraft seems to have accepted the ancient veracity of everything that *he* managed to collect, believing, like Richter, that a singular, still existing "mythology" "furnishes the best clue to their hopes and fears, and lies at the foundation of the Indian character" (*Indian Legends* 10).[17]

This is not necessarily a perception shared by Jane Johnston. The closest one can come to finding her voice "alone" is in Schoolcraft's earliest published anthropological research — a self-published magazine that he called *The Literary Voyager* (1826–27). *The Literary Voyager* was an idiosyncratic grab bag of random Amerindian lore (stories and customs), family poetry, personal information (issue 14 is devoted to the death of Schoolcraft's and Johnston's child, Henry), and humor (acrostics and conundrums), with various family members providing material under numerous pseudonyms. One of Jane Johnston's several *Literary Voyager* pseudonyms is "Leelinau," and it is under this name (and in the magazine's first number) that she published her only attempt to speak to the problems of cultural anthropology and, more particularly, of historical upstreaming.[18] In "Character of Aboriginal Historical Tradition," Johnston writes:

> Now the stories I have heard related by old persons in my nation, cannot be so true, because they sometimes forget certain parts, and then thinking themselves obliged to fill up the vacancy by their own sensible remarks and experience, but it seems to me, much oftener by their fertile flights of imagination and if one person retains the truth, they have deviated, and so the history of my country has become almost wholly fabulous. (Schoolcraft, *Voyager* 6)

Johnston, as Leelinau, argues that with the possible exception of "one person," the recording of Amerindian tradition is an impossible task. People forget, of course, and quite unremarkably, each storyteller retells the tale according to new lived experience. The tales that Henry Schoolcraft, Jane Johnston, her relatives, and others collected for *Algic Researches* were, at least to begin with, told by these same "old persons" (perhaps fifty such elders, perhaps more), among whom new versions and new meanings proliferate so endlessly that only the "almost wholly fabulous" exists. *Algic Researches,* from this perspective, is just another collection of whoppers.

But who is the "one person" of truth to whom Leelinau refers in her sketch? It is, quite strangely, Leelinau's supposed father, "descended from one of the most ancient and respected leaders of the Ojibway bands" (Schoolcraft, *Voyager* 6).[19] Now Johnston's actual father, as noted earlier, claimed no Amerindian identity, and this other father, then, is sheer make-believe — a phantom conjured by Jane Johnston in order to assert the bare fact that, yes, some truth, somewhere, exists.[20] But perhaps not here, because Leelinau also explains that her father is dead. Will Leelinau, with her memories of her father, be able to pass on to Schoolcraft the "ancient traditions and customs," the old stories? (7). "I should strive to," she says, provided she could write her own letters (which she cannot do because she is Amerindian, raised within Amerindian culture). At the end of the sketch, therefore, the "truth" of Amerindian life remains unknown.

It is possible to read Jane Johnston's text as part of a microbattle for authority within Schoolcraft's and Johnston's joint proto-anthropological project. For example, when Leelinau returns to the pages of *The Literary Voyager* in January 1827, Henry Schoolcraft frames her tale of "The Origins of the Robin" in a way that does violence to her original narrative. According to the editorial frame, she is now able to write English, and Schoolcraft says that she is descended partly from "European parentage" (38). So "The Origins of the Robin" is *not* pure Amerindian legend, says Schoolcraft. Rather, Leelinau's story "derives additional interest" because of "the position she [Leelinau] occupies between the European and aboriginal races" (38–39). Leelinau is here interesting as a hybrid storyteller, and Schoolcraft's frame at least hints, in a reversal of Johnston's argument in the first Leelinau piece, that it is *Johnston* who is not quite Amerindian enough to speak the pure truth of the Amerindian mind.[21]

Again, as with the Lyons/Mohawk/Gill impasse, these arguments are abyssal. Or, more precisely, the rhetorical figure that describes this conversation is *aporia*; two roads diverge, and both are blocked. On the one side, according to Jane Johnston, Schoolcraft cannot know the truth of Amerindia because all of the figures he has interviewed are radically cut off from the "traditional" past. And, on the other side, according to Henry Schoolcraft, Leelinau (and Johnston too, of course) cannot speak with a singular cultural tongue about Amerindia because of her partial European birth and background. In this case, if one accepts both narratives, both arguments, as true, no one can say anything for certain about the Amerindian past. There is literally no entry point — no access to it.

One more turn — a kind of coda — on the relationship between Schoolcraft and Johnston: A number of *The Literary Voyager* texts, including Jane Johnston's folklore contributions, were reprinted in *Algic Researches,* and Henry

Schoolcraft added yet more matter, including the tale "Leelinau; or, The Lost Daughter." It is hard to resist reading this text, and its later transformation in Schoolcraft's revision of *Algic Researches* (published in 1856 as *The Myth of Hiawatha* in order to cash in on Longfellow's acknowledged debt to Schoolcraft), as Schoolcraft's attempt to have the final word on Jane Johnston's authority, her auto-anthropology. In "The Lost Daughter," Leelinau is described as a young girl, both "pensive and timid," and "dissatisfied with the realities of life" (*Indian Legends* 155, 156). Leelinau is, in short, prone to "fancy" of the most odious sort (157) — communion with the fairies of the woods — and on the evening before she is set to be married and enter the world of adult responsibilities, she retires to her favorite "fairy haunted grove" and disappears forever, presumably turned into a spirit or sprite by the chieftain of the wood fairies (158). Schoolcraft, as per his usual habit, turns this into a moral tale about parental supervision: Leelinau was "a daughter whose manners and habits they had not sufficiently guarded, and whose inclinations they had, in the end, too violently thwarted" (158).

Two things should be noted about this portrayal of Leelinau. First, it is an act of representational violence against Jane Johnston that Schoolcraft literally makes her pseudonymic incarnation vanish; it disappears from the world. This is the precisely the action of *Algic Researches,* which, unlike *The Literary Voyager,* does not acknowledge Jane Johnston's contribution to the collection and production of its texts; for example, *The Literary Voyager* attributes "Mishosha, or The Magician and His Daughters" to "Bame-wa-wa-ge-zhik-a-quay," another of Jane Johnston's Amerindian pseudonyms, and *Algic Researches* prints it, and indeed every story in the book, as the product of Henry Schoolcraft's own researches.[22] In "Leelinau; or, The Lost Daughter," as in the Schoolcraft-Johnston folklore corpus, Jane Johnston's presence is effaced, and the necessarily joint Anglo-Amerindian production of anthropological discourse is completely erased.

Second, the moral frame makes clear that Leelinau, and therefore Johnston, lives in a world of make-believe; this is precisely the charge that Schoolcraft leveled again and again at David Cusick's book, as I will show later. This infantilization is Schoolcraft's preferred method for contextualizing, and thereby neutralizing, the large fact, and therefore the truth claims, of auto-anthropology. Though Schoolcraft acknowledged the Amerindian presence in his work—

he was, after all, a folklorist and cultural anthropologist *in the field,* and he depended primarily upon Amerindian informants for information—he at the same time denied that the Amerindian mind might be able to fathom the depth of or ferret out the truth of their own identities. It is up to the Anglo anthropologist, finally, to make historical, cultural, and racial sense out of the welter of confused data that, admittedly, only Amerindians can provide.

Finally, Schoolcraft's greatly shortened poetical rendering of the Leelinau tale in *The Myth of Hiawatha* (as the book's final story, "Leelinau: A Chippewa Tale") further etherealizes Leelinau by poeticizing language and form. This final version of the story ends thus:

> Night came but Leelinau was never more seen, except by a fisherman on the lake shore, who conceived that he had seen her go off with one of the tall fairies known as the fairy of Green Pines, with green plumes nodding o'er his brows; and it is supposed that she is still roving with him over the elysian fields. (*Hiawatha Legends* 236)

In this rendering, Jane Johnston is frozen in a sentimental pastoral: a magical but insubstantial girl wandering distant landscapes (*Hiawatha Legends* 235–36). She is, in short, turned into an Indianism—romantically banished and vanished. At one and the same time she is rendered less likely than ever to contribute to knowledge of the Amerindian and is turned into a dehistoricized, mythic subject fit for Schoolcraftian analysis.

THE CUSICK PROBLEM

David Cusick's *Sketches of the Ancient History of the Six Nations* suggests a way of thinking through the aporia produced by Schoolcraft's and Johnson's critiques of one another. Henry Schoolcraft knew of Cusick's short book. In fact, one might go so far as to suggest that he brooded upon it. Between 1847 and 1855, Schoolcraft addressed the problem of the very existence of the Cusick text at least six times. Here was a book, an Amerindian book, written in English, that took up all the topics that concerned Schoolcraft: Amerindian folklore, culture, history. Matters of expertise and authority mark every turn in Schoolcraft's recurring reference to *Sketches.*

Schoolcraft republished several pages of Cusick's text in 1847 in his *Notes on the Iroquois*. He prefaced the text by suggesting that Cusick's "full blooded Indian" nature and his book's "style, or grammar" were "evidence of the authenticity of the traditions recorded" (*Notes* 475). Yes, this was an "Indian book." Considered as such, Schoolcraft said that Cusick's *Sketches* was "remarkable," but he also summarized his feelings about the work by calling it a "curious publication," as if something about the book was cause for wonder. But what might that be? After all, Schoolcraft is quizzical about a text written almost entirely within the terms of his own emerging discipline. Other than the fact that it is written by an Amerindian, what is so strange or odd about a text that in so many ways resembles Schoolcraft's own works on Amerindian legend and lore?

Schoolcraft's answer to this question did not come to him right away. A reading of Cusick emerged over the course of the next decade as Schoolcraft began production and publication of his monumental *Historical and Statistical Information Respecting the History, Condition, and Prospects of the Indian Tribes of the United States* (1851–57; six volumes with seven hundred oversized pages each). Though the volumes include a number of contributions from contemporaneous scholars, Schoolcraft wrote the bulk of the work, digesting, abstracting, and rendering judgment upon hundreds of works about Amerindians in general and about their various races, nations, tribes, and language families.

Schoolcraft virtually ignores auto-anthropology in these volumes. There is no mention of Jane Johnston (perhaps not surprisingly), but, strangely, there is also no reference to William Apess's or George Copway's anthropological works, which were then available, nor to Ely S. Parker's work, even though Parker was one of his correspondent-informants during the writing of *Notes on the Iroquois*. (Schoolcraft's major section on Amerindian writers, in volume 4 of *Historical and Statistical Information* [1854], is devoted exclusively to translations of scripture, school primers, and hymns into Amerindian languages — safe enough to acknowledge).[23] But Cusick's name comes up five times over the several thousand pages, and with increasing attention. This process culminates in volume 5 (1855), where Schoolcraft reprints the whole of Cusick's book, with an extended comment (*Historical* 5:632–46). Cusick's text, then, represents the problem of auto-anthropology for Schoolcraft, and a careful look at Schoolcraft's remarks here is quite revealing.[24] Finally, School-craft's critique (for that is what it is) centers on the matter of writing *history*.

In volume 1 (1851), Schoolcraft writes that Cusick's "mind" was "replete with traditions"—a point in Cusick's favor—but that

> his ignorance of general chronology, and of the very slow manner in which the dialects and languages of the human race must have been formed, was profound; and his attempts to assimilate the periods of the several Atotarhoes or lead-ing magistrates of that famous league of aboriginal tribes, are utterly childish and worthless. Not so with his traditions of events. When he comes to speak of the Indian mythology, and beliefs in spiritual agencies, the monster period, and the wars and wanderings of his people, he is at home,—and history may be said to be indebted to him for telling his own story of these things in his own way. So much for Cusic. (*Historical* 1:125)

"History" is indebted to David Cusick, but only so long as he stays "at home," telling the stories that he knows without historical context, without method: "in his own way"—that is, an Amerindian way of knowing the world. For Schoolcraft, the "genuineness" of Cusick's text depends upon his presentation of belief without an overarching understanding, upon his presentation of "a mass of incongruous details" that remains unassembled in terms of chronol-ogy or race theory (*Notes* 63).

In volume 4 Schoolcraft again refers to Cusick as the author of "that curious publication" by a "native archaeologist." The issue of history is again fore-grounded: "The chronology and dynastic terms of his pamphlet are believed to be conjectural, or faulty" (4:137). Finally, in volume 5, as a preface to his reprinting of Cusick "*verbatim et literatim,*" Schoolcraft begins by noting that "this extraordinary piece of Indian penmanship . . . is, specially, left in the lit-erary garb in which it came from his hands." Yet at the same time Schoolcraft claims that

> like many writers of far higher pretensions, he falls into the error of trying to generalize and systematize matter which

would be better if left in its accrete state. The greatest merit of such traditions consists in their being told in a simple manner, without any attempt at chronology or embellishment. By putting the time-frame of a suppositional chronology to the traditions, he entered on quicksands where stouter feet have sunk. This part of the narrative may be regarded as a mere excursion of a North American Indian into the fields of imagination. The assertion that there had been *"thirteen"* Atatarhos, or presiding rulers, at Onondaga, the seat of the confederacy, may be regarded as the tradition; although, if we regarded each Atatarho as ruling thirty years, it would carry the antiquity of the confederacy a century farther back than is generally conceded. (*Historical* 5:631)

Schoolcraft, in short, accuses Cusick of upstreaming without a paddle: He "put[s] the time-frame of a suppositional chronology" onto a collection of folklore in order to produce a history of undocumented eras. Curiously, the "fields of imagination" within which Cusick tarries are, according to Schoolcraft, only "a century" removed from the "generally conceded" truth of Anglo historical reconstruction. (At the end of this passage Schoolcraft inserts a footnote instructing the reader to refer to his own work, *Notes on the Iroquois*—meaning that Schoolcraft himself is the "generally conceded" expert on such matters.) One hundred years: Schoolcraft's rhetorical tone—"childish," "worthless," "faulty"—borders on the hysterical, given the minimal magnitude of the mistake (if it is one) which he discovers.

But consider matters from another angle. The two longest remarks on Cusick in *Historical and Statistical Information,* both partially quoted above, focus their attention on Cusick's reconstruction of the chain of thirteen Iroquois Atotarhoes, or rulers, and of the events that occurred during each successive reign. One might well agree with Schoolcraft that it is this very feature of Cusick's text that most clearly distinguishes Cusick from other midnineteenth-century anthropologists. It is at these moments in *Sketches of the Ancient History of the Six Nations* that ethnic or racial history is most dramatically reworked. It is at these moments that one can locate and identify a previously unthought methodological difference between Schoolcraft and Cusick: whereas Schoolcraft understands Amerindian and Anglo identities as separate and distinct, Cusick figures them as necessarily relational.

A passage from *Algic Researches*' "Preliminary Observations" makes explicit Schoolcraft's view that Amerindia and Europe have shared nothing, exchanged nothing — that no borders have ever been crossed, much less crossed out. Schoolcraft says that the history of the "contest" for North America

> has been anything but favorable to the production of right feeling and a reciprocal knowledge of real character on both sides. The Indians could never be made to appreciate the offers of education and Christianity by one portion of the community, while others were arrayed against them in arms. Their idea of government was, after all, the Eastern notion of a unity or despotism, in which everything emanates from the governing power, and is responsible to it.[25] Nor has their flitting and feverish position on the frontiers been auspicious to the acquisition of a true knowledge of their character, particularly in those things which have relation to the Indian mind, their opinions on abstract subjects, their mythology, and other kindred topics. Owing to illiterate interpreters and dishonest men, the parties have never more than half understood each other. (*Indian Legends* 17)

This very complex narrative makes it clear that a long string of contingencies has prevented anything but a "half" knowledge of the other. With Amerindians "flitting" on the "frontiers" and Anglos either "illiterate" or wildly divided in their presentation, it seems, more than 230 years after Samuel de Champlain's arrival, as if the colonial encounter has not yet taken place.

Of course, there is little truth to this narrative, and within a few pages *Algic Researches* produces a quite contradictory argument, chastising the Amerindian because "he does not seem to open his eyes on the prospect of civilization and mental exaltation held up before him" (22). Schoolcraft now argues that "these scenes have been *pictured before him* by teachers and philanthropists *for more than two centuries*; but there has been nothing in them to arouse and inspire him to press onward in the career of prospective civilization and advancement" (emphasis added; 22). Instead of taking this good advice, says Schoolcraft, the Amerindian "pines away as one that is fallen, and despairs to rise," while meditating upon "a sort of golden age, when all things were better with them than they are now."

This is hardly the Amerindian who does not know the European, nor is this the Amerindian untouched by colonialism, "flitting" beyond the space of contact. This is, instead, a portrait of a mind transformed by massive redefinitions of physical and psychic space, albeit in the tragic mode. This is, absent the tragedy, Cusick's Amerindian. Cusick begins his narrative, however, with a "cross-cultural" trope that essentializes cultural difference. "I have taken much pains," he says, not only "procuring the materials" for the book but also crossing the cultural divide and "translating it into English language":

> I have been long waiting in hopes that some of my people, who have received an English education, would have undertaken the work as to give a sketch of the Ancient History of the Six Nations; but found no one seemed to concur in the matter, after some hesitation I determined to commence the work; but found the history involved with fables; and besides, examining myself, finding so small educated that it was impossible for me to compose the work without much difficulty. (In Beauchamp 1)

Cusick's reference in his first line to the Tuscaroras as "my people" makes it clear how he comprehends his own identity and that he understands his audience as other, Anglo. It is his very identity, it seems, that makes for "difficulty" in the writing of a book for "the public." Crossing over a cultural divide with an entire people's history on his back hurts — it comes with great "pains."

This same paragraph, though, also gives the first indication of a counternarrative at work in the *Sketches,* when Cusick starts to undermine his attempt to write "history." It is all "involved with fables," he says, which suggests the same problem for historical upstreaming that Leelinau raised. And though it is true that *Sketches* claims to reproduce the mental world of the "ancients," just as Schoolcraft did, at the same time Cusick's various sketches are deployed less as historical truths than as political fictions that make recurrent, specific reference to the politics of Amerindian removal.

Cusick makes it quite clear, in the "tale of the foundation of the great island (now North America)," that the earth is a "possession" of the Amerindians,
the "real people":

> When he [the "good mind," Enigorio] had made the universe
> he was in doubt respecting some being to possess the great
> Island; and he formed two images of the dust of the ground
> in his own likeness, male and female, and by his breathing
> into their nostrils he gave them the living souls, and named
> them Ea-gwe-howe, i.e., a real people; and he gave the Great
> Island, all the animals of game for their maintenance. (In
> Beauchamp 3)

One might note that Cusick seems primarily to be recounting the Christian
creation myth — and Cusick may or may not be aware of this — but what is
more interesting is how this story, read as a tale of original Amerindian possession, resonates throughout the short book.[26]

Relatively late in the text, Cusick tells of an ancient Tuscarora prophecy by
this "good mind" (who has taken the form of an old man) in which he says that
Europeans "would in some future day take possession of the Big Island, and it
was impossible to prevent it" (in Beauchamp 31). But Cusick finishes this tale
by recounting that "the aged man died among them, and they buried him; but
soon after some person went to the grave and found he had risen, and never
heard of him since." In this passage, again marked by Christianity (and, some
might argue, the "culture hero" myth), it is clear that even though the "Big Island" will be lost, the creator of the "real people" has symbolically promised
them a resurrection. And right at the end of the *Sketches,* in the next to last
paragraph, "Holder of the Heavens" appears in a dream to an Iroquois prophet
and advises the tribe "not to comply with the wishes of the whites, lest they
should ruin themselves and displease their Maker" (37). To invoke Schoolcraft,
these are "remarkable," potentially dangerous words — *"not to comply with the
wishes of the whites"* — written, as they were, in the middle of the removal
debate.[27]

But so far, all that has been suggested is that Cusick, who foregrounds the
fablelike or "fabulous" ground of ancient Amerindian history and identity (much

as does Jane Johnston) uses this to his advantage and explicitly constructs a history in the shape of a politics, thereby intervening in the ongoing, asymmetrical conversation about removal.[28] More "curious," though, is the way in which Cusick's versions of Iroquois and hemispheric history converge. Iroquois history points toward the successful military and political conquest of all area tribes following the founding of the Iroquois Confederacy, "after which the kingdom enjoyed without disturbance for many years" (in Beauchamp 38). Cusick explains that at the very same moment of peace, however, Columbus arrived on the continent and shattered the Iroquois dream. "Columbus" and the successful "confederacy" happen at the same moment, and this is not a coincidence in Cusick's narrative. This is, instead, the determination of a History with a capital H, a History with a vector and a *telos*. Twelve times throughout the *Sketches* Cusick connects Columbus to events in his Iroquois history:

> This fate happened probably about two thousand five hundred winters before Columbus discovered the America. (9)

> Perhaps about two thousand two hundred years before the Columbus discovered the America . . . (10)

> Perhaps about 1250 years before Columbus discovered the America . . . (15)

> Perhaps 1,000 years before Columbus discovered the America . . . (16)

> Perhaps about 800 years before the Columbus discovered the America . . . (20)

> In the days of King Ototarho VI, perhaps 650 years before the Columbus discovered the America . . . (23)

> In the reign of King Atotarho VIII, perhaps 400 years before the Columbus discovered America . . . (27)

> In the reign of King Atotarho IX, perhaps 350 years before the Columbus discovered the America . . . (31)

> In the reign of Atotarho X, perhaps 250 years before Columbus discovered America . . . (36)

> Atotarho XI, perhaps about 150 years before Columbus discovered America . . . (36)

In the reign of Atotarho XII, perhaps about 50 years before
Columbus discovered America . . . (37)

In the reign [of] Atotarho XIII, in the year 1492, Columbus
discovered the America. (38)

Undoubtedly, several things are happening in these repeated intonations.
For one, the use of the term "discovery" should be understood ironically, since,
each time, the term appears in a sentence that documents either complex tribal
history or kingly consolidation and rule. More important for my purposes,
however, this constant locking together of Columbus and the Six Nations makes
it impossible to think one without the other. In the *Sketches,* the very ability to
"sketch," the very ability to narrate "ancient history," is entirely dependent upon
the presence of Columbus. Put another way, it is "the Columbus" that enables
the discourse of folklore anthropology, that makes it possible in the first place.
"The Columbus," in this sense, literally produces the past in the Cusick text,
in that the "ancients" can only be narrated with reference to him.

"The Columbus" and whatever he stands for literally appears at the same
moment as do Cusick's Amerindians and their project of peace. They are born
together. They must mean everything to each other. Which is why, in the first
place, the Gill and Lyons-Mohawk texts stand in such strange relation to each
other. The very possibility that these figures can make their claims with *any*
degree of credibility supports a massive revision of their understanding of
identity. It is not a question of Mother Earth or democracy belonging to one or
the other; rather, the point is that each is produced within sight of the other,
with reference to a site for the other.[29]

Interesting, too, is the type of precontact Iroquois identity that Cusick constructs. His narrative, as noted, is primarily one of conquest and consolidation: The Iroquois were centralizing empire builders, intent on bringing an entire world under one stable rule through battles with cannibal giants, stonish
giants, flying heads, giant mosquitoes, and tribe upon tribe of indigenous peoples. A god, in fact, has taught the Iroquois to agglomerate territory:

The Holder of Heavens visited the Five Families and in-
structed them in the arts of war, and favors them to gain the
country beyond their limits. (In Beauchamp 16)

In a manner that might best be described as Cortésian, they raid and conquer beyond their territories and "make incursion upon the enemy that may be found within the boundaries of the kingdom" (23). And the Iroquois, according to Cusick, also go out on "expeditions" to "explore" the world, and discover, like Columbus, strange, unevolved "others" who seem to be more animal than man. Cusick writes that when the Iroquois met the "Dog Tail Nation," "they were astonished that the people had short tails like apes; a hole was made through their seats where they put their tails" (24). This is similar to the incident reported in Columbus's letter concerning his fourth voyage, which reports: "A crossbowman wounded a creature that was like an ape, only much larger and with a human face. He had pierced him with an arrow from the breast to the tail but had to cut off the fore and hind paw because he was so fierce. . . . The hunting of this animal was so strange and splendid that I have had to describe it" (Columbus 298).

In these ways, Cusick's Iroquois are a kind of mirror for Columbus or Cortés, and Cusick provides no rhetorical resources with which one could sketch significant identity differences between Anglo and Amerindian. The importance of the *Sketches* for identity politics is that, unlike *Algic Researches,* Cusick's book constructs an Amerindian identity entirely circumscribed by colonial relations and in which the Iroquois are colonizers every bit the equal of the Europeans. Amerindian identity is, in Cusick's text, both relational and decentered, and at the same time it is curiously identical to Anglo identity.

SPANISH IROQUOIS AND A(NTHRO)POLOGY

Of course, it would be tempting to reintroduce Cusick's nearly unknown text to wider readership as part of what Edmund Wilson aptly referred to as *Apologies to the Iroquois* (1959) and to Amerindia in general. But this would be repeating a very old colonial gesture, a gesture made as early as 1827, when Dr. D. B. Coates introduced Hendrick's Aupaumut's "A Narrative of an Embassy to the Western Indians" (c. 1794) to his Historical Society of Pennsylvania audience as an authentic product of the "sons of the forest" and as compensation for the fact that "no apologists have arisen to celebrate and exalt their [the Indians'] great actions" (Coates 63). Here apology for conquest and the "discovery" of auto-ethnic narrative are conjoined in a way that should remind one of the entire history of European "othering," from Cortés's pity for the conquered, even as he produces Moctezuma's voice, to Cooper's attempt, in *The Last of the Mohicans* (1826), to salvage the vibrant masculinity of Amerindian semiotics while reciting a funeral oration for "real" Amerindians.[30] As David E. Johnson points out, anthropology of the other is always in the form of an apology of one sort or another, and the "primal scene" of the production of otherness involves tears.[31] The word itself—"a(nthro)pology"— is framed by an "apology."

So rather than recover Cusick's text within, for example, a multicultural framework, which might comprehend it as an anthropological counternarrative or auto-ethnic account of identity (making Cusick either nineteenth-century anthropology's inventor or interlocutor),[32] Cusick can be configured as an identity dissenter—arguing from entirely different grounds. Simply put, he shows the border effects that Schoolcraft hides, and this border production destabilizes the very possibility of *Algic Researches.*

And Cusick's most general writing strategies and his identity politics, far from finding a ready home within anthropological discourse, even in this century, are *still* on the margins of anthropology.[33] Even a good deal of postmodern ethnographic practice and postmodern critique of ethnography does little more than foreground the subjectivity of the anthropologist at the expense of the other, forcing the other into the position of maximum alterity, of the occult—when, in fact, it is possible to argue that the great scandal of our lives is that "our" so-called differences hold no meaning.[34] Identity difference, then, may be at maximum relational and is often closer to the realm of the trivial— blank custom and habit masquerading as significance. One need only think of Schoolcraft's random accumulation of cultural oddities in his "grab bag" texts (*The Literary Voyager, The Indian in His Wigwam*) to understand this anthropological model: the compiling of lists of Amerindian food, clothes, implements, places, ritual, words—a strategy that multiplies the principle of othering but that adds up to nothing in particular. In these Schoolcraft compendiums, anthropology is presented in an "accrete state." But furthermore, if the Iroquois are fundamentally protocapitalists *and* anticapitalists *and* democrats *and* ecologists—then what's the difference?[35]

One thing more with reference to this problematic: I noted earlier that Cusick's notion of Amerindian identity rings and rhymes with accounts of Anglo identity. Yet it is not precisely *Anglo* identity that is at stake but, rather, *Spanish* identity, since Cusick's text refers to conquest and colonization only through "the Columbus." This seeming anomaly in Cusick is, on closer inspection, a more general Iroquois conceit. Iroquois materials from before and after Cusick sometimes evidence the same interest in Spaniards and Columbus. Richter notes that on 2 September 1723 an Anglo transcriber of a treaty negotiation reported what an Iroquois orator told his white and red audience:

> Formerly We lived alone and were Masters of this Land. Afterwards one came over the seas from afarr who had a skin like one of us and Entred our land and was Master of our Rivers Who We had discursed with and was welcome to us, he was a Spaniard. (Quoted in Richter 278)

A second text, the epilogue to the volume of essays *The State of Native America,* is from 1992. The book as a whole presents a summary of various sorts of modern Amerindian struggles over law, land, water, religion, gender, education, and the military service. The epilogue is written by John Mohawk and is entitled "Looking for Columbus: Thoughts on the Past, Present, and Future of Humanity." "Looking for Columbus"—the very title tells us something. Mohawk, a member of one of the Iroquois Confederacy tribes, whose home grounds are upstate New York and Canada, is searching for "Columbus" in order to comprehend his own "state." And even though this brief text criticizes a European tendency to imagine all of the peoples of pre-encounter America as just one—"Indians"—he himself bases all of his arguments about "Europeans" and "Eurocentrism" on only Spanish source materials: texts by Columbus and Sepúlveda (Mohawk, "Looking for Columbus" 440). For Mohawk, these two figures produce the two possible models for all European colonialism. Therefore, the Spanish alone set the tone and terms for conquest; they make the largest arguments to and on behalf of this thing called "Europe." To understand American colonialism in general and to combat it, one must "find the real meaning of Columbus" and "bury it" (443).

What can one make of Cusick's "the Columbus?" And of the anonymous Iroquois speaker's "Spaniard," "who had skin like one of us?" Why is "he" "here," in Massachusetts, at such a great distance from New Spain? And what can one conclude about Mohawk's ongoing fixation with Columbian discourses — a topic he has repeatedly raised in other work?[36] What does it mean that in this Senecan account of colonization and its consequences, the names of people like Samuel de Champlain do not appear, much less the names of Dutch or English — nor is there reference to northern European colonial records or to evidences of northern European home country debates over the fate of the Amerindians?[37] The trope of the "Spaniard" in Iroquois discourse — or, more broadly, the production of the identity of the "Spanish Iroquois" — is a curious problem for the project of comparing, contrasting, and, finally, distinguishing the colonialisms in the Americas. At stake are complex questions of colonial identities — strategies of Amerindian self-definition that, at one and the same time, strategize self-identity in ways that cut against the historical-anthropological work of Anglo investigators and produce, in certain specific ways, more revealing accounts of the very process and possibilities of the self-fashioning of identity.

The hundreds of years of Spanish Iroquois, finally, are not strange identity anomalies; rather, they are as "real" as anything else in this world; they are a necessary possibility and a reminder of the intellectual limitations that come with the project of determining *particular* identities or even *local fields* of identities — the sheer poverty of demarcating and explicating identities based on a reading of particular material practices or conditions. A historian might describe it as a pan-Indianism that predates most historical accounts of such, might explain it as an early and enduring dissemination of the stories of Spain and the "Black Legend," or might argue that it is a manifestation of modernity's world economy, with signs and texts in constant, turbulent interaction.

All of this may be "true," as far as causal explanations go, but the significance, in any case, is that there are not, nor have there even been, any Amerindians (or Anglos, for that matter) *as such.* Push the colonial record back to its beginning, and in the beginning Amerindians comprehended themselves as Amerindians only through the mechanism of — the text that is — Europe. Which is to say: Amerindia has always been Spanish (*"skin like one of us"*), and Anglo, and whatever else was conceptualized and embodied at time of contact. This is not a detour, not a colonized subjectivity or mentality: this figure or trope marks the limit of self-representation.

And if the rhetorical strategies of Cusick's *Sketches* have anything to tell us today, it is that, far from living in a world of singular cultures and their borders and contact zones, "we" are stitched together and shot through with all of "our" others. "Our" condition is critical, borderline — a network of dis-positions. And the hope for any "other" world is tied not to rediscovering precontact Amerindia, to upstreamed longings and imaginations, but rather to the limit recognition that "our" so-called differences are part of a more encompassing yet in principle never closed sketch; figures without a center, drafted in pencil; remains on a yellowing sheet of paper.

2. Destructuring Whiteness: Color, Animality, Hierarchy

If an honest white man could look into our private affairs and know
what wrongs we have suffered, it would change his complexion to
a hue redder than the Indian's.

—WILLIAM APESS, *INDIAN NULLIFICATION* (1835)

The study of "whiteness" is one of the most significant developments in "race" and ethnic studies over the course of the last few years, rivaled only, perhaps, by the rise of "border studies." An impressive body of literature has developed with the explicit aim of exposing the contours of American white identity and working toward the development of nonvirulent forms of whiteness, or even the elimination of whiteness as such.[1] As one example, Noel Ignatiev's journal *Race Traitor* uses as its motto: "Treason to whiteness is loyalty to humanity."[2] But in the first place what is "whiteness"—and "white," the "white race," and "whitening"? What precisely is being confronted in these texts?[3] Frankly, it is everything and nothing, and this is partly a problem of our lack of a genealogy, much less competing genealogies, for the very word "white." Most of the literature on whiteness tells us almost nothing explicitly about "white" as an analytical category and seems to make two unspoken assumptions that are historically insupportable: first, that "white" means "race," and second, that "race" means the scientific racism of the nineteenth century, with its attendant blood-based, polygenist speculations upon the mysteries of the body's interior. In other words, "white" equals "Caucasian." The hope of whiteness studies is to produce a reading of Europeans' nearly unremarked and seemingly invisible subjectivities, but to begin with this premise is to necessarily miss the mark, or at best to misname the object of study. Many of the current readings of whiteness, for example, make little or no reference to color as such.[4] And though the deployment of the term "white" in, for example, the nineteenth century sometimes does signify racialist thinking, the already presumed connection diminishes the project of exploring "whiteness" as such.

The discourse of whiteness historically precedes that of race. A hierarchical language of color differentiation ("white," "red," "gray," "black," and all points between) is one of the most enduring legacies of colonialism, far older and more pervasive than a language of "race," for example, which later absorbs and redeploys color language (see Jordan 4–7). Color, in the early history of colonialism, is in fact a separate analytic, not necessarily articulated with other contemporaneous discourses of distinction, such as those of religion or civilization. Jack D. Forbes's study of the multiple colonial languages of color and their contingent connections to other ways of thinking the other is perhaps the most careful work available on the subject.[5] He argues that over the course of the age of conquest, through to the eighteenth century, whiteness is thought in relation to a bewildering number of categories:

> We have a sequence in which first the Europeans began with very general color terms (*loro, pardo, baço*, etc.); second, when they coined many more color terms (*membrillo cocido, moreno*, etc.); thirdly, when they invented or adopted terms for various mixed-bloods *as* mixed-bloods (*mamaluco, mestizo, mulato, zambo*, etc.); fourth, when they attempted by means of such terms to individually categorize most types of mixed-bloods; and, fifth, when it all became so complicated that they fell back upon very general terms such as *pardo* or made ones like *mestizo* very nebulous. Finally, all of this occurred within a reality where the great mass of colonial people probably used all these terms in pragmatic ways based upon appearance and culture rather than upon actual ancestry. (Forbes 130)

This list includes only Spanish-language versions of the problem, but at least it is a beginning. The texts of the Spanish conquistadors, for example, are filled with elaborate and hazy traditions of color talk.[6] A sixteenth-century traveler like Cabeza de Vaca, for example, marched across most of the southern border of the present-day United States, distinguishing Amerindians from each other and from himself by referring to many gradations of color, with whiteness linked to other indicators of attractiveness: "They are a people of fine forms, pleasant features, and whiter than any of the nations we had so far seen" (Cabeza de Vaca 1983, 103). The records of Columbus's voyages, too, work this way, with straight-haired "fairer" figures living closer to Paradise and dark, cannibalistic "Caribs" inhabiting shadowy islands. Forbes's point about "appearance and culture" being of greater significance than bloodline is underlined and expanded in Alejandro Lugo's recent work, which intriguingly argues that "whiteness" for precontact America was a matter of face paint and that sixteenth-century Amerindian texts concerning the conquest and the "whiteness" of the Spaniards must be read according to a ceremonial logic entirely different from the logic of European colonial color discourse.

And as the history of American empires proceeds, "white" is articulated with almost anything that has to do with the production of psychic and political borders, including anthropological discourses of blood (polygenism), geography (monogenism), and culture (postrace thinking). Older distinctions of color, then, are often folded under and encapsulated within new rubrics. The point is that whiteness is a more enduring and complicated category of analysis than strictly anthropological ones, and we must carefully learn the histories and possibilities of whiteness's articulations (and nonarticulations and disarticulations) if the specific question of "whiteness" is to be examined.

At stake is more than a genealogy of a concept. At stake are matters of modernity, colonialism, and bourgeois identity, as well as judgments regarding such formations. For example, if one simply assumes that whiteness, in its early to postcolonial formations, is always a matter of race, then one's understanding of the last five hundred years is necessarily monological: modernity has one face, one shape, and it is racist. The shapelessness, the indeterminateness, the inchoate quality of "white" as a signifier in the early modern period is lost. And on the twentieth-century side of things, one loses the sense of the transformation of "race" to "culture," of evolutionary anthropology and its sense of "progress" to post-Boasian "pluralism" and "cultural relativism." And again, without the differences, modernity becomes a contourless blur. The fact that color talk has survived the general demise of scientific racism goes unnoticed and unremarked. There may well be philosophical or political advantages that come with advancing such a narrative, but what is needed in the first place is a more reflexive and analytically rigorous use of the intellectual entry point "whiteness."

In the following sections, I analyze the use of a specific language of color — white, red, and black — in two crucial early-nineteenth-century texts: William

Apess's "An Indian's Looking-Glass for the White Man" (1833) and James Fenimore Cooper's *The Last of the Mohicans* (1826). And Cooper's link between color and animality leads, in this chapter's final section, to an examination of the relationship between nineteenth-century studies of Amerindians and of beavers, in the work of both Cooper and Lewis Henry Morgan. In these pages, for once, color is not presumed to be "race," and it is understood, instead, as a more recalcitrant *and* more mobile category of differentiation than race ever was or will be.

Color Inversion and the Critique of Race

Apess's text is, today, one of the better-known Amerindian writings of the antebellum period; it is increasingly anthologized and analyzed. And William Apess (Pequot) is one of the two most prolific Amerindian writers in English during the Indian removal era.[7] The son of a Pequot father and a perhaps part African American mother, Apess as a young man served several white masters as an indentured servant. Later, he wrote and published five books, including an autobiography, a sermon, a eulogy-history of the seventeenth-century Pokanoket leader King Philip, and a work of political science regarding Amerindian sovereignty, from a Southern, states' rights perspective.[8]

"An Indian's Looking-Glass" has a curious textual history, which is recounted by Apess's modern editor, Barry O'Connell. It was appended to Apess's third book, *The Experiences of Five Christian Indians of the Pequot Tribe*. Some 1833 first editions of this volume include a subtitle — *or, An Indian's Looking-Glass for the White Man* — and others do not. And the 1837 edition of the book omits the text and any reference to it, substituting a quite different and much shorter piece addressed to a white audience called "An Indian's Thought" (Apess 325, 161). "An Indian's Looking-Glass" may or may not have been considered by Apess to bear a relation to his five confessional narratives about conversion, may or may not be a separate piece of writing, may or may not have been externally or even self-censored at time of the republication of *Experiences* — but its phantomlike status is at least part of the reason that it was not reprinted between 1833 and 1982 (Apess 325).[9]

The text is typically read as an unusually strong and ironic rebuke of white "principle" and hypocrisy — that is, as a political tract of "militant consciousness" to be read alongside Cherokee editor Elias Boudinot's removal-era speeches and writings, for example, or African American writer David Walker's *Appeal* (1829).[10] A good deal of attention has been focused on whether the text's values are truly Indian (in either a cultural or political sense) or co-opted (that is, acculturated Christian).[11] But this relatively brief text is also fundamentally anthropological in its attempt to thematize the question of color. "White," "red," "black," and "colored" are Apess's chosen formulations for analyzing the problem of distinction. And this is because prejudice, in the last instance, is founded upon what Apess says are "outward appearances" (Apess 155).

In order to begin to comprehend the complexity of Apess's thinking on these matters, it is useful, as Murray does, to think through the implications of the text's title. "An Indian's Looking-Glass for the White Man": the choice of words "allows us to visualize either an Indian looking at himself for the benefit of whites, or an Indian holding up a mirror so that the white man can see himself" (Murray 61). Yet neither of these interpretations quite captures what Apess is after, with his constant reference to what surfaces reveal or do not reveal — that is, to pigmentation. And the profound ambiguity of the title allows for at least one more interpretation: an "Indian's looking-glass" may be, in fact, "an Indian": the Indian *as* looking glass for the white man. The "looking-glass" is Apess's text — a "red" piece of writing. If this is so, the white man gazes at the text of color and sees himself. How can this be? One possible implication is that the white man reads the text only to understand *himself* as colored in some fashion or other, and this is precisely Apess's point.

"An Indian's Looking-Glass" is organized around a series of five reversals of color definition, and these reversals hinge upon an axis of distinction defined by the difference between interiority and exteriority. In other words, Apess begins with the binary distinction between whites and everyone else; as O'Connell notes, one of the hallmarks of Apess's prose is his figuration of "all . . . groups whites categorized as 'nonwhite,' including the Jewish people . . . under the single rubric, people of color" (Apess xiv). But whites, according to Apess, are really "colored" in their "heart" or in their thinking — black or red as the case may be. And the text's concern is with making this color manifest, with bringing it to the surface.

The first time he does this occurs when he analyzes why whites praise Indians in certain ways yet deny them American "rights and privileges":

> Is it not because there reigns in the breast of many who are
> leaders a most unrighteous, black principle, as corrupt and un-
> holy as it can be — while these same unfeeling, self-esteemed
> characters pretend to take the skin as a pretext to keep us
> from our unalienable and lawful rights? (156)

Skin versus that which lies within the "breast" — this is Apess's crucial distinction. Whites are "black" in their feelings toward others. He reiterates a
version of this same color problem in the next paragraph: "I am . . . merely
placing before you the black inconsistency that you place before me — which
is ten times blacker than any skin that you will find in the universe" (157).
Hypocrisy is a form of "blackness," and no one is blacker than a white man.

The next two times Apess describes the white man's character, he fantasizes that white peoples' colored qualities might be made visible. If all of the
people of the earth were brought together, notes Apess, one would see that
colored people outnumber whites by fifteen to one:

> Now suppose these skins were put together, and each skin
> had its national crimes written upon it — which skin do you
> think would have the greatest? . . . I should look at all the
> skins, and I know that when I cast my eye upon that white
> skin, and if I saw those crimes written upon it, I should enter
> my protest against it immediately and cleave to that which
> is more honorable. And I can tell you that I am satisfied with
> the manner of my creation, fully — whether others are or not.
> (157)

Whites, if their acts were made visible — if the results of their "principles"
were shown on their skins — would be bodies covered with ink, tattooed to a
"blackness" far darker than the skin color of any Indian. The writing of a historicist anthropology of white persons would render them morally colored. This
is perhaps to say that the determination of who is *really* colored in this world
is a product of representational practices, and not something natural. It is something that cannot be determined without anthropology and its attendant analytics and judgments.

As Apess produces his list of white crimes, of white violations of their own
religious and legal traditions, he tells his white audience, "I do not wonder

that you blush, many of you, while you read" (159). Here, white recognition of culpability for Amerindian poverty and abuse produces flushed skin; in the Indian looking glass the white man becomes, on the surface of his body, the red man.

One might usefully compare this text's nearly unique strategies to those of Wallace (W. D.) Fard and Elijah Muhammad in the construction of Black Muslim theology. Their "inversion" of "the arbitrary symbolism of light as essentially good and dark as essentially bad" led to the conclusion that "Darkness shines in the Light, and the Light cannot comprehend it. Black is good, white evil" (Wills, "Three Leaders" 66). Garry Wills argues that this reversal was "virtually begging to be made," and one might argue that Apess's reversal, too, is a logical and necessary response to the color field, to white/black hierarchies. In Apess's case, the first important point to be made is that white and black, white and red, white and colored remain inflected in precisely the same way that he found them. White is still "good" and dark colors "bad." In this way, one might suggest that "An Indian Looking-Glass" merely *reinforces* the prevailing color analytic; at best it opens onto a debate over the best way to define the linkage between color and persons. That is, in Apess's text it is impossible to imagine anything but a world in which whiteness reigns.

And though Elijah Muhammad's understanding of color manages to go so far as to rethink this moral color order, his reversal too is a logic trapped by original parameters. "Begging to be made": The very distinction between white and colored undergirds a network of reversals and inversions — positions within a field of possibilities — that, even if not apparent or immediately instantiated, are necessary to the constitution of the field. White-skin chauvinism engenders black-skin chauvinism, white-heart chauvinism, and the like. Columbus, Apess, and Muhammed thus occupy a discursive hall of mirrors — indeed, a series of looking glasses. Mutually supportive, each of these different readings of color lends credence to the others. Each demands recognition of the significance of color, and each calls out to the others as its logical interlocutors. What goes relatively unremarked, then, in these texts is color distinction itself, unless one were to attempt a reading of such texts as ironic or parodic. And there may be room in Apess for such a reading: The fifth time that Apess refigures the question of color he does so colloquially, punningly: "By what you read, you may learn how deep your principles are. I should say they were skin-deep"

(Apess 160). Here Apess refers to all of the seventeenth- and eighteenth-century maxims or aphorisms assembled around the trope of "skin-deep," from "All the beauty of the world, 'tis but skin deep" to "Many a dangerous temptation comes to us in gay fine colours that are but skin-deep."[12] Apess shifts the focus of such aphorisms from the depth of good looks to the depth of "principle." White skin conventionally marks his readers as good people, Apess suggests, but whites are all darkness beneath the surface. And yet the invocation of the familiar warning about surface appearances — and the violence of its introduction here as a kind of rhetorical slap in the face — suggests that Apess is not entirely serious about his redefinition of color. "An Indian's Looking-Glass" can at times be read as tactical wit: an exposure of the absurdity of color logic.

One more point: Apess's redefinition of color across an axis of outside/inside mimics the logic of nineteenth-century scientific racism, which translates older methods of distinction based on judgments of "surface" beliefs, behaviors, and appearances (for example, white/black, Christian/non-Christian, savage/civilized) into an account of difference that begins with the blood, with the internal workings of the body. The crucial text for understanding this act of translation is Thomas Jefferson's *Notes on the State of Virginia* (1787), in which Africans and Indians are figured differently. They are measured in terms of their relationship to white civilization by separate criteria. Jefferson begins his acount of Indians, for example, by citing the Comte de Buffon's list of Indian characteristics: feeble, small organs of generation, neither hair nor beard, no activity of mind, and the like. He dismisses some of these, and working from what remains, he argues that Indian difference is situational, not natural — a product of living conditions, not biology: "The causes of this are to be found, not in a difference of nature, but of circumstance" (Jefferson 186). That is, their comparative savagery — their nearness to the state of nature — accounts for any difference. For example: "He is neither more defective in ardor, nor more impotent with his female, than the white reduced to the same diet and exercise," and "his vivacity and activity of mind is equal to ours in the same situation" (184, 185). Jefferson argues that though there are "varieties in the race of man, distinguished by their powers both of mind and body," Indians are "probably... formed in mind as well as in body, on the same module with the 'Homo sapiens Europaeus' " (189, 187).

But as is well known, Jefferson centered his account of Africans on the significance, the primacy, of color:

> Whether the black of the negro resides in the reticular membrane between the skin and scarf-skin, or in the scarf-skin itself; whether it proceeds from the colour of the blood, the colour of the bile, or from that of some other secretion, the difference is fixed in nature, and is as real as if its seat and cause were better known to us. And is this difference of no importance? Is it not the foundation of a greater or less share of beauty in the two races? Are not the fine mixtures of red and white, the expressions of every passion by greater or less suffusions of colour in the one, preferable to that eternal monotony, which reigns in the countenances, that immoveable veil of black which covers all emotions of the other race? (264–65)

Jefferson goes to great lengths to discount any understanding of African difference, including intellect, as a product of "situation," of slavery. Here the question of color proper — the aesthetics of appearance — is directly linked to some organ of the body: "membrane[s]," "bile," or "blood."[13] Just as in what Reginald Horsman calls "the first significant classification of the races of mankind" — François Bernier's work in the late seventeenth century — classification is "based on physical characteristics, mainly color" (Horsman 46). That is, theorists of whiteness may well have good reason to suggest that color talk is race talk, but it is an articulation, a historically contingent jointure rather than a necessary identity or conflation. Analytics of the outside worm their way inside in *many* rather than *every* account of race. "Fine mixtures of red and white": these beauties — "red and white" and all points between — are a natural thing in Jefferson's text and are naturally linked to human potentialities, whatever the evolutionary actuality.

In short, Jefferson's text is monogenist (or committed to a view of single human creation) when it comes to Indians, with its insights organized in a manner consonant and consistent with midnineteenth-century evolutionary anthropology, and polygenist with regard to Africans. And Jefferson uses color, the oldest modern category of differentiation, to secure or ground race theory. Early scientific racism, then, penetrates the body, searching out linkages between "color" and the mysteries of fluids and living tissues. Apess's text works precisely this territory: color is an index, or a symptom, of a more fundamental, interior matter or substance. But Apess's crossing of the color line — showing that bad people can manifest white skin, for example — potentially turns the text into parody of scientific racism. "An Indian's Looking-Glass" presents to a white audience that which is literally unthinkable in order to score the point that the linking of surface to depth — the project of racialist theorizing — is intellectually bankrupt. Apess perhaps only underscores this point by reference to the "heart" as the crucial organ or faculty of the interior, subtly and slyly shifting the ground on bloodline accounts of essence. "Yes," he seems to say, "it's the blood, but only to the extent that it regulates your affect with regard to people of color." The significance of Apess's text is further underlined in that it appeared in the same decade as Samuel Morton's *Crania Americana* (1839), the crucial text for — the "large fact" of — polygenist interpretation. The dissenting voice of "An Indian's Looking-Glass" emerges at the very moment that scientific racism entered the American anthropological mainstream.

All of which is to acknowledge both the dangers and subtleties that Apess negotiates. His is an extremely difficult position: accusing all of his readers of hypocrisy, flirting with reverse racism, maintaining a nearly undecidable tonality so as to border on mere eccentricity. And yet, granting Apess everything — granting his text the power to critique and perhaps destabilize color's instrumental relationship to race theorizing in the name of a "leveled" "distinction" (160) — one might wonder whether Apess, in the end, breaks with all anthropological thought or perhaps advocates some other, already existing version of anthropology. One can answer this latter question affirmatively, and perhaps Apess's anthropology is not so far from Jefferson's account of Indian personhood.

Apess urges his "civilized" white readers to consider the plight of the Indian trapped in a relatively undeveloped and stultifying mode of political economy — primitive communism:

> They are made to believe they are minors and have not the abilities given them from God to take care of themselves, without it is to see a few little articles, such as baskets and brooms. Their land is in common stock, and they have nothing to make them enterprising. (Apess 155)

He imagines a future in which Indians will be educated to take part in the competitive individualism of civilization—a time when "the brightest and first-rate talents [among the Indians will be] put forward and held up to office" (156). In other words, even though Apess's text makes clear that the Amerindians' current "mean, abject, miserable" condition is the result of the white man's greed and indifference, it also inevitably works a version of the savage/civilized dichotomy—a version familiar from many nineteenth-century white anthropologists, and one put in the service of cultural condescension, hierarchization, and exclusion.

Four years later, in the second edition of *Experiences,* the substitution of "An Indian's Thought" makes this investment quite clear: Christian whites have a duty toward "all the race of mankind"—a duty to respond to Indian "ignorance" and to "educate the Indians" (Apess 161). Apess is a monogenist in his emphasis on a single human "race" and a hopeful evolutionist with regard to his prescriptions for "ignorant people." Apess's text, then, dismantles a "modern," emerging mode of distinction (race) in the name of an "older" one (savagism). "Prejudices" and "distinction" reemerge in another form. The result of Apess's "militant" critique of white discourse is Pyrrhic.[14]

THE COLORED FOUNDATION OF WHITENESS

James Fenimore Cooper's *The Last of the Mohicans* is an equally complex account of color, which may seem a strange claim to make given the novel's reputation as straightforwardly racist through and through. In Gary Ashwill's comparison of Apess's and Cooper's texts, for example, Cooper's Indians are read as "ineradicably, *racially* different [and] unequal" (Ashwill 213). Frequently remarked are the text's "imperialist nostalgia" for the inevitable decline of the Indian and the narrative's seeming prohibition against racial amalgamation (the blonde heroine is saved from Indian rape; the part-Caribbean, dark heroine, Cora, and the novel's good young Indian, Uncas, are killed before they can actualize their sexual desire for one another). But it is rarely noticed that Cooper's language of differentiation, in *Mohicans,* is primarily one of color. And even though Cooper's text is highly overdetermined in this regard, and certainly the word "race" is used in the text, the terms "white" and "red" are ubiquitous. This language is decidedly not a code or mask for an idea of race, and in the novel the normative and seemingly natural boundary of white and colored is crossed in a way that is even more confounding than the strategies of "An Indian's Looking-Glass," producing another kind of identity politics — what one might call "an-other to othering."

It is possible, however, for the reader to be beguiled by the speech that Cooper's "bad" Indian, Magua, makes before the old chief, Tamenund, in chapter 29 — the novel's single longest remark on the topic of differentiation. The speech distinguishes not only between red and white but among red and white and animal:

> "The Spirit that made men, coloured them differently," commenced the subtle Huron. "Some are blacker than the sluggish bear. These he said should be slaves; and he ordered them to work for ever, like the beaver. You may hear them groan, when the south wind blows, louder than the lowing buffaloes, along the shores of the great salt lake, where the big canoes come and go with them in droves. Some he made with faces paler than the ermine of the forests: and these he ordered to be traders; dogs to their women, and wolves to their slaves. He gave this people the nature of the pigeon; wings that never tire; young, more plentiful than the leaves on the trees, and appetites to devour the earth. He gave them tongues like the false call of the wild-cat; hearts like rabbits; the cunning of the hog, (but none of the fox,) and arms longer than the legs of the moose. With his tongue, he stops the ears of the Indians; his heart teaches him to pay warriors to fight his battles; his cunning tells him how to get together the goods of the earth; and his arms enclose the land from the shores of the salt water, to the islands of the great lake. His gluttony makes him sick. God gave him enough, and yet he wants all. Such are the pale-faces.
>
> "Some the Great Spirit made with skins brighter and redder than yonder sun," continued Magua, pointing impressively upward to the lurid luminary, which was struggling through the misty atmosphere of the horizon; "and these did he fashion to his own mind. He gave them the island as he had made it,

covered with trees, and filled with game. The wind made their clearings; the sun and rains ripened their fruits; and the snows came to tell them to be thankful. What need had they of roads to journey by! They saw through the hills! When the beavers worked, they lay in the shade, and looked on. The winds cooled them in summer; in winter, skins kept them warm. If they fought among themselves, it was to prove that they were men. They were brave; they were just; they were happy." (Cooper, *Mohicans* 300–301)

Color serves as the prime marker of distinction, and color has a racial character. At the bottom of the scale of value are the black bear and beaver. At the top is the "brighter and redder" skin of the Indian. And somewhere in between are people with "faces paler than the ermine," or "pale-faces." Each has a quite separate and distinct way of being and purpose in the world, according to Magua. Each was created separately by the "Spirit" and has a unique relationship to labor and property.

Magua says these things, but there is no good reason to trust to the wisdom of Magua, since color does not work this way in the rest of the novel. In Cooper's world, color is not something that one is simply born into, no matter how many times Hawk-eye, or Natty Bumppo, says that he is the "man without a cross." Hawk-eye himself, for example, has been able to alter his physical color, and this is cause for some pride even as he demands that he be considered white: " 'The worst enemy I have on earth, and he is an Iroquois, daren't deny that I am genuine white,' the scout replied, surveying, with secret satisfaction, the faded colour of his bony and sinewy hand" (31). Many times, too, the novel notes that Indian color is nothing but a product of a life lived outdoors, under the sun—a monogenist argument about geographic dispersion and adaptation.[15] The novel's epigraph, from *The Merchant of Venice,* says as much: Amerindian "complexion" is just "the shadowed livery of the burnished sun" (Cooper, *Mohicans* xxvii).

Color in general in the novel is a code for something akin to "culture." The language of color is deployed in paragraphs that treat the topics of styles of manhood (31), Christianity (78), and methods of battle (138), for example. Two particular examples concerning central characters in the novel make it abundantly clear that color is culture. If Magua is correct about color and character, then the Mohican brave Uncas should be "red." Hawk-eye, however, tells Uncas that he has been modified by their friendship, that he is no longer quite the same red man as his blood relatives, the Mohican Tortoises: "the same blood runs in your veins, I believe [as in the Tortoises]; but time and distance has a little changed its color" (272). And Cora, who is clearly explained to be the product of a marriage between a white man and a mulatto mother (159) and who is described as having a complexion "the color of the rich blood, that seemed ready to burst its bounds" (19), is said more than once near the end of the novel to be "white." First Hawk-eye says it, noting that her spirit is that of a "pale-face," and then Cooper reiterates the point, saying that the story of Uncas and Cora is "the tale of the white maiden, and the young warrior of the Mohicans" (346, 348). If Cora, for Cooper, is white, then color must be mutable in the novel. It is possible to be born with whatever blood, whatever skin tone, and become the color of another through experience.[16]

This is the project that the book develops for the one character who undergoes a major transformation or development over its course—Duncan Heyward, the British army major forced into an encounter on the forest's border with two sorts of Indians, as well as the British scout Hawk-eye, in order to protect the women he loves. Heyward is, according to Cooper, an "adventurer in empiricism" (246), which means that, like Hawk-eye, he is engaged in some sort of significant experience that involves interacting with Indians in the wilderness. That experience is an important one, according to Cooper's elliptical remark in his 1831 preface to the novel and according to his longer comment in his 1850 preface to the *Leatherstocking Tales*. In the former, Cooper suggests that Hawk-eye is "perhaps more improved than injured by the association" with Amerindians (*Mohicans* 7). In the latter, Hawk-eye is said to be "too much a man of the woods not to imbibe as much as was at all desirable, from his [AmerIndian] friends and companions":

> Removed from nearly all the temptations of civilized life, placed in the best association of that which is deemed savage, and favorably disposed by nature to improve such advantages, it appeared to the writer that his hero was a fit subject to represent the better qualities of both conditions, without pushing either to extremes. (352)

Cooper in neither case is specific about just what would "improve" someone by contact with Amerindia, but Duncan Heyward's particular improvement from living among red men is bound up with issues of gender (learning how to be a real man and friend to other men) and violence (drawing blood and witnessing death). And these are not separate matters: they are intertwined because blood is a man's business, and a good deal of the blood spilled comes from women's veins.

Heyward is a trained soldier educated in the white world, and he is capable of many things, as the novel demonstrates. He is good with words, knows foreign languages, is clever in his deployment of reverse psychology when confronting Magua, and is an excellent fighter in a conventional sense. But, blind to his own limitations, he makes fun of the psalmster David Gamut because the latter is not a professional man (24).

Though a "manly figure," Heyward nevertheless makes endless mistakes as he journeys through the wilderness (27). He lets up on "active watchfulness" of the forest around him at the very beginning of the novel (27), and as his situation worsens he makes the reverse error, letting his "imagination" delude him. He "converted each waving bush, or the fragment of some fallen tree, into human forms, and twenty times he fancied he could distinguish the horrid visages of his lurking foes, peering from their hiding places, in never-ceasing watchfulness of the movements of his party" (45). At the beginning of chapter 9, for example, Duncan finds himself helpless in the wilderness. He is "ignorant," in "painful doubt," and attempting "fruitless" "inquiry" into the fate of his friends and enemies alike (81). Hawk-eye has little respect for Heyward's abilities and makes fun of his "schooling and passing a boyhood in the settlements" (220). Hawk-eye tells Heyward at one point that "in the darkness, and among the signs of the wilderness, your judgment would be like the folly of a child" (128).

But Heyward catches on, now and then, to things that can be taught in the wilderness through interaction with Indian warriors and Hawk-eye. He assists the latter in reading the signs of nature at a critical point on the trail (217). He also successfully (and appropriately) masquerades as a fool in order to rescue his beloved Alice from the Huron — thereby learning Indian "cunning." And he is permitted to take an important part in the battle between Delaware and Huron that ends the novel.

These all are matters of the empirical, or the "really real." Heyward goes to the wilderness in order to ground himself in the reality of life, to learn that "life is an obligation which friends often owe to each other in the wilderness," as Hawk-eye says (73). Life, finally, is about the "stern and unyielding morality" of us against them: " 'Tis their scalps, or ours!" (75). And the blood, drenched on the landscape, is that which is ultimately real about life in this world, as in the passage that describes the ground around Fort William Henry after the massacre:

> Here and there a dark green tuft rose in the midst of the desolation; the earliest fruits of a soil that had been fattened with human blood. The whole landscape, which, seen by a favoring light, and in a genial temperature, had been found so lovely, appeared now like some pictured allegory of life, in which objects were arrayed in their harshest but truest colours, and without the relief of any shadowing. (181)

Richard Slotkin has noted that a crucial part of "the American myth" is the attempt to "get back to the primary source of blood-knowledge of the wilderness," and in Cooper's novel, life is blood; anything else is merely a shadow (Slotkin, *Regeneration* 17).

The question of the spilled blood is several times directly connected to matters of color in the novel. The topic of bloodline is referred to at moments of bloody conflict, and the notion of original color or racial difference is undercut through reference to the spilling of blood — the opening up of the human body to see what is inside. In chapter 8 Natty implores, "let us teach these natives of the forest, that white blood can run as freely as red, when the appointed hour is come" (77). And Magua, after the massacre, holds up his bloody hand and taunts, "[The blood] is red, but it comes from white veins!" (178). In both cases, the very idea of whiteness is undermined by the fact that whites, under their skin, are really red. Their blood, like Amerindian blood and skin, is red, too. The repeated trope suggests that under the skin all whites are really "red."

One might usefully compare this strategy to Apess's: in Cooper, all bodies' interiors — the site of exploration for scientific racism — are red. A racialist account of bloodlines is undercut by recognition of the blood's constant, universal coloration. Cooper's text, like Apess's, is thus a parody of racialist appropriation of color talk; it is a critique of the founding of a discourse of otherness on imaginary connections drawn between the body's inner and outer halves. Unlike "An Indian's Looking-Glass," however, *Mohicans* privileges redness, not whiteness, as base, foundation, ground.

And what Heyward learns in *The Last of the Mohicans* is precisely this: Through the course of the book, he finds his redness. He journeys dialectically backward into the wilderness in order to seek that which is already red within him, in order, finally, to be better at being white. He is more fit to return to the settlements once his redness is uncovered, made explicit. Cooper figures a proper male, white identity as necessarily incorporating Amerindian masculinity and its semiotics and epistemology (reading nature's signs rather than books, for example).[17] In *Mohicans,* then, one can be a white man, ready to assume the tasks of the white world, because one is always already red. Heyward becomes at least a bit like an Indian in his practicality, his cunning, his reading of the signs of nature, and his ability to draw blood. He undermines the concept of bloodline by becoming bloody red.[18]

Recognizing this intermingling puts one at odds with some of the most distinguished works of Cooper criticism of the last couple of decades. For example, John McWilliams argues that upon the "individuals who exist outside of the fixed social types and classes" in Cooper's fiction (and he is thinking here about Hawk-eye, among others) "fall[s] the burden of loneliness and the necessity to make the crucial decision — to acquiesce or to revolt, to remain or to flee" (McWilliams, *Political Justice* 14). There is no place in Cooper's world, argues McWilliams, for hybrids, for in-betweener figures. And Jane Tompkins says much the same thing. Though she admits that *Mohicans* experiments with crossing the lines of "race, tribe, nationality," in the end, she says, "none of the characters risks his or her identity in the least": "In order to be fully human in Cooper's eyes, a person must belong to one class, one totem, one tribe" (Tompkins 115, 116, 118).[19]

But such conclusions miss something fundamental in Cooper's logic, even though this is not to say that Cooper doubts that whites are more moral and more socially advanced than reds. For him, it is quite clear that whites have moved further along a hierarchical scale of development or civilization. But whites, in the process, have lost something that can only be reclaimed by going back down the ladder of development to a forgotten ground for proper being-in-the-world. A sense of Indian culture must be saved and transmitted to white leaders like Heyward if they are to save themselves at the most fundamental level of right living.

BLACKNESS AND BEAVERS

Animals function much the same way in Cooper's text, and here one should note the long connection between racialisms and analogies between animals and people of color. Apes and Africans, for example, are frequently grouped together—contiguously related—in nineteenth-century polygenist race theory. Jefferson indulged this trope in his *Notes,* arguing that Africans favored white over black: "declared by their preference of them, as uniformly as is the preference of the Oranootan for the black woman over those of his own species" (Jefferson 265). Just as potent, but far less well known, is the linkage of Indians and beavers in the nineteenth-century imaginary. And, here again Cooper's strategies cut against the traditions of such "species-racialisms."

Though Magua argues that a sharp line separates the black animals from red and white human beings, the novel shows that no such sharp line exists.[20] Natty can become a bear and Chingachgook can be a beaver, for example. Uncas, too, figures himself as like a beaver when he describes his own capture: "He followed in the steps of a flying coward, and fell into a snare. The cunning beaver may be caught!" (*Mohicans* 241). And Magua's and the Hurons' inability to grasp this possibility—their failure to recognize Hawk-eye in bear disguise—is mocked by Uncas near the end of the novel: "Go, Huron; ask your squaws the colour of a bear!" (312). There is something to be claimed in this experience of animal masquerade—in the descent to the very depths of a human being's animal existence—and this is clearest in the novel in the many passages about the beavers. Beavers, in several remarkable passages, are shown to be far more ambitious than red men and to have some qualities that make them instructive to whites. When Heyward, from a distance, mistakenly identifies a beaver dam complex as an Amerindian village, Cooper notes:

A hundred earthen dwellings stood on the margin of the lake, and even in its water, as though the latter had overflowed its usual banks. Their rounded roofs, admirably moulded for defence against the weather, denoted more of industry and foresight, than the natives were wont to bestow on their regular habitations, much less on those they occupied for the temporary purposes of hunting and war. In short, the whole village, or town, which ever it might be termed, possessed more of method and neatness of execution, than the white men had been accustomed to believe belonged, ordinarily, to the Indian habits. (218)

Within a few more pages David Gamut and Heyward are again looking at these same "admirable structures," and immediately afterward Heyward finds the real Indian village. He notes that its buildings "were arranged without any order, and seemed to be constructed with very little attention to neatness or beauty. Indeed, so inferior were they, in the two latter particulars, to the village Duncan had just seen." Amerindians are dancing around rather wildly in the village, and according to Gamut, these are "idle antics," and "the wholesome restraint of discipline is but little known among this self-abandoned people!" (231). The beavers, whom Magua scornfully said were put on the earth to labor, are actually models of discipline, industry, and order.

The beavers' mentality is worthy of consideration by both whites and reds. Though Magua argues that beavers do not have much to offer in terms of the "virtue of wisdom" (282), one of Magua's companions on the trail talks to beavers and speaks "in words as kind and friendly, as if he were addressing more intelligent beings" (284). This Amerindian man hopes that beaver intelligence can be transmitted to his war party if he speaks respectfully to the animal. He "intimated, though with sufficient delicacy and circumlocution, the expediency of bestowing on their relative a portion of that wisdom for which they [the beavers] were so renowned" (284–85). Hawk-eye adds something on this score: "I have known greater fools, who could read and write, than an experienced old beaver" (222). More dramatically, Heyward thinks (concerning the beavers) that "even the brutes of these vast wilds were possessed of an instinct nearly commensurate with his own reason" (230).

Beavers certainly amount to something less than civilized men in Cooper's view, but they also bear a deep relationship to men—and, perhaps, to bourgeois men in particular. They picture a set of characteristics and values that remind men of what they should be, at bottom. Just as red men have something to teach whites about who they are, so too the black beavers' presentation of a sound grounding for human beings (for human being)—their instinctual wisdom, intelligence, and industry—makes them prime companions for woodlands slumming. It is, finally, a matter of real interest that Magua refuses to recognize his relationship to the beavers, whereas Chingachgook can be mistaken for one and demonstrates both "sagacity" and "reason" during his masquerade (285). And Heyward's mistaking black beavers for red men is instructive as well. In gazing down on beaver architecture, he imagines better, even ideal, Amerindia, where existing real advantages of being red might be secured by absorbing that which is black.

As point of comparison, James Kirk Paulding's *Koningsmarke,* published three years before Cooper's novel, in 1823, is an Indian captivity tale that includes side commentary on beavers and Indians.[21] Paulding's eponymous hero, who has been forcibly adopted by Indians, attempts to convince the "great warrior, statesman, and hunter" Ollentangi that his "philosophy and religion" are "nothing but the light of nature, which only served to lead people astray" (Paulding 210; 216). Ollentangi argues,

> "I see every day the bears, beavers, and all other animals, pursuing their natural impulses, by which they attain such a degree of happiness as they are capable of enjoying. . . . The beaver . . . builds better houses than we Indians, and the fox is better lodged in winter than we. Had we been naturally as reasonable as they, we should have made our habitations under ground, at least for the cold season. You white men, it is true, build better houses than the beavers, and are better lodged than the foxes, but in attaining to this you have become a miserable race of slaves, who do nothing but work all day long, and buy and sell every thing, from your Maker, down to the smallest article you possess." (216, 217–18)

Nature and the force of natural impulses teach the conditions for happiness, Ollentangi says, and therefore "the animals were wiser a great deal than men"

(217). But Koningsmarke will have none of this: He "would then undertake to explain the distinction between man and all other animals; the former being governed by reason, the latter only by instinct, and therefore of an inferior race by nature" (217). Koningsmarke gives up, however, when he recognizes the vast difference between his and Ollentangi's "state of society, as well as the progress of intelligence" (218). He cannot convert the "confined views and opinions" of a simple Indian. Paulding therefore denies the possibility of learning anything from either Indians or beavers or of teaching Indians anything about white "reason" (218). As in Magua's discourse, animals and reds are each locked into place, and their ways of being are at odds with those of whites.

Perhaps more usefully, one can relate Cooper to Lewis Henry Morgan on this same point. Morgan, in many ways the founder of modern anthropological research, wrote four foundational classics of anthropology between 1851 and 1881 (*League of the Iroquois* [1851], *Systems of Consanguinity and Affinity of the Human Family* [1871], *Ancient Society* [1877], and *Houses and House-Life of the American Aborigines* [1881]), as well as nearly fifty magazine and journal articles on Amerindians. In fact, Morgan wrote exclusively about Amerindians his entire career, with one exception: in 1868 he published *The American Beaver and His Works.*

Morgan does not generate a colored reading of beavers, and yet his beavers map out a clear alternative to Cooper's politics of identity. Morgan says that beavers are on a far lower level of intellectual development than either Amerindians or Europeans:

> The hiatus between man and the nearest species below him on the scale of intelligence is so wide as to disturb the symmetrical gradation of the several orders of animals. . . . Portions of the human family are still found in the darkness of ignorance, and in the feebleness of mental imbecility; and yet, although the distance is very great, it is much less than that between the latter and the most intelligent of the inferior animals. The difference expresses the superiority of his structural organization and of his mental endowments. (*American Beaver* 280, 281)

And yet Morgan's view is that the similarities between beavers and human beings in terms of what he calls their "psychology" far outweigh the differences.

There are differences of "degree" but not "in kind between the manifestations of perception, appetite and passion, memory, reason and will on the part of a mute [i.e., beaver]" (276). The beaver "is capable of sitting up erect upon his hind legs, and of walking upon them, his paws thus liberated," which means that beavers are more like men than almost any other animals: "Man's great superiority over the inferior animals is shown in nothing more conspicuously than in the freedom of his hands" (27). The freedom of beaver paws, in turn, permits the building of elaborate and thoughtful architectural structures that are "suggestive of human industry" and that demonstrate a *"free intelligence"* and "act[s] of progress from a lower to a higher artificial state of life" (viii, 146, 264). The "Supreme Being," according to Morgan, may even have endowed beavers with a "moral sense," a characteristic that Morgan presumes his readers understand as the ultimate distinction between man and animal (249).

If all of this is true, says Morgan, then God wants beavers to share this world with human beings: "It is not unlikely that God has adjusted a balance among the several orders of animals which cannot be overthrown except at the peril of the aggressor; and that in some mysterious way this balance is destined to be preserved" (283). Human beings must learn to respect the beaver, and grant it its place and even its "rights" (284). Morgan's book, then, is a nineteenth-century animal rights document, designed to encourage its readers to think of "our relations to them . . . in a different, and in a better light" (284).

But what can be learned from the beaver, if anything? Do the lower orders of being, as in Cooper, act as a kind of natural ground for purposes of constituting his readers' identities? Morgan, like Cooper, writes at some length about mistaking beavers for Indians:

> The cry of a young beaver resembles very closely that of a child a few days old. A trapper illustrated to the author the completeness of his deception by this cry, when he first commenced his vocation in the Rocky Mountains, by relating the following incident: he was once going to his traps when he heard a cry which he was sure was that of a child; and, fearing the presence of an Indian camp, he crept in cautiously through the cotton-wood to the bank of the stream, where he discovered two young beavers upon a low bank of

earth near the water, crying for their mother, whom he afterward found in one of his traps. On one occasion I was similarly deceived in an Indian lodge at the mouth of the Yel-
lowstone River, where a young beaver was lapping milk from
a saucer while an Indian baby was pulling its fur. It was not
until after several repetitions that I noticed that it was the cry
of the beaver instead of the child. (Morgan, *American Beaver*
134)

And Morgan relates a story about the successful domestication of the beaver
by an Indian woman, her trapper husband, and their "half-blood" boy. The
beaver "was particularly attached to the half-blood boy with whom he was
nursed and grew up—following him on all occasions wherever he went" (222).

But beavers do not instruct or ground human life in Morgan's work. All
they can do is mimic human beings in certain respects, reminding human beings that purposeful and even moral life does not begin and end with humanity. Knowing something about the beaver enlarges people's sense of the wonder and importance of all of God's creations. Morgan's view of beavers and
beaver life is, to put it simply, bare multiculturalism. Let us live with them, he
argues, and respect creation's common bonds as well as God's determination
of absolute differences between beings.

The whole of Morgan's work, including that on Amerindians, constitutes
nothing but increasingly complex chartings of differentiations and distinctions
among beings. In his first book, three wholly different states of being or
"spirit"—"the hunter, the pastoral and the civilized state"—provide the ar-
mature for distinction, and his later work simply expands and complicates this
scheme (Morgan, *League* 60). "Strongly teleological and bound to a system
of unfolding ideas," his work in general constitutes an "ordering" "in value-
laden stages" (Hinsley 29). Each step up the ladder of development is a matter
of pure progress, with nothing lost along the way. As Thomas R. Trautmann's
study of Morgan suggests, "The most encompassing of Morgan's ideas is that
the evolutionary process is a progressive, unilineal one. The evolving subject,
of course, is mind." (32).[22] In Cooper, on the other hand, a process is a work
by which the developmental leaps upward from animal to red to white come
at great cost, and the very idea of whiteness must be secured by remembering
the losses incurred—that is, by remembering the forgetting of redness (and it

may be, too, that an adequate whiteness or redness is secured by blackness in the same way). In this special sense, the very idea of whiteness is de-structured in Cooper's text. Only a person who senses that proper whiteness rests on a red foundation can escape Cooper's criticism.

But there are real limits to Cooper's imagination in this regard. For example, color identities are not complexly grounded in the opposite direction. Black identity is not dependent on red or white identity. It is merely black and ultimately servile if not combined with whiteness. Nor is an Amerindian identity dependent on whiteness. It is just red. (Uncas's whiteness is an *addition* to his redness rather than a grounding of it.) This is so because Cooper and Morgan are united in their belief that the developmental ladder points one way only: up. For Cooper, only higher states of being and identity are complexly shaped. Only whiteness needs other colors in order to comprehend itself.

And it is important to make clear what Cooper is not, in terms of his special identity politics. Cooper is not interested in preserving the actual lives of people of color; rather, he is merely interested in preserving their culture. Indians are disappearing from the scene as quickly as the beaver, and there is neither plea nor plan anywhere in the novel for red salvation. The loss of actual red (and black) bodies is simply an inevitability, as Uncas's death demonstrates. At most, Cooper hopes that the very ideas of redness and blackness will remain embedded within whiteness, even as the world turns blindingly, numbingly white in terms of skin color. Nor is Cooper a color leveler, even though Hawk-eye believes that whites and reds have a "common nature" (53) and Cora, Munro, Heyward, and Tamenund all serve (though some of them equivocally) as spokespersons for color blindness in the novel. At the end of the novel, Munro fantasizes a future life in heaven with fewer notions of difference, and Cooper significantly permits Hawk-eye to disabuse him of the idea. Munro hopes that "the time shall not be distant, when we may assemble around his throne, without distinction of sex, or rank, or colour!" (347). But Hawk-eye "shook his head, slowly." And he argues that this would be like hoping "that the snows come not in the winter, or that the sun shines fiercest when the trees are stripped of their leaves" (347). Munro reluctantly but finally agrees: "I understand you. It is the will of heaven, and I submit." Even in heaven there are no end of distinctions. And Cooper's novel ends by foreclosing blood amalgamation in this world in the crucial case of Uncas and Cora.

Though Cooper thus clearly "colonizes" color in order to secure white identities, his text points promisingly toward a larger project of the de-structuration of color scheming. Whiteness in *The Last of the Mohicans* is a necessarily and happily contaminated category from its beginning. And that very thought might be worth preserving. Whiteness is not something that needs mixing. Rather, whiteness needs to recognize its always premixed condition; that is, that it is already mixed if it is to be anything at all. And, just perhaps, it should not be anything at all.

3. Amerindian Voice(s) in Ethnography

We stand with them in many interesting relations.
—LEWIS HENRY MORGAN,
LEAGUE OF THE IROQUOIS (1851)

Lewis Henry Morgan and Ely Samuel Parker are linked together at what many historians of anthropology consider to be the foundational moment for modern American ethnography: Morgan's *League of the Ho-de'-no-sau-nee, Iroquois* (1851).[1] The joint production of this text is carefully foregrounded by the white Morgan, whose dedication indicates his "obligations" to Parker, a Seneca Indian, and describes the book's contents as the "fruit of our joint researches" (vi). The book's preface reiterates this debt to Parker's "invaluable assistance during the whole progress of the research, and for a share of the materials," and for his "intelligence, and accurate knowledge of the institutions of his forefathers" (xi). The precise terms of these two men's personal and intellectual interaction during the creation of *League of the Iroquois* can be assessed in great detail, given the huge number of letters and documents Morgan left behind and, more important, the hundreds of pages of ethnography, correspondence, and other work that Parker produced during their collaborative period, nearly all remaining to this day in manuscript.[2]

This is no small matter: in recent years ethnographic theorists have increasingly criticized the practices of more than one hundred years of fieldwork for its overwhelmingly Western, Anglo, "upper-middle-class professional" voice (Rosaldo, *Culture and Truth* 206). Renato Rosaldo, for example, has called for the production of "relational knowledge," in which the work of the anthropologist is aligned and contrasted with "the so-called native's interpretation of the ethnographer's conduct" (206):

> The study of differences, formerly defined in opposition to an invisible "self," now becomes the play of similarities and

differences relative to socially explicit identities. How do
"they" see "us"? Who are "we" looking at "them"? Social
analysis thus becomes a relational form of understanding in
which both parties actively engage in "the interpretation of
cultures." (206–7)

Rosaldo's claim is that all fieldwork has always inevitably involved the ongoing interplay of such voices, even though most of the resulting, predominantly
synchronic ethnographic accounts repress this drama and "exclude diachronic
processes as objects of fieldwork" (Clifford, *Predicament* 32). As David Murray reminds us, with reference to colonial encounters in the Americas, "Any
temptation to imagine an archetypal pristine moment of confrontation between
absolute others needs to be tempered by the almost ubiquitous presence on
the scene of someone, usually an Indian, . . . who has already made the connection, and who could act as mediator" (Murray 1–2). In Rosaldo's language,
this mediator serves less as an agent of "enculturation" — a kind of guide or
initiator for the "innocent" anthropologist — than as a participant in "a recurring conflict of interests, an agonistic drama, in mutual respect, complicity in
a productive balance of power" (Rosaldo, *Culture and Truth* 204, 205, 206).

A mediator such as Parker always produces ethnographic text in conjunction with and in struggle against the anthropologist, and this fact should in-
form readings of any literature that involves the "study of man" on the basis
of "lived experience" with the other. For example, the novelist James Fenimore Cooper had little or no interaction with Amerindians, yet a number of
his most significant conceptions of Amerindian life are drawn from anthropological literature that claims such interaction, including the Reverend John
Heckewelder's *History, Manners, and Customs of the Indian Nations* (1818).[3]
Although many American Studies–style interpretations of nineteenth-century
race literatures assume that works such as *The Last of the Mohicans* are nothing but a mass of stereotypes about Amerindian peoples, it is at least cause for
wonder that Ojibwa author George Copway, or Kah-ge-ga-gah-bowh, wrote
Cooper in the same year that Morgan's book was published that

of all the writers of our dear native land, you have done more
justice to our down trodden race than any other author. . . .
Many times in my travels . . . I have been asked the question

"Does Mr. Cooper give a true picture of the American Indians." I have universely [*sic*] had the pleasure of answering,
"yes." (Cooper, *Letters* 275)[4]

One might conclude that Amerindians such as Copway were brainwashed by
European conceptions of their nature,[5] but the joint foundations of anthropological thinking make Copway's remark inevitable. Anthropology in the largest
sense is not simply a disciplinary Anglo discourse — an extension of Western
cultural imperialism — but a practice that necessarily crosses and double-crosses
the color line. The subaltern voice, collaborative and countertextual, is lodged
at the very sites of the invention of the various anthropological discourses.

The novelty in the particular case at hand is that Ely Parker's intellectual
precocity and Western-style education permitted him to act not only as the
prime mediator, translator, and oral informant during Morgan's fieldwork but
as a long-distance collaborator on the actual text, providing by letter detailed
information on the Seneca and the Iroquois and composing extended portions
of *League of the Iroquois* — most particularly transcriptions and translations
of Iroquois speeches for the book's second section, "Spirit of the League."
This interaction was fraught with asymmetrical power relations: At the time
Morgan most sought Parker's assistance, he was holding over him the promise
of various state posts as a civil engineer on the New York canal system. More
than one of Morgan's letters contain both a request for detailed information and
a report on slow progress toward Parker's postings.[6] But Parker also produced
a large number of never-published materials about the Iroquois, clearly separate from Morgan's needs but inspired by his work with him. During the late
1840s and early 1850s Parker apparently planned his own volume on the Iroquois, which at one point had the working title "History of the Government,
Manners, Customs, Religion, and Literature of the Iroquois Confederacy, or
the Nations of Indians."

Strangely, the story of the collaboration between Morgan and Parker and of
Parker's own ethnographic and historical writings has yet to be told, even
though Elisabeth Tooker has written several important articles on the composition of *League* and two biographies of Morgan and two of Parker have appeared in this century. Typically, these scholarly assessments refer to little of

Parker's own ethnographic materials other than his transcriptions for Morgan. And even the more detailed of these assessments stop once they have judged just how much of Parker's material was included in Morgan's book: Tooker concludes that "neither Morgan's interviews with nor letters from Parker were as extensive as some have supposed" (31), whereas Parker's grandnephew, anthropologist Arthur C. Parker, argues that both Ely and his brother Nicholson contributed substantively to the text.[7] But no one has yet dealt with the significance of such contributions — that is, the status of Parker's "voice" and the ways in which Parker speaks in and through the text.

Such an analysis will reveal a great deal about ethnic voice — the ways in which Amerindian and Anglo voices figured themselves in the midnineteenth century — and will even, at times, problematize the very possibility of speaking with a singular tongue. Finally, however, a gap opens up between the texts of Parker and those of Morgan. Morgan's work, though undoubtedly ethnocentric,[8] is primarily dedicated to preserving the idea of the inherent connectedness of different cultures, whereas Parker's texts consistently insist, through various rhetorical strategies, that there are absolute gulfs between Anglo and Amerindian. The two voices make uneasy partners, even though together *they constitute what one might consider the two lobes of the modern, liberal mind on matters of race.*[9] In short, a reading of the Parker papers can reveal an agonistic struggle within liberal identity politics, very much akin, for example, to the difference between relational and antiassimilationist multiculturalisms, as I described in the prolegomenon. On one level, these are important *tactical differences,* and they speak differently to highly charged, nineteenth-century matters of late conquest such as political sovereignty and citizenship, just as multiculturalism does on slightly different, slightly more "cultural" (and slightly more presuppositionally incorporative) grounds. But on another level, these differences *have no value,* because neither Morgan's nor Parker's anthropology can provide an adequate framework for thinking around or beyond a more obviously exclusionary colonial anthropology — what Drinnon calls "the metaphysics of Indian hating."[10] And yet one is tempted to suggest that there are two Ely Parkers, and that a certain archival Parker, positioned against anthropology in general, at least provides hints toward something else: this Parker, as will be made clear, is a candidate for the canon of anti-anthropology.[11]

CROSSING GAMES

Although Parker speaks with the experienced voice of the auto-anthropologist in his later ethnographic fragments, he occasionally uses the cynical, deflating voice of what one, with qualifications, might call "the trickster"[12] when he addresses Morgan's early attempts to become "Indian" through adoption and assimilation. This Parker, commenting on the strategies and techniques of the ethnographer, appears not in *League of the Iroquois* but in the manuscripts.

The Morgan-Parker relationship is marked from its beginning by complex cross-ethnic identity gaming. By the time he met Parker in 1844 Morgan had founded the Order of the Gordian Knot, a men's secret society, and transformed it into the Grand Order of the Iroquois, whose initiation ceremonies involved turning Anglo men into modern-day representatives of dead Cayuga Indian warriors. The first version of the ceremony, which Morgan wrote in 1844, noted that the "Great Spirit" would be appeased when "men learn of them [the Indians], & admire them, & mourn for them." "To save their memory from the grave is our delightful task," the ceremony instructs, and it concludes with the organization's "prophet" telling the new initiate, "You are now a Cayuga warrior. . . . you have taken the place of the ancient Cayuga henceforth you must be known only by the name of ———." Morgan took for himself the name Skenandoah, "after an Iroquois friendly to Americans during the Revolution" (Resek 23). Morgan, then, was already a self-styled "Indian" by the time he met Parker in 1844, and he installed Parker into the society soon afterward. This is not as curious as it might at first sound, this transforming of a Seneca man into the embodiment of a deceased Cayuga warrior. When Parker wrote to Morgan during these years, he typically wrote from a "white" subject position, referring to the Iroquois in the third person.[13] This strategy may have marked his own understanding that he had crossed cultures over the course of his Anglo-style education, a point not lost on his biographers. Both emphasize Parker's partial self-transformation from "red" to "white," and both recount the story that his mother had received a prophecy in a dream during her pregnancy that Ely would be "a white man as well as an Indian" (Parker, *Life* 48; Armstrong 14).[14]

So Ely was born Seneca, became white, and then became Iroquois again, this time Cayuga. And Morgan, the budding Anglo anthropologist, turned himself Cayuga, and then became red again when, in October 1846, he asked, through Parker, that the Iroquois officially adopt him as an Indian. "The honor was not given freely," notes Morgan's biographer Carl Resek, and Morgan and his friends Charles Porter and Thomas Darling were made Seneca warriors of the Hawk clan only after promising to pay "for the expense of food and entertainment" for the annual corn harvest festival (Resek 37–38).[15] Morgan was renamed "*Ta-ya-da-o-wuh-kuh,* meaning 'One Lying Across,' which signified that he would serve as a bond of union between the Indians and the whites" (Stern 18).

But just how fluid were Morgan's and Parker's understandings of ethnic identity? Morgan, from all appearances, took his own initiations quite seriously. Parker, on the other hand, demonstrates some reserve — and even a sense of humor — regarding both Morgan's initiation as a Seneca and the initiations that took place in Morgan's Iroquois society. Parker's at times scathing written remarks may be responses to the colonial power relations at the heart of the Morgan-Parker collaboration. Two examples from Parker's papers can be cited. During the journey that Morgan, Porter, and Darling made to Tonawanda for initiation, Morgan and Darling met with a mishap while crossing the Tonawanda creek. Arthur Parker summarizes Porter's version of the event:

> Darling entered the canoe, wrapped himself tightly in his shawl, and then Morgan, famed student of Indian lore, grasped the paddle, shoved off the canoe and leaped into it. But alas, he no sooner leaped in than he leaped out, for his "shoving out" was also a shoving over. This was a sad plight for Mr. Darling, for he was wound in his shawl like an Egyptian mummy. (*Life* 83)

Arthur Parker's mirth is redoubled and the satire considerably sharpened in Ely Parker's version (written, significantly, from an Indian subject position):

> Now it has happened to us Indians that we are not as favored as our white brothers in many respects. We are not as civilized and enlightened, and therefore we do not enjoy the benefits of the many improvements that are daily brought before the public for their use. We do not yet comprehend

the mode of navigating the waters by steam, and of annihi-
lating space and time by the same method. We still retain
many of the primitive customs of our fathers, and among
them the art of navigating the water, save that the wooden is
substituted in place of the bark canoe. Now it was owing to
this that a sad misfortune happened to our brothers or rather
may we say to one, viz our Darling. (Parker, "A Report")

Ely Parker's version of the event contextualizes it within the familiar terms of
savagism and civilization, which was Morgan's basic model for comprehend-
ing human difference, as well as the model for most nineteenth-century anthropologists. The "primitive" Indians, Parker notes, occupy a position far below that of "civilized and enlightened" peoples. And yet his tongue is firmly
in cheek, and Morgan's woodlands slumming is undercut: Morgan and his
company do not belong out in the woods with the Indians and probably do not
deserve to become Seneca warriors. But Arthur Parker's account of this story
goes this far, too: Morgan, "famed student of Indian lore," cannot paddle a canoe. Ely's lines, however, additionally question the very distinction made between "savage" and "civilized" peoples. At the very least, civilization may come
at the cost of not being able to perform the simplest of tasks; Morgan and
Darling cannot cross a small creek without risking their lives. But it is only
the terms or significance of the distinction between Amerindian and Anglo that
is questioned, and not distinction in principle, because Parker's pride in being
Indian surfaces in these lines. The satire establishes a distance between Morgan and Parker that no purchased, off-the-rack initiation can change. Parker is
an "Indian," and Morgan is little better than what today Ward Churchill calls
"plastic medicine men."[16]

Parker's skepticism concerning Morgan's attempts at transculturation is
also evident in the former's 1847 revision of the Grand Order of the Iroquois
initiation ceremony, prepared at a time when the Grand Order was on the verge
of collapse. The ceremonies that Morgan had written—including his 1845 revision of the ritual, based on visits with Parker and other Iroquois—were
filled with one-dimensional, wooden-Indian language about the "Redman,"
the "Pale-face," and the "Young Warrior."[17] But Parker's version, the "New
Initiation of the Wolf Tribe of the Cayuga Nation," raises the stakes of this

identity narrative, tripling or quadrupling such stereotypes. Its depictions, like this one of Cayuga warrior life, thus read as satire:

> The blackness of despair surrounds him, as he sits in his lonely wigwam — it accompanies him during the chase, it returns with him at night, to rack his mind as he lies upon his bearskin, seeking that rest that he so much needs. Mighty Prophet — The braves of the Cayuga nation have brought into our wigwam, this young man who has wandered for many moons in the trails of the Pale Faces. ("New Initiation")

Perhaps most telling is Parker's reference to the Cayuga "wigwam." Parker knew full well that the Iroquois had long lived in large groups in wooden "long-houses" and not the "lonely" wigwams of certain Great Plains Amerindian groups. Parker, too, through reference to the daily "chase" after venison and "bearskin," plays up the stereotype of the Indian as primarily a hunter, an image that dogged Morgan's work, including *League of the Iroquois,* long after Morgan, too, knew that the Iroquois at time of European contact were settled agriculturalists. And the Indians who "wandered for many moons in the trails of the Pale Faces" might as well be characters created by Henry Wadsworth Longfellow, given the passage's forced Indian romanticism. One cannot with certainty call Parker's "New Initiation" a satire. But when compared to Parker's careful culling of ethnographic data during this period — on matters ranging from international relations to astronomy to arithmetic to medicine — the text appears to be, on one level, one great laugh at the naiveté of Morgan's Grand Order.[18]

In Parker's ethnographic letters to Morgan, he easily figures his subject position as white, or at least as being at some remove from Indian ethnicity. And yet in the two texts on Morgan's multiple Indian initiations, he erects a border between cultures that Morgan is not permitted to cross, and Parker's "Indian" voice has humiliating, trickster qualities. Parker understands his own voice to be cross-cultural, and yet it denies Morgan that same mobility.

The significance of this gesture becomes clearer the more one explores Parker's gestures toward racialism and their relationship to Morgan's narratives of Indian identity. Parker's racialist "identity dissent" finds one form of expression in his ethnographic fragments, some of which Morgan includes in *League of the Iroquois,* but Morgan frames such dissent in the context of a larger, more authoritative ethnographic narrative of identity. Parker's early satirical texts, on the other hand, chip away at the seeming authority of Morgan's ethnography.

THE UNCIVILIZED MODEL OF CIVILIZATION

League of the Iroquois uses multiple strategies to situate or explain "Indianness." When Morgan describes Indianness, he refers to color (the "red man"), to a somewhat indeterminate concept of "race," and to the notion of "spirit" or character ("characteristics").[19] Most famously, Morgan situates the Indian within at least three progressive, developmental schemes, foreshadowing the complex gradations of late-nineteenth-century evolutionary anthropology, including Morgan's own *Ancient Society* (1877).[20] The first scheme concerns political economy and hypothesizes three "states" through which all peoples have moved or are moving over time, "the hunter, the pastoral, and the civilized," much in the manner of Adam Smith's elaboration of the same theme (Morgan, *League* 60). The Iroquois, according to Morgan, exist in the "highest position among the Indian races of the continent living in the hunter state," the "zero of human society" (57, 143). The second scheme ranks types of governments, describing a "progression...from the monarchical...to the democratical, which are the last, the noblest, and the most intellectual" (129). In between is the oligarchical, which is a "low state of civilization" but which also has a "liberal character" to it (63, 105). The liberal Iroquois polity is only a single step from democracy (133): "It seems to have been the aim of the *Ho-de'-no-sau-nee* to avoid the dangers of a hereditary transmission of power, without fully adopting the opposite principle of a free election, founded upon merit and capacity" (114). The third, religious scheme ranks the Iroquois above the Greeks and below Christians in their knowledge of a "Supreme Being" (151).

In these three tripartite scales, then, the Iroquois rank high in the lowest and middling ranks, but in no case do they rise to the level of full "civilization." Human groups such as the Iroquois are capable of moving upward on their own, but Morgan says that the task is extremely difficult:

> If their Indian empire had been suffered to work out its own
> results, it is still problematical whether the vast power they
> would have accumulated, and the intellect which would have
> been developed by their diversified affairs, would not, to-
> gether, have been sufficiently potent to draw the people from
> the hunter into the agricultural state. . . . The Iroquois, at all
> times, have manifested sufficient intellect to promise a high
> degree of improvement, if it had once become awakened
> and directed to right pursuits. Centuries, however, might have
> been requisite to effect the change. (*League* 142, 143)

Given prodding by the State of New York, it might be possible to "stimulate"
the Iroquois to become "sufficiently advanced in the agricultural life"—that
is, the pastoral state—but this is as far as Morgan will speculate (36).

There are, however, other forces at work in Morgan's text that make one
wonder just how well his categories work, even for him. Particularly when it
comes to elaborating the second of the scales—which measures the sophistication of the Iroquois "system" or "structure" of laws,[21] as embodied in the
Iroquois Confederacy or the League of Six Nations—Morgan tends to collapse distinctions between Iroquois and Anglo governments and even at times
to praise Iroquois polity at the expense of "later" developments. Morgan does
this through his recurrent suggestion that Iroquois and U.S. government structures and values are astonishingly similar.[22] His tack in these passages stands
at the beginning of an intellectual tendency that today manifests itself in the
claims made by some Amerindian and an increasing number of Anglo historians that participatory democracy and democratic values were literally transmitted by the Iroquois to Anglo-Americans—that the Iroquois held the key to
successful, liberal governance.[23]

Sometimes Morgan says this directly, and at other times he merely implies
it by invoking key words from U.S. political mythology when he describes the
Iroquois system. In one instance of the former, Morgan says that the nations
of the Iroquois had for hundreds of years been "sustaining nearly the same relation to the League, that the American states bear to the Union" (*League* 62).
Obviously referring to the intentions of the framers of the U.S. Constitution,
Morgan elaborates:

> Something more lasting was aimed at, than a simple union
> of the five nations, in the nature of an alliance. A blending
> of the national sovereignties into one government, was sought
> for and achieved by these forest statesmen. . . . Yet the pow-
> ers of the government were not so centralized, that the na-
> tional independencies disappeared. (77)

The very structure of the League of the Iroquois, then, deeply resembled the
structure of the most advanced government on earth.

Morgan is also a master of tropological suggestion. His statement that the
Iroquois were assembled in "the most perfect union of separate nations" (81)
echoes the U.S. Constitution's goal of establishing "a more perfect union."
Even as Morgan defines Iroquois government as oligarchical, his rhetoric works
to demonstrate that its powers "rested upon the popular will" (76). The power
to wage war resided "with the people" (75), and near-democratic mechanisms
ensured the inclusion of "the people" in political decisions: "From the public-
ity with which the affairs of the League were conducted, and the indirect participation in their adjustment thus allowed the people, a favorable indication
is afforded of the democratic spirit of the government" (106). Such references
to "the people" circulate throughout Morgan's pages on government, recalling
the Constitution's "We the People" and Jefferson's "Right of the People."

Other Iroquois values, too, resonate with the language of the Declaration
of Independence and with Morgan's notion of the highest values any government can foster: "the just sentiment of 'political equality' . . . coupled with that
of 'personal liberty'" (131):

> In the language of Charlevoix, the Iroquois were "entirely
> convinced that man was born free, that no power on earth
> had any right to make any attempt against his liberty, and
> that nothing could make him amends for its loss." It would
> be difficult to describe any political society, in which there
> was less of oppression and discontent, more of individual
> independence and boundless freedom. (138–39)

One would suspect, given Morgan's developmental schema, that liberty, or
freedom, is a value that unfolds more completely with each step up the evolutionary ladder of government forms. An oligarchy, even in its most "liberal"

form, should logically preclude liberty more than would a democracy. But Morgan suggests that no political entity valued freedom more than the Iroquois: "The government sat lightly upon the people, who, in effect, were governed but little. It secured to each that individual independence, which the *Ho-de'-no-sau-nee* knew how to prize as well as the Saxon race" (77).

"Equality," too, is a touchstone value for the Iroquois, according to Morgan. Within the oligarchical framework there was an "equal distribution of powers" among the League's sachems, or legislators, and the nations "occupied positions of entire equality in the League, in rights, privileges and obligations" (93). Even "the people" were granted an equality with one another: the League's "higher effort of legislation" had the effect of "placing the people upon an equality, and introducing a community of privileges" (137). Though Morgan uses fewer superlatives in describing Iroquois "equality" than in characterizing their passion for freedom and liberty, these passages suggest that the Iroquois valued and institutionalized equality at the level of nations, legislators, and individuals.

Morgan's greatest burst of enthusiasm comes when he suggests that the Confederacy "is, perhaps, the only league of nations ever instituted among men, which can point to three centuries of uninterrupted domestic unity and peace" (141). For Morgan, the Iroquois League often seems to be a model for U.S. governance rather than a stepchild of it — rather than a mere glimmering or foreshadowing of democracy within a less civilized context. Morgan's strategy, at the very least, is one of incorporation, allowing his readers room to imagine a time when New York will be able to "raise" the Iroquois "to the condition of citizens of the State" (36). But this strategy puts tremendous pressure on Morgan's scales, and even vitiates them. Morgan's more macro interest in developmental differentiation is squeezed into his account of the details of Amerindian polity, and the result is that he makes nearly as many claims of Anglo-Amerindian sameness as of difference.

Ely Parker's most extensive contributions to *League of the Iroquois* move in yet another direction: toward full-blown racialism. In the section on Iroquois religion, Morgan carefully inserts thirty pages of Iroquois speeches (most of it a three-day-long talk by one of the League chiefs, Jemmy Johnson, which recapitulates the teachings of the New Religion of the turn-of-the-century Iroquois prophet, Handsome Lake) and fully acknowledges Parker's transcription and translation of the material. The second of these speeches, that of Onondaga leader Abraham La Fort, or De-ät-ga-doos', took place at a Mourning council of the Iroquois in October 1847. La Fort/Parker begins:

> Let us observe the operations of nature. The year is divided into seasons, and every season has its fruits. The birds of the air, though clothed in the same dress of feathers, are divided into many classes; and one class is never seen to associate or intermingle with any but its own kind. So with the beasts of the field and woods; each and every class and species have their own separate rules by which they seem to be governed, and by which their actions are regulated. These distinctions of classes and colors the Great Spirit has seen fit to make. But the rule does not stop here; it is universal. It embraces man also. The human race was created and divided into different classes, which were placed separate from each other, having different customs, manners, laws and religions. (231–32)

This speech, in which biological "class" difference is made universal, natural, and a product of a divine act, is polygenist through and through. From the beginning, "the human race was created and divided into different classes," and so, consequently, Indians and Anglos are inherently different, separated by a racial "boundary line" that has been artificially "crossed" by the incursion of the "white-skinned race" onto Indian land (232). The Indian race is "entitled to a different religion, a religion adapted to their customs, manners and ways of thinking" rather than a religion either related to or contaminated by white religion (232). Indian "laws," too, are separate and distinct. Neither Morgan's sense of developmental relations among all forms of government nor his more covert erasure of significant difference is countenanced by La Fort/Parker. To give a complex context for this passage, it is worth noting that it is startlingly similar in content to Magua's long speech in *The Last of the Mohicans,* cited in chapter 2, which Cooper's dialogical imagination serves up as a wrongheaded counterpoint to his own distinct version of evolutionism. Broadly, then, Cooper/Magua operates as a pair analogous to Morgan/Parker, which should give some pause to any attempt to culturally essentialize standpoints and positions.

The Handsome Lake/Johnson/Parker materials, gathered at several Condolence councils, including those of 1845 and 1848, and put into final form by Parker in 1850, are similarly positioned: "All men were made equal by the Great Spirit; but he has given to them a variety of gifts" (*League* 247).[24] And "He has made us, as a race, separate and distinct from the pale-face. It is a great sin to intermarry, and intermingle the blood of the two races" (251–22).[25] Though Morgan, in his later *Systems of Consanguinity and Affinity of the Human Family* (1871), would emphasize that "blood" is what Robert E. Bieder calls "the controlling or limiting factor in the transmission of culture," he also hoped that the "blood" or intellectual limitations of Amerindians might slowly be compensated for through the process of amalgamation (Bieder 223).[26] Johnson/Parker, on the contrary, asserts that any mixing of blood damages the Amerindian. Purity of blood is the only guarantee that a divinely created, "separate and distinct" people will endure.

"The pale-faces," however,

> are pressing you upon every side. . . . You must therefore live as they do. How far you can do so without sin, I will now tell you. You may grow cattle, and build yourselves warm and comfortable dwelling-houses. This is not sin; and it is all that you can safely adopt of the customs of the pale-faces. You cannot live as they do. (250–51)

Merely the smallest of variations of custom are permitted the Indian, and that only for reasons of survival, so that Amerindians can stabilize and protect themselves on the boundary line of white invasion.

Both the La Fort/Parker and Handsome Lake/Johnson/Parker materials radicalize the question of difference in a way that is familiar today in anthropological practice.[27] According to the culturalist paradigm at work in a good deal of twentieth-century anthropology, the world's peoples are nothing but different, and it is not possible to describe the moral or political significance of such difference. Although the significance of Amerindian difference is left entirely undetermined in the Parker transcriptions and translations in *League of the Iroquois,* other Parker papers tantalizingly address such matters and suggest reasons why Parker freezes out Morgan's hierarchies and strategies of incorporation.

It might be worth noting that Parker's perspective on such matters was rel-atively hard-won and that, based on the existing documentary record, Parker's editorial control over the Jemmy Johnson material, in particular, amounts to pure invention at the level of identity politics and is therefore best understood as *Parker distinguishing himself from Morgan.* The archival record includes four more-immediate Parker versions of Johnson's speeches, *not one of which conforms, in terms of its anthropological politics, with the version printed in Morgan's book.* Briefly, the Parker and Morgan archives include a full Parker "translation" of Johnson's 1845 version of the speech, Parker's brief 1847 *Batavia Times* newspaper report on yet another version, a Parker draft of the *Batavia Times* text,[28] and Parker's shorthand notes for the 1848 version — all of which predate the text Parker finally sent to Morgan for inclusion.[29] The 1845 text provides the only foundation for the remarks on the "whites" and the pro-hibition against their way of life, but it is far less pointed than the version Morgan published:

> The Great Spirit made the Indians to live by the chase. But he foresaw the day when the Indians would be deprived of their hunting grounds; therefore He has said it was not a criminal wrong to follow the example of the whites in some respects. He said that it was not wrong to build houses after the manner of the whites, to work your farms and raise do-mestic animals. But an Indian could not live and be happy when he exceeded these bounds. (Quoted in Parker, *Life* 261)

The *Batavia Times* texts reiterate that white settlement and white practices threaten Indian life: "He [the Great Spirit] saw that they had greatly decreased, and were grossly degenerating into the manners and customs of the pale faces, who were settling around them in great numbers. He saw the ravages of the fire water of the white man among them" (Parker, "Indian Council" 1).[30] But, significantly, Parker reports Johnson's religious doctrine as "not much averse to universalism," which certainly has a bearing on anthropological thought.[31] Universalism may only signify secure salvation for Indians, since the Batavia draft includes Parker's report of "Jimmy" Johnson's "peculiar idea" that, un-like Indian souls, "the souls of white people dying never passed from earth, but were continually wandering up and down to and fro" until the last judgment, with the exception of the soul of George Washington ("Indian Council" 2). But here one needs to underline that Johnson apparently distinguishes whites from Indians merely at the level of conduct and God's judgment, unlike, for example, Cooper's Hawk-eye, who insists that whites and reds occupy separate heavens. Parker, in other words, reports Johnson asserting in 1847 that there is one God, one religion, one standard of judgment.

Finally, Parker's shorthand notes from 1848, which are important because Morgan urged Parker to produce "a fine record of the proceedings" for incorporation into *League of the Iroquois* (Fenton 303),[32] have Johnson noting the "jail & Fetters and rope & whip" of the "white folks" and urging Indians to recognize that there is a "Great Sin in selling land," but the only strictly anthropological moment in the text is positively Jeffersonian, when Johnson says, "All men created equal, but different in property &c — & Mind this was intended by G[reat]. S[pirit]." (Fenton 308, 307, 309).

All of this at least suggests that the anthropological antiassimilationism laced throughout Parker's pages in *League of the Iroquois* significantly elaborates, heightens, and even swerves from actual field notes and reporting. *Something happens* at the moment when Parker must incorporate himself — and must incorporate his vision of Indians — into the Morgan text, and perhaps the most that can be said is that Parker's strategy amounts to a rejection of Morganism, but only on the basis of the most obviously available countertradition within anthropology.

RACIALIST ANTIASSIMILATION

Morgan, as has been noted, emphasizes freedom and equality as the root values within Iroquois political life (and on this point, the Parker/Johnson 1848 field notes tend to agree). Morgan adds to his list both "peace" and "supremacy" when he analyzes the "international" reasons for the construction of the league. The Iroquois partook of the Indian's "universal spirit of aggression" (*League* 8), and they produced their confederacy, in part, in order to be better conquerors. Raising "a colossal Indian empire," they "often established settlements or colonies of their own people, to exercise a species of superintendence over their acquired possessions" (15). The league was designed to "promote their prosperity, and enlarge their dominion," and "the great object of their confederacy was peace—to break up the spirit of perpetual warfare" through complete conquest of all adjoining territories (67, 92).

These are Morgan's Iroquois: embracing peace through strength, freedom and equality through oligarchy. Parker, on the other hand, emphasizes a word that does not appear in Morgan's text: "happiness"—itself, of course, another keyword in Jefferson's Declaration. Parker's notion of "happiness" is quite similar to Garry Wills's understanding of Jefferson's term. Not merely the private pursuit of pleasure, "happiness" is "a *political* goal," a public politics of mutual obligation between one person and another and between state and citizen: "a hard political test of any reign's very legitimacy" (Wills, *Inventing* 248, 251). Parker wrote about Indian "happiness" in greatest detail in a text from his school years: "A Composition Read by Ely S[.] Parker at Cayuga Academy November 18 1845." The "Composition" is an overnight response to a challenge Parker received in debate: "If the savage life is more condusive to happiness than the civilized, why has Mr. Parker abandoned that life?" Parker's reply is complex, but in it he writes about the benefits of Amerindian life:

> I have seen that the happiness of the savage consists in the gratification of his desires. Their appetites are few, and not being vitiated are easily supplied. Their happiness consists in their strong social affections, and the pains they use to cultivate this among themselves is great. Their happiness consists in the exercise of their physical and mental powers. Their happiness consists in their temperate habits & the great benedictions of health and ease. Their happiness consists in the principle discharge of their duties & responsibilities, which are comparatively few to those of the civilized. . . . Special laws are unnecessary for the restraint of their actions, for in their intercourse with one another, their actions are dictated by right reason, common politeness and civility. Their happiness consists in the contemplation of the great attributes, the mighty works and the well guided providences of the Great Spirit. . . . their happiness consists in . . . their virtue, benevolence and hospitality and a strict adherense to truth & duty, and a high regard of word and authority.

"Happiness," then, is a special combination of "duties and responsibilities" and the individual cultivation of "right reason" and moderation in both consumption patterns and emotional behaviors. Such things lead to a life of public "virtue," "ease," and personal "contemplation" — in other words, "happiness." Morgan explicitly rejects such a life in a comment in *League of the Iroquois* on desire and the " 'power of gain' ": "For the desire of gain is one of the earliest manifestations of the progressive mind, and one of the most powerful passions of which the mind is susceptible. It clears the forest, rears the city, builds the merchantman — in a word, it has civilized our race." Indians do not have such desires, he says, and therefore are stunted in their development, even though Morgan acknowledges that Indians have secured "an exemption from the evils . . . which flow from the possession of wealth" (139). But Parker refuses to accept this logic:

> I have read of civilized men possessing great wealth and riches, of civilized acquiring distinctions and greatness, of civilized acquiring power almost unlimited in its extent, & of men of learning & erudite wisdom, but I have never read of happiness existing among them. ("Composition")

And Parker concludes his composition by suggesting that if he continues to find that "happiness" does not exist in the "civilized" world:

> We will resume the blanket, the cap of feathers, the bended bow & the arrow, and tomahawk and scalping knife & . . . savage life in all of its wildness & then you may justly say "do what you will an Indian will still be an Indian."

This not-so-veiled threat to return to the "tomahawk and scalping knife" is Parker at his most racially exclusionist and militant, holding that Indians are the one true happy people and their lifeworld of "happiness" must be protected even if violent retribution is necessary. Here one can comprehend how Parker might believe that he himself is capable of crossing the line that separates races and cultures, but that such crossing is a dangerous game and perhaps should not be played at all.

Another, related site for Parker's dissent from Morgan involves the interpretation of Iroquois "family" relations or kinship, which Parker understands in "sentimentalist" terms. Jane Tompkins argues that nineteenth-century sentimentalism promoted a powerful, empowering, and self-willed transformation of the heart's "sorrows" into "sympathies" rather than "rage" and further promoted the subsequent communication of this ability "from heart to heart" (Tompkins 131). As Augustine St. Clare puts it in *Uncle Tom's Cabin,* "Any mind that is capable of *real sorrow* is capable of good" (Stowe 444). Although sentimentalism is always overtly concerned with crossing lines of race and gender on the basis of universal human sentiment, sentimentalism often houses, close to its heart, a politics of separatism that "has worked to institutionalize racial categories" (Brown 60).[33]

Parker's sentimentalist view of Indian social bonding is reflected in his ethnographic transcription of the story of the Iroquois Confederacy's founding—the crucial historical moment for Morgan's understanding of Iroquois political life. This tale is endlessly repeated by both Anglo and Amerindian anthropologists of the nineteenth century, but Parker's version is remarkably different from these other tellings. The tale involves two men, Tadodahoh and Dagonowedah. Tadodahoh is an Onondaga warrior with a head full of snakes; he had become a "military despot," ruling over the five Iroquois nations by force and "terror" (Parker, "Iroquois" 56). Dagonowedah is a visionary Onondaga man "renowned for his wisdom" who conceived the Iroquois League as a method to "take from Tadodahoh his power." Dagonowedah calls a council of the five nations, and

> he proceeded to divulge his plan when he was informed that his daughter had died whom he had left at home sick. He drew his robe about him, covering himself completely, and mourned for her.... He mourned night and day, and in his mourning which he did in a kind of song, he repeated the whole plan of Union. And when he had finished, no one of the wise men seemed to understand or comprehend his meaning and objects. (56–57)

Dagonowedah's plan of uniting the disparate nations in a peaceful "family organization" is conceptualized at a moment of family grief—interestingly, the death of a daughter. Dagonowedah's sorrows are turned to good account, and the Iroquois warriors are finally bound together in a sentimental community around the death of a young woman.

At times Morgan, too, emphasizes the "family" ties of the league, but in a nonsentimentalist mode.[34] He acknowledges that the league "was to bind the people together by the family ties of relationship, and thus create among them a universal spirit of hospitality, and a lasting desire of social intercourse" (*League* 171). But he in no way relies on Parker's version of the founding events. In Morgan's version, Dagonowedah merely has "an impediment in his speech," and the league is established through "a debate of many days" (*League* 101, 61). Morgan's interest in Iroquois family relations is, finally, coldly structural—concerned with the "complex, and even stupendous system of civil polity" based on the family ("Laws" 132). For him the crucial question is "What great object was sought by making the title of chief or sachem hereditary in the female line, thereby perpetually disinheriting the son?" ("Laws" 145). He concludes that it prevents the sachem from "perpetuat[ing] his power in his own family . . . until despotism would succeed to freedom" ("Laws" 147).

In other words, Morgan and Parker, in their recapitulation of the Iroquois League and its purposes, are playing out the very same themes—despotism and freedom, women and men—but for Morgan, women figure significantly at the founding of the league for a functional rather than a sympathetic reason. For Morgan, "freedom" is preserved through carefully planned custom and law. The Iroquois are advancing toward civilized—that is, Anglo—values by well-organized, thoughtful steps: the establishment of matriarchal descent in order to guard against monarchical tyranny. For Parker, on the other hand, "democratic" family feeling is the product of real family sentiment, of the emotions engendered by blood ties. It is specific, internal, and exclusive to Iroquois "family" life.

Morgan and Parker always work at cross purposes in the 1840s and 1850s. Although, as Morgan wrote, they pursued "joint researches," the fault lines in *League of the Iroquois* erupted into disputes that took place only in manuscript notes and fragments. Reading these fragments, one can ascertain that, had Ely S. Parker produced a full countertext to *League,* another view of Iroquois life would have emerged, framed by a significantly different form of identity politics. None of this is to suggest that Ely Parker's work is better than

Morgan's because he "actually was" Indian: Parker's frames of reference are deeply related to Morgan's and are marked by nineteenth-century Anglo ideals such as happiness and sentiment. Put most simply, Parker's ethnographic work in these years amounts to a hardening of racial or ethnic divisions, with the "indigenous" voice, always already vibrating at the heart of the history of ethnography, asserting its right to speak with a deceptively alterior race voice — the voice of blood, of nature, of romantic and wild contentment.

THE END OF ANTHROPOLOGY

But then again there is the *other* Ely Parker — the Parker who on occasion wrote about his suspicions of the whole nineteenth-century anthropological enterprise — indeed, of anthropology in its most general sense — in such a way as to undercut the significance of both Morgan's and his own researches. This skeptical Parker threatens to bury any version of the positive science of anthropology. Listening to this Parker provides an opportunity for "something else" to appear on the horizon, something "beyond anthropology" in any of its many formulations.[35] This other way of thinking, negative in character, attempts to find a way to the bottom of the liberal impasse that is called anthropology.

In an address probably written in 1847, shortly after he joined the Batavia Masonic Lodge, Parker tells his fellow Masons:

> To day, we say and write nothing that has not been said and written ages before. When we claim that an age has attained to a higher degree of civilization than the world[']s history has ever before experienced, we only mean that our common ideas are more generally diffused upon the face of the globe than it has ever been before. What we call the inventions and discoveries in the art and sciences and upon which our age bases its present enlightenment are but the application of natural laws that have existed ever since our universe had a being — In man[']s early history, were philosophers[,] poets[,] astronomers, legislators, theologians, naturalists, chemists, agriculturalists and mechanics cunning in all kinds of workmanship — What have we or do we now that they did not? They had governments and societies as we

have today. They had their national anniversaries and festival days, as we are now holding this recurring anniversary of our Grand Lodge. If you agree with me, my task this evening becomes easy. I cannot impart to you any new ideas. ([Address])

This text, teasing and even confrontational, challenges Parker's predominantly "white" audience's ethnochauvinism. "Natural laws," it argues, have always been available to all of the peoples of the world, and all have learned them and worked with them in equal measure of complexity. There are no "new ideas" in the world. There is no progress, no higher civilizations — only an endless round of different lifeworlds, organized around the same themes of contemplation, technology, literature, government, ritual.

Morgan's projection of developmental stages is necessarily a failure, and Parker's address points toward a late-century Boasian paradigm of "culture" and cultural relativism. More dramatically, in a March 1845 note to himself on "the study of man," written on the back of a list of school expenses, Parker proposes that "there is no study in which more real enjoyment can be found than in the study of man" because he is "endowed with a mind the very essence of divine nature." He continues, however:

> But when we attempt to solve the question how the immaterial thinking being is connected with the physical past of man we are introduced into a labyrinth of mystery which defies all human wisdom and skill to expound. And when we turn in upon our own selves and view our own structure, when we see the Mood of life growing from the great question of human existence to every part of the system, and when we see how tender the vessel which contains that upon which life is dependent, and unnending the power[,] wisdom and skill of that Infinite Being who created us, we can exclaim with the man of old, "I am fearfully and wonderfully made." ([Essay])

In this spiritually inflected fragment, Parker acknowledges, like Morgan, that there is "structure" and "system" to human life — there is a "Mood of life" that can be contemplated. But no end to this study is possible. "Man" and his "physical past" are a "labyrinth of mystery which defies all human wisdom and skill to expound." Taking Parker to the limit, anthropology in general may be a human science founded upon nothing securely "human" at all. It is, finally, an abyss, and without a ground. If *this* Parker is right, then the other, "Indian" Parker who speaks with such authority about significant racialisms is a political Parker—the product of a particular time and place, advocating positions that are fraught with the obvious political perils that all racialisms bring, even when embraced by a dominated fraction of the population and even when liberal in content.

And the direction of the most skeptical Parker—the Parker who undercuts Morgan's and even his own classifications—is the one worth remembering if there is to be a day beyond or, better, without anthropology. A day in which identity politics dissolves neither into cultural warfare nor into its intellectual partner, the doomed and equally fractious grin of multiculturalism. A day in which "the study of man" has become irrelevant in terms of both "study" and the object of study. A day, finally, in which the "labyrinth" that is "man" no longer appears as a puzzle asking to be solved *or* as an insoluble theological riddle. A day in which "man," quite literally, no longer appears.

4. Methodists and Method:
Conversion and Representation

Friends, Christians, your love of mankind extends beyond the
border. . . . May you not tire or grow faint.

— GEORGE COPWAY, *THE TRADITIONAL HISTORY*
AND CHARACTERISTIC SKETCHES OF THE
OJIBWAY NATION (1850)

In surveying the relatively small field of auto-anthropology in the antebellum
era, it is one of the larger surprises that not one but two Canadian-Amerindian
Methodist ministers, George Copway (Kah-ge-ga-gah-bowh) and Peter Jones
(Kahkewaquonaby), wrote book-length anthropologies of their own tribe, the
Ojibwa, at century's midpoint: Copway's *The Traditional History and Char-*
acteristic Sketches of the Ojibway Nation (1850) and Jones's *History of the*
Ojibway Indians (1861). Jones was twenty years Copway's senior and one of
his most important mentors within Methodism; Copway worked for Jones and
admired him, and Jones aided Copway's career in significant ways.[1]

Though Jones's and Copway's lives were linked together in numerous ways
(their wives, for example, were fast friends, even after the Copways' divorce),
Jones grew increasingly wary of Copway. In 1845 Jones wrote in a letter that
Copway "has not judgment to carry out any great undertaking. He is too hasty,
and withal neglects to seek the advice of those who have older and wiser
heads than his own" (Smith, "Life" 16). Copway was expelled from the church
in late 1846 after accusations surfaced of embezzlement of both church and
tribal funds, and his career as a professional writer dates from his subsequent
move to the U.S. East Coast (Smith, "Life" 16–17).

Jones's text, which was written primarily in the 1830s and had been abandoned by 1845, was unpublished at the time of his death in 1856 (Smith,
Sacred 188). The work was published posthumously, edited and with additions
by his wife, Eliza, and other friends. (These additions include a deathbed in-
terview with Jones on matters that would have been covered in the final, un-
written chapters.) Though Jones, in all likelihood, knew of Copway's text and

perhaps had even read it (Smith, *Sacred* 229), nothing supports the conclusion that Jones wrote any of his *History* as a countertext to Copway's. Nor is there any evidence that Copway had read Jones's work in manuscript before producing his own anthropology. Neither author, for example, refers to the views of the other: Copway is mentioned once in Jones's account, and only as a matter of fact; Jones acknowledges the "Indian missionary" Copway's translations of the Gospel of Luke into the Ojibwa language (Jones, *History* 189). Copway, in turn, refers to Jones only as a successful missionary (Copway, *Indian Life* 178–79). The two of them exclusively cite Anglo anthropologists in situating their discourse: Copway cites Washington Irving, Thomas L. McKenney, Henry Rowe Schoolcraft, and John Lloyd Stephens, among others; Jones cites Samuel Morton, Ephraim George Squier, Jonathan Carver, Jedidiah Morse, the Book of Mormon, and the like.

These, then, are independent Indian accounts of the same matter. In assessing the relation between these texts it is difficult to find points of contact; seldom do they cover the same material. For example, both texts contain chapters on Indian language, but Jones's chapter is early nineteenth-century linguistic-ethnological and is concerned with determining the relation between the various Indian languages and dialects, whereas Copway's lens is romantic-ethnographic, focusing on the natural poetry of Indian words and expressions. There are implications that one can tease out of such strong thematic choices, certainly, but one must go outside Copway's book in order to secure a moment when both authorities confront precisely the same matter.

Two Types of Horseradish

From 10 July to 4 October 1851 Copway edited and published a New York–based newspaper, *Copway's American Indian,* in which, typically, his own contributions consisted of excerpts from his three already published books. In each issue, however, he contributed a bit of new matter—typically squibs, Indian sayings, or news paragraphs. In the 26 July issue, however, Copway printed an anecdote, and a very similar anecdote appears in Jones's text. It concerns horseradish. It is a little thing, this "Causes Not Always Apparent, or Horse Radish and Religion." And the same story—or, better, a version of it—is also of little overall consequence in Jones's book, where it is included as one of several bits of Indian "Wit and Shrewdness." But the two reports of the same horseradish reveal a great deal about the differences between Copway and Jones.

The story concerns John Sunday, whom Jones elsewhere in his text identifies as a "well-known Indian Missionary" (*History* 110).[2] But other than this reference to a particular man, a converted Amerindian whom both Copway and Jones knew personally, the two texts display many of the conventions of folk tales. When Copway begins "Some years since, not over a thousand miles from the city of Albany" ("Causes"), he may as well be writing "A long time ago, in a land far away." Two men are traveling: Sunday and a minister, whom Jones identifies as "the Rev. W. Case" (Jones, *History* 205) and whom Copway refers to as an English missionary from "one of the dissenting bodies." Here the stories diverge slightly: Copway writes that the two men stopped at a lodging house and ate with the landlord; Jones says the two men visited with another minister from the United States in order to dine. According to Jones, their host

> was talking to John about religion, feeling truly thankful to see a converted Indian. Among other eatables before him was a dish of finely-scraped horseradish: John, not knowing what it was, and supposing it might be something very sweet, took a spoonful of it into his mouth; presently tears came into his eyes; the minister observing them, and supposing John was weeping for joy at what was the topic of discourse, began to shout, "Glory! glory! glory!" John, as soon as he could, raised his hand and pointing to the dish of horse-radish, said, "O, it is that, — it is that!" (Jones, *History* 205)

The story that Copway tells changes a few structural details: It is Sunday's old friend who tells the landlord about converted Indians, who watches Sunday cry, and who mistakes the effects of horseradish for religious sentiment. But Copway's piece is distinguished from Jones's by the behavior of both Sunday's friend the minister and the Indian. Copway emphasizes that John Sunday paid no attention to the minister's overripe discourse: "He was too busy loading his plate to think of clapping his hands, or in any way signifying his approval of the Doctor's remarks."

And when Copway's minister concludes that "his Indian friend, when he thought of his former barbarity, was *happy* at the thought of his present condition," Sunday corrects him in a manner tonally distinct from Jones's anecdote:

> Just then he relieved himself by swallowing his horse radish, and having wiped his eyes, turns to the Doctor, his face wearing a comic expression, and with a roguish laugh, says, "Doctor, tis not that, (was not happy,) but it is this!" pointing to the radish. "O! very much fire," rubbing his mouth at the same time, when the Doctor took up his knife and fork, and resumed his former occupation with as much zeal as any one around the table.

Copway emphasizes Sunday's general disinterest in his friend's discourse and his "roguish" and "comic" reaction to it, as well as the minister's final disinterest in the Indian. Food is more important than conversion—either talk of it or its signification through tears.

Jones, on the other hand, suggests a sentimental-religious moral to the story, but only through reference to a third burning-sauce anecdote (actually, an analogue of the same tale):

> It is related that two chiefs came from the West to the city of Washington, on business with the government. While they were there, a gentleman invited them to dinner. They went,— and being seated for the first time at a white man's table, they began to eat such things as were set before them, and to help themselves to such as were within their reach. One of them seeing some yellow-looking stuff (mustard), took a spoonful, swallowing the whole. Tears soon ran down his cheeks. His brother chief, seeing him weep, said, "Oh! my brother, why do you weep?" The other replied, "I am thinking about my son who was killed in such a battle!" Presently the other chief took a spoonful of the same stuff, which caused his eyes to weep as did his brother's; who in return asked him, "Why do you cry?" Upon which he replied, "Oh! I weep to think you were not killed when our son was." (*History* 204–5)

Jones's point: The mustard-eating Indians, who are not converts to Christianity, are both liars and obfuscators, and at least one of them has a cruel sense of humor; he is, to use Copway's term, a "rogue."

Jones's Indian missionary, though, by comparison (and Jones presents the stories one after another so that the point is clear), demonstrates what he calls "the difference between a pagan and a Christian Indian's veracity" (*History* 205). In the Jones text John Sunday is too honest to take the compliment when he is praised for his tears by the minister he has just met. It was only horseradish, after all. Jones's Sunday is, finally, so Christian that he cannot accept undeserved praise for his sensibility. He demonstrates, in the process, true Christian honesty and humility. Copway's John Sunday, on the other hand, is a prankster. His "friend" is shown up as pompous and fatuous. Christian tears — which Jones's Sunday takes seriously, even when crying for an altogether unrelated reason — are laughed at.

What, then, is one to make of these horseradish tales? Perhaps two things are useful to note, with reference to folklore tropes and folklore narrative patterns: first, tales about naiveté concerning food are quite commonplace. Versions of such stories exist in nineteenth-century American literature, told by Anglos in order to laugh at the lack of sophistication of various working-class and ethnic figures. Jones's and Copway's cases are interesting because they involve Indians telling such stories about *themselves,* and with the Indian figure emerging triumphant in the end by trumping the Anglo interlocutor through sarcasm (Copway) or humility (Jones). Second, and relatedly, as several dictionaries of folklore note, the symbol of horseradish "signifies the bitterness of the house of bondage" at the Passover seder.[3] The horseradish in Jones and Copway may foreground the fact that their stories emerge out of conditions of colonization. Though eating the hot sauce makes the Indian at the table appear uncivilized, it also triggers remembrance of the Anglo conquest of Amerindia and becomes a "weapon," perhaps, that can be turned back against the oppressor. In Jones the Indian is revealed to be as true a Christian as any Anglo, and in Copway, the savvy and unwilling recipient of Christian religion. Jones and Copway, the two Methodist missionaries, are united in their attempt to humorously resignify the Indian as the equal of or as more sincere or clever than the Anglo. Their stories equally depend upon what folklorists refer to as an "esoteric" representation (that is, a representation of what one thinks the other thinks of oneself). But, then again, their strategies — their Amerindian identity politics — could not be more diametrically opposed.

Let these two stories stand as a petit version of the problem that is presented by the texts of Jones and Copway. As has already been made evident, the two men share many things: both were self-identified as Ojibwa Indians, both lived in the same geographic region at the same time, both were Methodist-trained, both were students of their own culture. But they have passed on to posterity two books, two narratives, that do not easily cohere around a single notion of "Indianness." The disaccord between the two preoccupies the foremost student of Jones and Copway — their recent biographer, Donald B. Smith — who forces himself to make a decision about the relative truth value of the two texts.[4]

Smith argues that Jones's *History* is a "marvelous" account of the detail of Indian life and that "Eliza [Jones] presented it well" — that the *History* is an accurate record of Jones's voice (*Sacred* 246). In order to secure this reading, however, Smith must dispose of Copway's anthropological account. "Even a cursory investigation of his [Copway's] past reveals that historians and anthropologists must use his work with great caution," Smith says ("Life" 5). Smith presents Copway as a kind of con man; he exposes one of Copway's books — a Longfellowesque, book-length poem of forest life — as the work of another man, and a white man at that.[5] He notes that Copway's *Traditional History* is "not annotated, nor are the author's sources of information always identified" ("Life" 22).[6] And he suggests that large parts of the book could not "really come from Copway's pen," arguing that "an outside helper [his better-educated white wife, Elizabeth Howell Copway] is even more evident here than in his earlier autobiography" ("Life" 22). Finally, Smith says that Copway's rose-tinted presentation of precontact Amerindian life is belied by his having chosen to live among whites, in the city: "As an adult he did not return to such a life" ("Life" 6).[7] In other words, Smith implies that Copway's *Traditional History* is not an authentic Ojibwa-Amerindian text in at least two ways: Copway interpolates too much Anglo writing into the book, including Elizabeth's, and *he himself* is not much of an Indian by the time he writes the text.

But many of the same charges could be leveled at Jones and at his book. How "Indian" was this Methodist minister who traveled to Europe and lived in a manner quite unlike that of his Indian ancestors?[8] And why is it that Eliza Jones does not contaminate Jones's text through her editing and additions to his notes? How is it possible to claim that this mediator-editor merely "presented" Peter Jones in such a way so as to perfectly "preserve" his voice? Finally, and on a level of argument that Smith avoids altogether, Copway was born of two Amerindian parents, whereas only Jones's mother was Ojibwa (his father was a white surveyor). By Smith's own account, Jones grew up biracially and biculturally, living at different times with his mother and then his father. What makes Jones's voice "Indian" in the first place?

Authentic Amerindian "voice" seems to be determined in Smith's reading by poor, or at least inelegant, English and by a relative lack of conceptual sophistication.[9] One might justly conclude that Smith's reading of the truth value of the Jones and Copway texts is produced from very thin air—or, at least, from and through romantic anthropology. But what is of greater interest here, however, is Smith's penchant to *decide* the case between Jones and Copway. This is the mind of the classic social scientist, the seeker of anthropological knowledge, inflected by recent, liberal-ethnic critiques of white writing. It sees the discourse of the "insider" with "experience" as having a greater claim to "authenticity" than that of the "non-native." If Jones's text—the perceived insider's text for multiple, tenuously argued reasons—is "marvelous," then the other must be approached "with great caution." If Jones's text accurately represents Amerindia, then the other does not. If Jones is an Indian, the other cannot be. The largest curiosity that Smith's determinations raise concerns the fact that it is Jones's work that apparently is more deeply committed to a Christian-Methodist conversion frame of reference—a frame that an admiring Indianism generally regards with suspicion and reads as a sign of the contamination of pristine Indian culture.[10] It is at least cause for wonder that Copway's borrowings from other sources, his wife's assistance, and his absence from home place the status of his oeuvre—and his voice within it—in doubt, whereas a lifelong career as a Methodist minister does not.[11]

There are strange logics of addition and subtraction at work here that are nonetheless symptomatic of larger tendencies in scholarly Indian studies (whether ethnohistory, ethnocriticism, or multiculturalism in general) and that can be more fully elaborated. The project is one of legitimation: who is an authentic Amerindian, what is authentic Amerindian culture, and, perforce, what is not? Indian worlds are presumed to be, at bottom, enduring monads. Something or some network of concepts and symbols holds together—retains the essence of—the very idea of the "Amerindian." Locating this essence is the limit condition for establishing grounds of representing, and then respecting and admiring, the Amerindian—the limit condition of, for lack of a better term, multiculturalism. The addition of contaminating terms—all the problems of Copway and his texts, for example—is always potentially cause for expulsion or exclusion. These are additions that are thematized as crossing out and deleting the identities that multiculturalism's project of representation intends to preserve. No longer "Indian," not even a "bicultural" figure, Copway must be held at arm's length. Interestingly, however, Jones's grounds for inclusion within a network of Amerindian texts depend, as well, on addition—the manipulation of his texts by Eliza and his friends, the ability to write in English, conversion—without which there would literally be no "Jones" to read. In this case, additions do not amount to subtractions. Additions somehow preserve the "Indian" and make possible the entrance into a multicultural canon and community. One should conclude that multiculturalism is always and necessarily calculating such sums: what counts, and what counts one out. In the largest sense, the most crucial and yet least recognized addition is the representational lens itself: multicultural method, which mandates minimally that cultures be located, identified.

But what would happen if one thought questions of identity on entirely different grounds? What if Indian cultures did not, in themselves, add up? What if "Indian" does not begin from essence? "Addition," for example, might be reconceptualized as merely an effect—and a continually shifting one, at that—of "long division," which is the decision, taking place again and again over centuries, to determine two separate objects of study: Indians and Anglos. One could only conclude, from such a premise, that there is no Indian literature and no Indian identity, as such. The narrative pattern for Copway's and Jones's horseradish jokes, for example, is hardly an example of something identifiably "Indian." Nor are they presented in the text as enduring oral or folk Amerindian tradition. They are, rather, tales born of contact, and, more important for purposes here, fables of division in their own right. In both cases, decisions are rendered regarding what constitutes "good Indians" or "true Indians," and the Anglo-Amerindian border is constituted—*in the first place.* The two texts present "different" borders, certainly, and yet, in many ways, "similar" borders. These things can be said, if "one" chooses. Together they add up neither to "one" "Indian" (the same, or one true and one false) nor "two" (competing accounts: two kinds of Ojibwa). They generate an indeterminate figure, shifting along a concatenating dividing line. The examples of Copway and Jones are remarkable for making just this point: Indian auto-ethnographers have no greater access to the "truth" of Indian life, to particular tribal or national life, than do Anglo observer-participants. They merely—as all textual accounts of race do necessarily—divide and multiply.

THE TIMES OF INDIGENOUS CHRISTIANITY

Jones's and Copway's anthropology is inextricably bound up with their understandings of the relationship between Amerindians and Christianity. And what is at stake in the remainder of this chapter is the relationship between conversion and anthropology. For both Jones and Copway, conversion becomes the central event of—*the centering event for*—Ojibwa history. In this way, Jones's and Copway's work is reminiscent of European anthropological models of greatest significance between the fifteenth and eighteenth centuries, in which the method for distinguishing Amerindians rotates around the axes Christian/non-Christian and savage/civilized—preracializing formations. For Jones, conversion marks the threshold between Indian misery and happiness:

> I have often heard my brethren, both in public and in private, give utterance to the sentiments just expressed; and it must be acknowledged that they were much better off in their former comparatively happy state, when they could feast unmolested on the abundance which nature had provided for them. It should also be remembered that the pagan ideas of bliss are almost entirely sensual, and related to the unrestrained indulgence of the animal appetites. Alas! they know nothing of that real peace which the world can neither give nor take away. From experience of my early life, I can truly say, that their imaginary bliss is so mixed up with every-

thing that is abominable and cruel, that it would be vain to look for real happiness among savage tribes. "The dark places of the earth are full of the habitations of cruelty." (Jones, *History* 28)

In this passage, as in Jones's hot-sauce anecdotes, the themes of Christianity and civilization are intertwined in such a way that Christian conversion brings with it the "happiness" of civilization — that is, a moral world no longer shackled to the "abominable and cruel" (remember the hateful and dishonest jokes that pass between the two chiefs over the dish of mustard). Of importance in the passage as well, but not coincident nor coterminous with conversion, is white contact and conquest: "When they could feast unmolested" refers to a time before white incursions and white violence on the land, and the spreading of alcohol among Amerindian populations. Unlike a good deal of relatively contemporaneous literature produced, like the Jones text, by self-identified persons of color for a predominantly white audience, Jones's work does not treat the whites as benevolent agents of Christ and civilization, nor does he gloss over or mute the problems of contact-conquest and resource appropriation.[12] The generally "unprincipled white man" is, for Jones, "an agent of Satan in the extermination of the original proprietors of the American soil!" (*History* 29).

The implication of all of this is that contact and conquest have no necessary or even contingent relation to conversion, which is at odds with the most typical ethnohistorical narrative: "Religious conversion is related to social, economic, and political conversion" (West 33).[13] In Jonesian history, precontact Amerindia was "comparatively happy," though mistakenly so. The era of conquest and consolidation was recognizably miserable — full of unspeakable hardships — and the time of mass conversion of the Ojibwa brings with it the possibility of "real peace" apart from worldly suffering. This is a recognizably Christian history of falling and rising again, in which, finally, the Amerindian must accept the largest burden of blame: yes, it says, the whites' introduction of alcohol "contributed to the rapid decrease of the Indian tribes," but always because, at the time, Amerindians were "following their native mode of life," and therefore "all of the savage passions of [their] nature assume entire control" (*History* 30). The alcohol, in other words, merely accentuates the inherent "cruelty" of savage life.[14] There was no Amerindian golden age or "paradise"; precontact Ojibwa were "naturally depraved" and under the spell of witchcraft and "the evil spirit" (93, 147–50).

In Jones's history, however, Christianity *belongs* to Amerindians. It is neither a cultural imposition nor a white gift but, rather, the legitimate and inevitable goal for existing Amerindian faith and belief. Though Amerindians had "dark minds," they were "ready to receive the light of the gospel" (166). Indian folklore, for example, narrates versions of biblical stories, such as the tale of Noah and the flood (35–36). This thematic has a long history in Amerindian discourse, and James Treat assigns it to the history of "the global liberation theology movement" (Treat, "Introduction" 1).[15] And although Christianity teaches that all men are of "one blood" (Jones, *History* 32) and although Jones believed that all men were the product of a single, first creation, the thrust of Jones's anthropology (and his practical politics) is culturally separatist. Christianity belongs to Amerindia, therefore, in *its own way*—as a bulwark for Indian culture and survival. Amerindians are conceptualized throughout Jones's work as *not yet Indian enough*. Before Christianity, according to Jones, Amerindian culture was subject to a "law of nature" not sufficiently strong to constitute a functioning, limiting structure. With conversion, Amerindians have the power to master themselves and their passions and to control their own destinies and lifeways (Christianity brings with it moral responsibility, the work ethic, and so on). As a political activist, Jones worked at every opportunity to define a distinctly Indian geographical space, and the laws governing it, within which the Ojibwa might have the requisite resources to do just that. In other words, the implication of Donald B. Smith's reading of Jones is entirely in line with Jones's own conception of Amerindian identity; Indianness and Christianity are both positively inflected because, together, they constitute the positive limit—and the proper sum—of Amerindian identity.

George Copway's anthropology, on the other hand, cannot be mistaken for that of his mentor's. What bears emphasizing in Copway's horseradish story, for example, are the words in parenthesis in John Sunday's final remark: "Doctor, tis not that, (*was not happy,*) but it is this!" When this line is read to its limit, it is, potentially, a broad rebuke. Christianity has not brought Sunday out of misery and into happiness, and far from reflecting Amerindian reality, the minister's belief belongs to the Anglo imaginary. Copway's discourse in his explicitly anthropological text bears all the marks of the romantic, the Indianist. "I love my country; and will any of my readers condemn a child of the forest for loving his country and his nation?" (Copway, *Indian Life* 25). Jones writes of "nature's law" in describing the Amerindian savage state; Copway of "Nature" with a capital *N:* "The mountains, rivers, lakes, cliffs, and caverns of the Ojibway country, impress one with the thought that Nature has there built a home for Nature's children" (14). Amerindians, left to themselves, were a legitimately happy people, "the happiest creations of the Great Creator" (24). Precontact was "that happy time," "the day of their [Amerindians'] glory and prosperity" (20, 23). Unlike Jones's cruel and evil Ojibwa, Copway's are models of honesty and honor (60) and are great lovers of beauty, as evidenced in their onomatopoeic language (123, 125).

As earlier noted, conversion is crucial to this anthropology, but in such a manner that one cannot bring together Copway's history with that produced by Jones. Copwayesque history unfolds in three eras, just as does Jones's, but these epochs are precontact times, when Amerindians always already were true Christians; the denigration of Indians at the hands of the whites; and the gradual learning of "cultivation" from European examples. Original Amerindian Christianity is, one might say, Thoreauvian in character, "governed by the pure rules of christianity, with less coercion than the laws of civilized nations, at present, impose upon their subjects" (Copway, *Indian Life* 141). "Law" is the world's greatest evil, and the less the better. Law brings the "bad signs" of "prisons, penitentiaries, and poorhouses." In the absence of law, Amerindians are guided by an internal censor, an inner persuasion based on notions of honor: "They would as men be persuaded to the right" (141). Law is divisive; the absence of law is inherently communitarian: "Whatever we had was shared alike. In time of gladness all partook of the joy; and when suffering came all alike suffered" (141). The Ojibwa provide a model of Christian charity. This is precisely opposite to Jones's portrait of pre-Columbian times as an era of pure, idlike cruelty of one man to another, which demands social structuration — including Christianity, of course, but many other things, too — in order to produce beings of internal depth, of conscience and judgment and care.

Even more than in the Jones text, then, Christianity is disarticulated from Europe and whites. Copway nowhere suggests that white Christianity serves as a model or even as an influence upon Amerindia. If anything, as in the horseradish tale, white Christians are ethnochauvinist, condescending dunces, puffed up by their blind, smiling charity. They are missionaries bearing spiritual gifts to those who neither need nor want them. As a result, in Copway there is almost no sense of Christian time in the strict sense; there is no moment of fall from grace, no special time reserved for the soul's salvation. The Amerindian relationship to the creator is unchanging.[16] Copway presents instead a secular fall: the history of Amerindian proto-Christians being conquered and then struggling to achieve strictly temporal goals involving the practices of "civilization."

In Copway's *Traditional History,* and unlike in Jones's *History,* Christianity and civilization do not go hand in hand. Copway sees the latter — which includes all forms of education and knowledge building, including the learning of English — as an Amerindian import, grafted onto native Christian practices. As several of Copway's headnotes emphasize, original Amerindian Christianity is Edenic in the sense that it is a time of "garrulous innocence," a time of the "Fantastic, frolicksome and wild / With all the trinkets of a child" (97, 49). Conquest, then, is ambivalent in Copway — "evil entered with the good during their intercourse with the whites" (160).

On the one hand, as in the Jones text, Anglo civilization is criticized in *The Traditional History* — but across a wider front. Amerindians suffered full-scale "dissipation" upon contact (x). They devolved under the pressures of contact; traders took advantage of the Ojibwa, and the tribe was forced by whites to abandon their homes and an agricultural life and move west in order to collect furs for survival (downshifting from the pastoral to the hunter state, in social-evolutionary terms) (241–42; see also 32). Copway adjusts the stereotype of the nomadic, forest-loving Amerindian, presenting it as a product of white/red relations.

On the other, whites in general (and Americans in particular) are a "good influence" on the Indians — helping them toward the "employments of peace," for example (*Indian Life* 64). Cultivation and "improvement" are of crucial concern to Copway's Amerindians (172). He loudly demands: "We want Light! We want Education!" (194). Even though Amerindians enjoyed a "musical flow" of "natural language" before contact, there was a want of "fine discriminating taste" in rhetorical matters (125). And even though the Ojibwa were perhaps the world's most Christian people in spirit, they were "without the means of religious education" (193):

The present state of the Ojibways renders them fully ripe
and ready for great advancement in religion, literature, and
the arts and sciences of civilized life. Multitudes have left
their wigwams, their woods, and the attractive chase, and are
now endeavoring to tread in the footsteps of worthy white
men. (172)

To partially reiterate: all of this situates Copway within the discursive parameters of what today can be called "Indianism." *The Traditional History*
loves precontact Amerindians; *The Traditional History* condescends to precontact Amerindians. It is this ethnochauvinist romanticism that connects Copway's text to Know-Nothing and nativist discourse in midcentury (see Knobel).
Copway's practical political plan — the moving of Amerindians to a western
territory, the granting of American citizens' rights within this territory, and the
eventual absorption of Amerindia through statehood for that territory — deli-
cately links antimonious ideologies: U.S. removal *and* inclusion (see Copway,
Organization).

Neither Copway nor Jones, perhaps, is precisely on the same ground as
Methodism's founder, John Wesley. Wesley also took up the question of Indianness and wondered, when comparing "the bulk of the nations in Europe and
those in America, whether the superiority lies on the one side or the other"
(Wesley 1:617). Wesley's one conclusion is that "the heathen has far the pre-
eminence" when it comes to following Jesus' command to "lay not up for
yourselves treasures of the earth." Unlike Jones' moral abominations and Copway's moral models, Wesley's Indians are constituted by the good "nothing":
"He desires and seeks nothing. . . . He reserves, he lays up nothing." (Wesley
1:617). Besides a certain "non-Wesleyanism," however, Copway's and Jones's
decidedly different historical-anthropological speculations share more important characteristics.[17] The two texts are linked by the telos of a certain kind of
subjectivity: the self-policing subject — that is, the subject that attains a certain, internal distance by expanding itself outward from a one-dimensional drive.
Indians are truly *themselves,* according to these two auto-ethnographers, only
when such self-reflection is possible.

This is the moralizing self, the self-examining self — which is, following
Michel Foucault in *The History of Sexuality,* Volume 1, the modern self par
excellence. Foucault describes a medieval moment in which Christian confes-

sion—"the obligatory and exhaustive expression of an individual secret"—produces such subjecthood, "the basic certainties of consciousness" (Foucault 61, 60). Anthropology, too, is organized according to the logic of the secret, as David E. Johnson suggests, and this is true of auto-ethnography perhaps more than of any other form of anthropology because it alone promises the insider's unmediated story, the hidden truth ("Accounting"). And this logic is only accentuated in the cases of Copway and Jones because theirs are explicitly Christian accounts of Amerindian being with confessional narratives of individual conversion looming at their borders. In both cases, the stories of their conversion are contained within other sets of covers—for Jones, the *Life and Journals of Kahkewaquonaby (Rev. Peter Jones)* (1860), and for Copway, *The Life, History, and Travels, of Kah-ge-ga-gah-bowh (George Copway)* (1847).[18] One might conclude that these are necessary precursor texts to the anthropological matters taken up in the national histories and that, furthermore, these national histories are nothing but versions of conversion literature. One's own secret must be known to oneself—one must come to individual, modern consciousness—before the secret of the group (the individual writ large) can be articulated, released.

By situating the self-reflexive subject—the subject of conscience—at the center of their projects, they therefore reproduce the very conditions of identity, which is why, in the first place, their version of Christianity (Christianity understood as the production of an internal discrepancy between acts and a moral code, for example) coincides with the production of authentic Amerindian personhood. Christianity as such is irrelevant to this question, as are the pathways along which such personhood is achieved (for Jones, out of a time of undisciplined human anarchy, and for Copway, from the beginnings of Indian time) and as are the threats to such personhood (for the former, savagism, and for the latter, law). The point is that Jones's and Copway's shared notion of full Amerindian personhood is a modern identity politics through and through, in the sense that the self-regulated and self-regulating production of "who one is" is the precondition for right living, for the examined life. And, relatedly, the telling of such secrets—the enunciating of one's identities—is linked over many centuries to themes of freedom. In Jones's and Copway's texts, this operates at a personal and national level: for example, only by speaking the truth of Amerindian identity, by sketching it in all of its specificity and uniqueness, can one begin to liberate Amerindians from white or other oppressions.

Foucault's point was, though, precisely to question the very process by which one becomes oneself—to consider the ways in which self-constitution through reflection produces the necessary conditions for a domination that does not have to depend upon the unwieldy machinery of law and punishment, of direct coercion.[19] Foucault's point is that confession/identity does not come out of oneself; rather, it "unfolds within a power relationship," and "the agency of domination does not reside in the one who speaks (for it is he who is constrained), but in the one who listens and says nothing" (61, 62). The implication is twofold: First, identity itself is a domination in that it produces internalized prohibitions, rules of conduct (precisely Jones's and Copway's points, and why they affirm the process). But Foucault's second insight is perhaps more important: identity is subject to manipulation and control "by virtue of the power structure immanent in it" (62). The construction of identity in general—according to any analytic, inflected in whatever manner—is necessarily to leave oneself open to the technics of state control. *Every* identity formation justifies internal and external regulation; every word that one speaks about oneself provides purchase and leverage for another. In terms of Jones's and Copway's metahistories, the hierarchical organization of the concepts "Christian/non-Christian" and "civilized/savage" underwrites a number of possible readings of all or some Amerindians: as holders of a zero-degree identity (Jones's "flat" precontact Amerindians); or an identity that lacks, that is deficient, that needs paternalistic care; or a dangerous identity.

None of this is to argue that, tactically and strategically, the Jones and Copway texts do not attempt to progressively reconfigure white anthropological commonplaces, particularly with regard to Christian matters (the very appropriation or near-appropriation of Christianity, for example, as red), but also concerning the relationship between colonialism and identity. It is evident from the foregoing analysis that the thrust of their metahistories, for example, is to undercut various aspects of white versions of the progressive evolutionary narrative.[20] The major challenge for texts such as *The Traditional History and Characteristic Sketches of the Ojibway Nation* and *History of the Ojibway Indians,* however, is whether the establishment of Indianness in any manner, according to whatever history and anthropology, can free itself from the dominations inherent in identity formation. Foucault's largest point is that all identity resistances are, finally, "transitory" and subject to shifts in strategic redeployment of the technics of power. There are petit epistemological-political questions at stake (for example: the problem of any anthropological account, including Jones's and Copway's, working to cancel others out, to silence others), and grand ones as well: what, if any, account of racial or ethnic identity is inherently "just," inherently outside or beyond hierarchical accounts of difference? Given the importance of this question, Donald B. Smith's choosing between these texts is premature, but these issues can be taken up in a mid-nineteenth-century context by returning to the work of James Fenimore Cooper and subjecting the particularities of Jones's and Copway's formulations to another sort of Christianity.

THEORY'S RACISMS

Cooper's *The Oak Openings* (1848), the last of his Amerindian novels and perhaps the least known and most disliked,[21] works all of the same territory as Jones's and Copway's texts and provides a unique and superbly relevant countertext and counterdiscourse: the novel is set in northern Michigan, the Indians are Ojibwa, the theme is Methodist conversion. Cooper's race rhetoric had undergone massive shifts since the publication of *The Last of the Mohicans,* and these shifts — nearly sea changes — can be measured, one step at a time, along the arc of his eight Amerindian novels.[22]

The most complex and revealing text of the intervening years is *The Pathfinder* (1840), in which elaborate debates about the foundations of knowledge serve to undermine any number of the conclusions reached in Cooper's earlier texts. The book, which like *Mohicans* is set during the French and Indian Wars, consists of long dialogues about the "nature" of "gifts": calling and the division of labor (and therefore class), race, color, culture, nation, and gender. Natty Bumppo is typically positioned, in these debates, on the side of natural differences and respect of limitations imposed by such difference. In short, Natty is a condescending, racializing pluralist: the "Mingo" Indians are his enemies, for example, and he does not like the characteristics of the tribe, yet one must simply accept that they are living out their "gifts" to the best of their ability and that they are placed on this earth, in this condition, for some yet-unknown reason.[23] Charles Cap frequently serves as Natty's interlocutor. When it comes to race/color/culture issues, for example, Cap is a monolithic culturalist—that is, monogenist and evolutionary in his assumptions: he insists that "a man is a man" but that all Indians, for example, are horrible "savages" (*Pathfinder* 210, 28). Cap flat out condemns Amerindians as unfit to share a white world.

Though both characters are, in the largest sense, racists, an ongoing stand-off between Bumppo and Cap is crucial to the text's dialogic style, and Cooper's text, it might be argued, does not resolve the dispute in either's favor. What is one to make of this impasse? Long metacommentaries in the text frame these encounters. In one, which occurs relatively late in the text, a version of this same problematic emerges with reference to British and French coercion and use of Amerindians in the war. Two other figures take part in the ensuing discussion: Serjeant Dunham, Cap's brother, and Mabel (Magnet) Dunham, the serjeant's daughter. The serjeant argues that though it is legitimate, or at least excusable, that the British "consort with" and "employ" Indians, it is "a very different thing" when the French do so (306, 307). Natty, unsurprisingly, argues that the French and Mingoes "are not to be blamed for following" their "gifts:" "Natur' is natur', though the different tribes have different ways of showing it" (307). And Cap, true to form, simply argues that French kings as a group are "humbugs" (307).

The arguments made during this conversation are increasingly odd and arcane, at least from Mabel's perspective: "This is all unintelligible to me," she notes at one point, and it only gets worse after that, as Cap lectures the others, ignorantly and incorrectly, concerning the meaning of the word "*caput*"—producing etymological proof, finally, that the whole line of French kings deserves to be beheaded (307). At this point, Cooper intervenes:

> As all parties, Mabel excepted, seemed satisfied with the course the discussion had taken, no one appeared to think it necessary to pursue the subject. The trio of men, indeed, in this particular,...much resembled the great mass of their fellow creatures, who usually judge of character equally without knowledge and without justice. (308)

This is the narrator's reading of *The Pathfinder,* and a potentially radical one at that: All of the major characters, all of its social theorists (Mabel, perhaps, excepted), are fools. Neither Natty's nor Cap's approach—and, together, they represent the major strains of race thought in the midnineteenth century—is anything more than mere "judgment." They are decisions without foundations, or, at least, without the foundations of knowledge and justice. Cooper's spoof is made more apparent by representing the monogenist as being borderline genocidal, and the polygenist as being patronizingly tolerant. Though degrees of racism are not necessarily connected to particular scientific racial theories, it is generally true that monogenism reflected a deeply held commitment to a biblically inspired account of Adamic ancestry for all human beings and resonated with a politics of Amerindian melioration and conversion, whereas polygenism did not even attempt to distance its hard scientific method (the statistical study of skulls and bones) from the politics of removal and extermination.[24] Cooper's reversal of the typical polarities subtly reveals the illogic, as well as the racist politics, of the whole enterprise.[25]

The Oak Openings thus begins with the ground cleared of the gamut of nineteenth-century race theorizing, of scientific racism—both monogenism and polygenism and all of their possible historical accouterments: progressive evolutionary, lapsarian, cyclical, migratory. The most remarkable feature of the novel is the constant, recurrent ethnological (that is, comparative) focus across specifically *cultural* lines that few anthropologists ever—and no other contemporaneous ones—permit themselves to cross: that is, the border between First and Third World, between Anglo and Amerindian.[26] And, in the crossing, *The Oak Openings* makes it increasingly difficult to distinguish Amerindians from Anglos or to count upon judgments about the border itself.

Perhaps this is all the more remarkable given the potentially charged historical events that served as the seeds for the fictional tale: the rise of pan-Indian resistance on the white frontier. One might call this the "Pontiac matter" (Scalping Peter, or Onoah, is a figure for this Amerindian leader and is the focus of Cooper's Indian interests here), and it is this same matter that, three years later, Francis Parkman would fashion into a far better remembered text, *The History of the Conspiracy of Pontiac* (1851). Parkman's rendering of Pontiac is racist through and through. He imagines Pontiac as a "thorough savage" with all of the "faults of his race" (Parkman 483). Parkman constitutes a white/red border that cannot be crossed.

On the other hand, *The Oak Openings'* Anglo hero and bee-hunter, Benn "Buzz" Boden, inaugurates a far more complex line of inquiry in a modest way when an Ojibwa Indian,[27] Pigeonswing, asks him whether he belongs to any "tribe." Boden responds, "I have my tribe, as well as another" (*Oak Openings* 28). This sentence can be read in at least two ways. First, as an Indianism: although Boden does not think of the United States as a "tribe," he uses the term "tribe" condescendingly in order to communicate at Pigeonswing's conceptual level. This is a possible reading, for throughout the novel Boden often plays to what he perceives as the Amerindian's mental limitations, and often to gain some sort of advantage. But the other reading is more intriguing and is equally defensible: "tribe" is a legitimate ethnographic term to describe political alliance, whether Amerindian or Anglo. From this perspective, the United States is a "tribe." Since "tribe" is a colonial term through and through — a term of art both imposed on Amerindia in order to organize and map it, and a part of a vocabulary of hierarchical social relations ("tribe" versus the more civilized "nation" or "state," for example) — Boden's phrasing holds the potential to destabilize the project of colonial representation, along cultural lines. Boden, in nascent form, proposes not a multiculturalism but, rather, a transculturalism: at the level of form and structure, all cultures are radically alike.

The narrator of the *Oak Openings* performs this sort of work — breaks down commonplace distinctions — again and again. In war, Amerindia, France, England, and the United States are all equally "savage," and all equally concerned with "honor" (30–31, 107), so much so that Cooper calls this a "code of international morals . . . in which the student shall be at a loss to say which he most admires — that which comes from the schools, or that which comes direct from the wilderness" (108). Political-miltiary "insignias" of "authority and rank," too — whether tattoos and stones or crosses and medals — are equally prevalent and similarly symbolic across the red/white divide (164).

As noted, there are a number of moments in the text where Boden takes advantage of Amerindian ignorance of this or that, and no more so than when it comes to the triangulations of bee vectors involved in hunting wild honey, which Boden presents as a kind of necromancy or powerful magic in order to awe the Indians (including Scalping Peter) into submission. Boden thinks that he manipulates the subintelligence of primitive peoples, and Margery "Blossom" Waring—the book's only Anglo female character and the object of Boden's affections—chastises him for resorting to such a strategy. But the narrator puts another perspective on the Indians' supposed ignorance, and in a way that needs to be quoted at length:

> In his [Peter's] ignorance, how much was he worse off than the wisest of our race? Will any discreet man who has ever paid close attention to the power of the somnambule deny that there is a mystery about such a person that exceeds all our means of explanation? That there are degrees in the extent of this power; that there are false as well as true somnambules, all who have attended to the subject must allow; but a deriding disbeliever in our own person once, we have since seen that which no laws, known to us, can explain, and which we are certain is not the subject of collusion, as we must have been a party to the fraud ourselves were any such practiced. To deny the evidence of our senses is an act of greater weakness than to believe that there are mysteries connected with our moral and physical being that human sagacity has not yet been able to penetrate.... Why, then, are we to despise the poor Indian because he still fancied Le Bourdon [Boden] could hold communication with his bees? We happen to be better informed, and there may be beings who are aware of the as yet hidden laws of animal magnetism, —hidden as respects ourselves though known to them,— and who fully comprehend various mistakes and misapprehensions connected with our impressions on this subject, that escape our means of detection. (440–41)

At least two deflations of white cultural conceits snake their way through this passage, both circling around an odd and fascinating tentativeness regarding singular and progressive scientific knowledges. Peter's understanding of honey finding is equivalent to Cooper's own regarding séances and spiritual mediums: both believe without comprehension. But "manliness" demands that one be open to the world's "mysteries." In this sense, Peter is a real man and not a superstitious Indian. On another level, although the whites may know something that Peter does not ("poor Indian"), the tables may some day be reversed, and "animal magnetism" may prove to be legitimate science. In that case, Peter's credulity may open onto a separate horizon of scientific investigation: triangulation may locate honey, but so may mental control over insects. Perhaps, finally, Boden *is* psychically influencing the bee's behavior and misunderstanding his own process of hunting honey. Cooper here issues a linked pair of warnings to those who make the most basic assumptions regarding technical-scientific superiority. Judging inferiority risks relative ignorance.

The male Amerindian's attitudes toward women may be a more problematic cultural matter. Boden tells Blossom that male Indians are characterized "by not even thinking of treating his wife as a woman should be treated" (152), and the narrator reiterates this point: "No advocate of the American Indian has ever yet been able to maintain that woman fills her proper place in his estimate of claims" (153). Patriarchy rules in Amerindia (wives are not worshipped as ladies but are beasts of burden and near-slaves), and Indian men can be judged — using universal moral principles regarding gender — as wrong.

But Pigeonswing notes, preemptively, that at least Indians are honest, in that they say what they mean about women, whereas the Anglo cult of the maiden "bess not take nobody in" for fear of fooling the unknowing (152): white men are hypocrites in their dealings with women, putting them on pedestals but treating them as inferiors. Even Boden is forced to admit that "there may be some truth" in Pigeonswing's account. And Scalping Peter, upon whom so much of the text's energies are focused, has, before conversion, "a great many of the essentials of the gentleman" in his dealings with Blossom: "a lofty courtesy," "gentleness" in "deportment," "a benevolent and kind interest" in her welfare (213). Again, one might suggest two readings of this passage. If it is interpreted as racist, Peter's manners are gentlemanly *only because* Blossom is white — a superior woman. But *The Oak Openings* in no way supports this reading; it seems, rather, that Peter is a true man in the best sense. He is either an exception to the Amerindian rule, or the rule is yet another distinction without content, merely a racist or cultural supremacist judgment. (This is not to say that Cooper's text in any way presents the same complications and qualifications at the level of gender, because it does not.)

This recurrent transcultural focus casts a cold eye on all of the world's peoples and their judgments. More dramatically than in *The Pathfinder,* all of the characters in the novel are at the mercy of the state as the War of 1812 opens onto the frontier: there is no figure in *The Oak Openings* for the state or nation — not even a military officer. All such persons (and they are discussed throughout) are out of range in the novel: up in the northern forts, off in the east, in Europe. *The Oak Openings* deals exclusively, then, "with the credulous and ignorant at a distance" from an understanding of the state's interpellations and manipulations. Even Buzz, the novel's ostensible male hero, is portrayed in the book as absurdly xenophobic: Though he is "not . . . certain of ever having seen a Jew in my life," he admits, "I have a sort of grudge against them, though I can hardly tell you why" (278). And, as far as Indians go, Boden adopts a jaunty, casual attitude toward racial supremacy: "The Bible says nothing about any colors; but we suppose the man first made to have been a pale-face. At any rate, the pale-faces have got possession of the best parts of the earth, as it may be, and I think they mean to keep them. First come, first served, you know" (229). One way or another, by right or by might, the world belongs to the white. And it is virtually impossible, given the forms of cultural analysis in which the text engages, to treat Boden's views seriously. The narrator of the novel goes so far as to suggest that Boden is a budding despot (309).

Even clearer, however, is the text's critique of the views of the proselytizing Methodist minister, Parson Amen, and it is here that one can begin to confront matters of Christianity and conversion in the text. As Amen enters the novel, the narrator notes his respect for the "humble and untiring efforts" of Methodist missionaries in general (161). Amen, however, is described as "zealous but slightly fanatical," and the contours of this fanaticism — wholly anthropological in character — will prove to be Amen's undoing (163). Amen is a benevolently minded racial theorist, intent on proving the twelfth-tribe thesis: Amerindians are the first diasporic Jews — an extremely conventional if minoritarian thesis that persisted and at times flourished from the era of conquest through the nineteenth century.[28] Amen hopes, in fact, to accomplish two tasks at once: Amerindian conversion and identification. In fact, the former is premised upon the latter, because it is only when the Ojibwa are convinced of their Jewish heritage that they can be brought to God.

The Oak Openings mercilessly satirizes Amen's thesis, which Amen proves by reference to a bewildering mishmash of biblical citations and interpretations. When Boden first asks Amen how he can be sure that Peter is Jewish, Amen responds:

> "I turn to the 21st verse [of Gen. 49] for the tribe of Peter. Nephthali — Naphthalis, the root of his stock. 'Naphthalis is a hind, let loose: he giveth goodly words.' Now, what can be plainer than this? A hind let loose is a deer running at large, and, by a metaphor, that deer includes the man that hunts him. Now, Peter has been — nay, is still — a renowned hunter, and is intended to be enumerated among the hinds let loose; 'he giveth goodly words,' would set that point at rest, if anything were wanting to put it beyond controversy, for Onoah [Peter's Indian name] is the most eloquent speaker ear ever listened to!" (171)

This reading of Jacob's blessing of the leaders of the families of Israel is tenuous, to be sure, on every level.[29] And Amen repeats this sort of reading many times over in the book, "endeavor[ing] to bend every fact and circumstance connected with the Indians to the support of his theory touching their Jewish origin" (262). As Amen notes: " 'I see in the redmen, in their customs, their history, their looks, and even in their traditions, proofs that they are these Jews, once the favored people of the Great Spirit' " (261). Cooper produces a limit interpretation of anthropological speculation such that the very positing of relation — such that *relation itself* — becomes cause for laughter.

One might argue that Cooper's critique is relatively circumscribed: Biblical interpretation of history is problematic (a typically polygenist argument found, for example, in Josiah Nott's contemporaneous work), or it elaborates relation from mere resemblance (as does John Lloyd Stephens's argument in his study of the Mayan ruins). But the text offers no purchase for such a reading. Amen is "mystified by his own headlong desire to establish a theory," which implies that theory in general, or theory itself — in this particular case, theory that situates "man" historically and geographically — is the source of his confusions (199–200). Cooper's text is progressive — "the world as a whole is advancing towards a better state of things" (413) — but not according to nineteenth-century cultural-evolutionary models. Human history is of negligible consequence in determining "who" "we" are and whither "we" go. "If the course is onward, it is more as the will of God than from any calculations of man; and it is when the last is most active, that there is the greatest reason to apprehend the consequences" (414). Human beings' senses of agency and ability, in general and in principle, do the world harm.

The most extreme question that *The Oak Openings* might posit concerns the relationship between theory and racism. Some scholars have argued that all elaborations of ethnicity and culture, even the most multiculturalist or pluralistic in outlook, find their roots in earlier racial theorizing and are therefore racist at their core.[30] Cooper may be making an astonishingly similar point. On the one hand, he regularly notes Amen's good intentions: his gestures of Christian inclusivity, his rejection of anti-Semitism, his Christlike suffering and eventual crucifixion at the hands of the Ojibwa (252, 278, 405–6). But on the other hand, Amen's narrative of color is condescendingly hierarchical:

> "[God] divided [men] into nations and tribes. It was then that he caused the color of his creatures to change. Some he kept white, as he had made them. Some he put behind a dark cloud, and they became altogether black. Our wise men think that this was done in punishment for their sins." (251)[31]

According to Amen, Amerindians are a "suffering" people who have endured great "hardships." As descendants of the Israelites, the Methodist says, they have the "honor" of being one of God's original chosen people (267). But Amen cannot disguise from the Ojibwa the fact that, as a logical consequence, he presumes them to be sinners—a *fallen* race (263, 267). Peter responds that the Jews

> "are a people who do not go with the pale-faces, but live apart from them, like men with the small-pox. It is not right for my brother to come among the redmen and tell them that their fathers were not good enough to live and eat and go on the same paths as his fathers." (266)

Acceptance of Amen's seemingly loving and benevolent thesis would involve trading one racist imposition for another. In addition, Peter slyly notes the cultural imperialism inherent in a white man telling Amerindians who they are and suggests a practical motive for creation of the twelfth-tribe thesis: if

Amerindians are lost Jews, then logically they should return home and leave the Americas, leave the white frontier (263). Peter brands the Indians-as-Jews tale as a removal narrative.

Of all the things Amen does in the novel, only his martyr's death bears fruit (Peter's witnessing of it aids his eventual conversion to Christianity). His project of identification and conversion is understood as racist, disastrously stirring the anger of those he most wants to help. The twelfth-tribe thesis also perturbs the auto-ethnographers Jones and Copway, and both of them believe that they have found an acceptable alternative: a truthful and value-neutral identity politics. Peter Jones relates a story concerning Indian attitudes toward the Book of Mormon, one of the crucial early nineteenth-century texts that linked Indian and Jew. In the story, a converted Indian at a Mormon meeting stands up to tell the congregation his version of the origins of the Book of Mormon:

> When the Great Spirit gave his good book to white man, the evil spirit Muhje-munedoo try to make one too, and he try to make it like the one the Good Spirit made, but he could not; and then he got so ashamed of it, he go into the woods, dig a hole in the ground, and then he hid his book. After lying there many winters, Joe Smith go and dig it up. This is the book this preacher has been talking about. I hold fast on the good old Bible, which has made my heart so happy. I have nothing to do with the devil's book. (Jones, *History* 198–99)

Even more specifically, Jones presents a brief rejoinder to the claims that Elias Boudinot made in his well-known work *A Star in the West* (1816) regarding the Jewish origin of Amerindian peoples.[32] Jones writes that he was "strongly inclined to favour the theory" on first encountering it but later found strong reason to doubt the connection:

> They [AmerIndians] have no Sabbaths, no circumcision, no altars erected, and no distinction between clean and unclean animals. It would seem almost impossible for the descendants of the Israelites ever to have lost the recollection of their Sabbath days, and the rite of circumcision, both of which were so solemnly enjoined upon them. (Jones, *History* 37)

George Copway agrees with Jones on this point: "Could it be possible, that, had we sprung from any of the Hebrew tribes, we should be so completely ignorant of a Messiah, a Sabbath, or a single vestige of the Levitical Law?" (Copway, *Indian Life* 44).

Jones and Copway, then, reject existing modelings of Amerindian identity as demonstrably social-scientifically false and, perhaps, politically coded and motivated, given Christian antipathy toward Jews. Instead, another model takes its place. Jones—and probably Copway, too—endorses the Bering Strait thesis: "I am inclined to favour the opinion that the Indians are descendants of the Asiatic Tartars, as there appears to me a more striking similarity in features, customs and manners, between them and my countrymen than any other nation" (Jones, *History* 37).[33]

But the remodeling of Amerindian identity—and, likewise, the positivist refashioning of any identity—is always a double-edged sword. For example, the Bering Strait thesis comes with its own problems and complications, as the famed critic of anthropology Vine Deloria Jr. (Sioux) has recently pointed out: "If Indians had arrived only a few centuries earlier, they had no *real* claim to land that could not be swept away by European discovery" (Deloria, *Red Earth* 82). Deloria's critique of the Bering Straight thesis is the same, then, as Scalping Peter's last point concerning the twelfth-tribe thesis. And Deloria, in turn, rejects migratory accounts of settlement of the Americas in the name of Amerindian authorities and their stories about original American creation. Here, the wheel turns full circle: Scalping Peter, Copway, and Jones reject Father Amen; Deloria rejects Copway and Jones; and Deloria parallels (again) Cooper's Scalping Peter, who argues, "The Manitou has made us different; he did not mean that we should live on the same hunting grounds" (*The Oak Openings* 252). This presents as large a problem as one might encounter in attempting to secure any version of the difference between Amerindian and white identities: Deloria's discourse is nearly identical to that spoken by Cooper's final Indian protagonist, in Cooper's presumedly most racist novel, and Deloria is at odds with the warp and woof of nineteenth-century indigenous anthropology.

And the equally large problem of locating a nonracist Amerindian identity is far from solved, since Deloria's and Scalping Peter's discourses locate them within Samuel Morton's polygenist camp—a remarkable appropriation given polygenism's racialist and separatist history and its necessarily racist implications.

CONVERSION AGAINST ANTHROPOLOGY

Interestingly, the whole thrust of Cooper's conversion narrative rejects Peter's claim of independent Indian creation and the need for a distinct cultural identity. And the alternative to the round of problems just sketched remains Cooper's. In *The Oak Openings* Cooper resists the temptation to replace racialist falsehood with truth, except to the extent that he believes all people seem to behave the same way, for bad or good. The closest Cooper comes to representing Amerindians as being in any way distinct comes in an aside midway through the novel, where he writes that Amerindians are "wonderful people...set apart," who, in some mysterious way, will "enact their share in the sublime drama of human events" (251).

Cooper's conceptualizations in *The Oak Openings,* interestingly, coincided with his own religious renewal — a topic of some mystery for Cooper scholars, given that he left behind no record of what led to it or the manner in which it occurred. Cooper is utterly silent about his late 1840s reconversion. What is known is that he proposed the novel to his publisher in November of 1847, and his journals indicate that he began avidly rereading the Bible on 1 January 1848, starting with the Gospel of St. John.[34] Beyond that, all that one has are the late novels, and it is clear that Cooper is taking great pains in *The Oak Openings* to stake out a particular vision of Christianity — one that is nonsectarian and whose content is very narrow indeed.

In Cooper's most focused conversion novel, *The Sea Lions* (1849), written immediately after *The Oak Openings,* Cooper emphasizes the simplicity of his reborn Christianity: "Love of God," for example, is the "one great test of human conversion" (*Works* 4:27).[35] And the definition of this love, the thing that lies at the core of Cooper's Christian vision, is "humility," which Cooper says "is the stepping stone of faith and love" (4:130).[36] Humility means that one must "honor and defer" to Christ (4:15) and to God's overarching Providence; in the process, one reduces the "self" and its schemes. (The plot of *The Sea Lions* pits faith in the Lord against financial calculations and scientific reason, in the shape of a South Pole adventure for profit.)

Cooper writes, "Of all the idols men worship, that of the self was perhaps the most objectionable" (*Works* 4:209).[37] This line has multiple implications,[38] but significant for this analysis is Cooper's undercutting of humankind's secular ambitions for knowledge. (As one such tactic, the narrator of *The Sea Lions* notes more than once that he will keep the latitudes and longitudes of the voyage a secret from the reader.) In this sense, Cooper's text resonates with Ely S. Parker's early, Christian-inflected texts, which warn about the limitations of the project of anthropology in its largest sense. In Cooper's late novels, such as *The Sea Lions* and *The Oak Openings,* humility involves a scaling back of many kinds of false desires, including the desire to *enlarge* and *develop* the self. Therefore, Cooper's *method* of conversion is not secured or grounded by the social sciences — one of the prime breeding grounds for self-development. Cooper's late-found Christianity, instead, empties out "man" as a necessary or even useful concept — hence the broadly based critique of anthropological-historical knowledges. The implication is that race, ethnicity, color, and culture are the products of human pride and prejudice, and not of nature. In short, conversion vitiates anthropology because man himself — in all of his self-creation, in all of his false sense of agency and capability produced through various narratives of the self — disappears in the process. The model for anthropology and history, to the extent that *The Oak Openings* presents one, is entirely organized around born-again conversion, in the face of which Peter's Indianness, his and his people's history, has no significance, does not amount to anything: "It was assailing his besetting sin; attacking the very citadel of his savage character, and throwing open at once an approach into the deepest recesses of his habits and dispositions" (414). The only thing that registers in *The Oak Openings* is what one will *not* be, not what one *is.*

Cooper's sense of Christian subjectivity is minimal indeed, and it perhaps has something in common with Wesley's "nothing" Indians. *The Oak Openings* ends with a sentimentalist moment of humility, when Scalping Peter announces that the Holy Spirit has turned his "heart of stone" to "de heart of woman" (476). This is an unprecedented moment in Cooper's Amerindian oeuvre, and it is dramatically distant from *The Last of the Mohicans,* where the worship of masculinity borders on the cultist. Certainly, this moment can be read as sinister-benevolent colonialist discourse: Peter's heart has been rendered quietistic, and he will no longer fight, nor even protest, white incursions into the middle states.³⁹ This is, then, the moment of "Uncle Tomahawk": It is similar to the sentimentalist conversion of the angry ex-slave George Harris in Harriet Beecher Stowe's novel. But Stowe's text is undergirded by a racial and racist theory so pronounced that it is difficult to understand Harris's portrayal in *Uncle Tom's Cabin* as anything but prescriptively dominating. Stowe's vision of the world is white to the end.

Cooper's version of the cultivation of the feminine heart—that is, the submissive and humble heart—is a different matter altogether. This Christian heart is that which minimizes self-identity and the history and anthropology that support it. The word "conversion" is related to the Latin verb for "transform" or "translate"—*convertere*—and, according to the *Oxford English Dictionary,* in one of its earliest English usages "convert" meant "to transport, carry, take from one place to another." It is, in many respects, a perfect term for the way in which relatively pacific, colonial relationships typically are represented: linguistic translation, followed by cultural transformation—that is, by a transporting of the Indian into the world of constricting whiteness: cultural imperialism. But in *The Oak Openings* conversion is actually a renunciation of problematics and logics of secular translation and transportation. The book's Christianity, then, is not that of the continent's conquerors; the Christianity premised, from the start, upon anthropological knowledges; the Christianity that divides and separates the chosen from the heretics, the whites from people of color. And, therefore, it is not the Christianity of Copway and Jones; it produces neither modern, expanded subjecthood nor, relatedly, races, ethnicities, and cultures. Rather, it is a version of a radically "Protestant" vision (reminiscent of that of Martin Luther or Jonathan Edwards)—a nearly Zen Protestantism—of the self at war with itself, undermining itself, reducing its individuality *and* its typicality to the smallest size possible and flirting with becoming nothing that matters—nothing that counts.⁴⁰

This is one way that one might read a third Ojibwa-Methodist anthropologist from midcentury, Maungwudaus (George Henry, to Christian friends), who wrote three short texts and whose brief Ojibwa "book," *Remarks Concerning the Ojibway Indians* (1847), is so peculiar (for one thing, so attenuated) that his work has gone all but unnoticed in the recent rediscovery of nineteenth-century Amerindian literatures. Donald Smith mentions him in passing, in part because Jones was his friend and (unknown to Jones) his half-brother

(Smith, *Sacred* 317, n. 78). Early in life, "Henry" was a candidate for the Methodist ministry, but by 1844 he had tired of Methodist strictness, founded an Indian dance troupe that paraded the "wild Indian" before audiences in England, and converted to Roman Catholicism. Henry's actions horrified Peter Jones, who believed that such presentations lowered white estimation of Indian character among religious audiences (Smith, *Sacred* 187–88).

Henry's text, published under his Indian name, might also have distressed Jones. It is twelve pages long, and the section that Maungwudaus wrote is all of three pages (the rest consists of testimonials from Anglo writers concerning the good character of Canadian Indians). It is really little more than a set of hastily scribbled program notes to accompany and promote his troupe's performances. The text is interesting, however, because of its seeming inability or unwillingness to speak to the matter of Amerindian identity. The contents of *Remarks* are easily abstracted:

> We belong to a Nation called Ojibway. . . . We inhabit a very large country. . . . We fast a great deal . . . that the Great Spirit and his agents might reveal themselves to us while suffering from hunger and thirst. . . . Our teachers are the aged. . . . We worship the Great Spirit, in offering sacrifices to him. . . . All our tribes practice the same mode of carrying their infant children for several months from their birth upon a flat board, resting upon its mother's back, as she walks or rides, suspended by a broad strap passing over her forehead. . . . Our women are far from complaining of their lot. . . . Red, green, black, white, and yellow, but chiefly red, are the colours mostly used by the Indians for painting the face and person. (Maungwudaus, *Remarks* 3–5)

Nothing more, nothing less: this is an extremely abbreviated list — presented under six topic headings — of some things Ojibwas do, without a recognizable analytic, sense of organization, or pretense of coverage. Christianity does not center this account; in fact, nothing does. It is not even clear which (if any) of Henry's remarks are meant to distinguish Amerindians from whites, and which (if any) are meant to demonstrate cultural similitudes. The Ojibwa live somewhere, they worship a creator and transport their children on their backs, they are patriarchal, they like the color red. But it all makes no difference: this is, truly, an anthropology from which the very idea of *significance* is absent. No racial or cultural or even theological theorizing of any sort takes place. Maungwudaus, it seems, makes nothing of the Ojibwa. He has nothing to say, nothing of any positive value or consequence. His work does not broach the border, does not constitute persons. Rather than constituting Indian time and space, this text is in the time before such decisions. This is to say that he, even more dramatically than Cooper, presents the most interesting possible alternative to the problem of nineteenth-century methods.

Do not then wonder, my dear friends, at my bold and unpolished
statements, though I do not believe that truth wants any polishing
whatever. And I can assure you that I have no design to tell an un-
truth, but facts alone.

—WILLIAM APESS, *EULOGY ON KING PHILIP* (1836)

Not accounted for to this point is the prominence of the word "history" in the
texts of the nineteenth-century Amerindian auto-anthropologists: Cusick's
Sketches of the Ancient History of the Six Nations, Parker's unfinished "History... of the Iroquois Confederacy, or the Nations of Indians," Copway's *The
Traditional History and Characteristic Sketches of the Ojibway Nation,* Jones's
History of the Ojibway Indians, Apess's *Eulogy on King Philip.* In very broad
terms, a historicist inclination in these texts resists the emergence of what was
understood as a decidedly nonhistorical, anthropological science. McGrane
notes of nineteenth-century white anthropology in general that it "constituted
a historicizing of the different" (93), but only according to a logic of separately
developing cultures. For the majority of Amerindian auto-anthropologists, "history" means the history of contact, conquest, and colonialism, and sometimes
the history of particular practices, rather than the broad conceits of evolutionary anthropology. One way to conceptualize this argument is to imagine the
interlocutors as historical "fact" and historical "theory."

In other words, and for example: when historical science deems the Amerindian to be debased and fallen, William Apess agrees, but he blames it on the
European treatment of indigenous Americans. And auto-history is a belated
response to a white writing that erases the marks of conquest, as Apess so often observes:

Indeed, had the Indians, on their part, been able to answer in
writing, they might have formed a contrast between themselves and their mortal enemies, the civilized subjects of
Great Britain. They might have recapitulated their conduct

in the persecution of *Indians, witches, and Quakers* in New England. — *Indians* and *Negroes* in New York, and the cruelty with which the aborigines were treated in Virginia. (Apess 58)

Cooper's novels are structured dialogically so as to reveal the same framework of argument: When white characters speak of Indian nature, the red characters often respond by "speaking truth to power" by emphasizing colonial relations and colonial history.[1] In these cases, the answers to questions turn on an axis defined by the poles of "racial nature" and "colonial culture."

No more startling example of this is provided than in the writings of John Rollin Ridge (Cherokee), whose Indian name was Yellow Bird and who was a prominent California poet, journalist, and newspaper editor. James W. Parins, Ridge's modern biographer, notes that Ridge's early life and his family's life were intimately bound up with the large fact of Indian removal. Ridge's father and grandfather were crucial signatories to the Cherokee removal treaty in the 1830s, and both were assassinated in 1839 by the majority, antiremoval Cherokee forces. John Rollin Ridge witnessed his father's murder, and in the 1840s, while living in Indian Territory, he killed one of his family's opponents. He remained involved in Cherokee politics even after the Civil War, taking part in their relatively unsuccessful treaty deliberations with the U.S. government. With Ridge, then, one is also dealing with an auto-anthropologist as broadly and deeply involved in U.S.-Indian struggles as was possible.[2]

In 1862, relatively late in Ridge's writing career, he began publishing a historical-anthropological series, "The North American Indians: Where They Have Been and What They Are," in the California women's magazine *The Hesperian*, a monthly journal that "featured fashions as well as literature" (Parins, *Ridge* 76–77).[3] Three articles — the first installments of an intended book — were published, but he abandoned the project, it seems, when new newspaper editing responsibilities beckoned (Parins, *Ridge* 189). The first of the three articles directly addresses the problem posed by scientific racism, and physical anthropology in particular, through an extended comment on Amerindian skull shape and size. By the 1850s, it was perhaps a commonplace in polygenist circles that skulls could be classified according to racial type through the emerging science of craniology and that Amerindian skulls betrayed marked inferiorities, compared to European skulls, in overall size or in the size of parts of the skull.

The allied science of phrenology was brought to bear in order to suggest the significance of craniology's findings. The seeming slope of the Amerindian forehead, for example, was reason to believe that the anterior cavity of the Amerindian skull—the supposed seat of the intellect—was markedly smaller than that of whites. Ridge, in the first of his texts for *The Hesperian,* is the only midcentury auto-anthropologist to address these claims head-on, as it were. It is one of the most remarkable of moments in nineteenth-century Amerindian writing—a direct refutation of one of the main branches of anthropological speculation, and one that looks forward to Amerindian anti-anthropological writing of one hundred years later:

> It is not generally known to the popular reader that the custom of flattening the head, or compressing it into unnatural form, which is now practiced alone by the Chenooks and a few other tribes of Oregon and British Columbia, once prevailed among many of the aboriginal tribes, both of North and South America. The ancient Mexicans and Peruvians were in the habit of moulding the head into forms of the most grotesque and sometimes frightful character. In the old Catacombs of Mexico and Peru, cranial distortions are found which would set at defiance the profoundest phrenologist who ever undertook to measure the human intellect with a pair of compasses—heads conical, long heads and square heads, heads triangular, heads elevated and heads depressed; heads with the moral faculties towering up like a mental Chimborazo, others again with the bump of benevolence utterly annihilated; here the lofty arching brow, and there no brow at all! The phrenologist, after running over a hundred or two of these heads, would be apt to come to the conclusion that the mind is capable of working in almost any sort of hole, and that the elastic brain of man would perform its functions as well, stretched out like a string of sausages, as if it were domed by the brow of an Apollo. ("Indians 1" 12).

Scientific racialisms, according to this somewhat sarcastic Ridge, forget history and culture only at their peril, and the return of historically based knowledges to anthropology is an antidote to, or perhaps a poison for, the project of science.

The writing of history, then, is a tactic in the struggle between red and white anthropology in the nineteenth century, and assessing its epistemological and political significance is crucial for the analysis of auto-anthropology. In Ridge's case, for example, his unparalleled resistance to "hard scientific" inquiry does not amount to the theorization of an antianthropology. Like polygenist scientific racialists or extreme, separatist monogenists, Ridge believes that Amerindians are a unique people, with "differences [from others] so wide, radical and striking as to settle the rational mind in the conclusion that this people are either indigenous to the continent, or that the period of their arrival is so remote in the past as to have effected, through climatic, geographic and other causes, a complete change in their primordial character" ("Indians 1" 6).

So although Ridge is fully capable of and willing to satirize the knowledge claims of anthropology (in his survey of anthropologists' claims of resemblances between Amerindian and European and Mediterranean cultural practices, he notes that acceptance of such claims would mean that Indians are "descended from *all* the branches of the Old World stock at one and same time" ["Indians 1" 7]), he indulges in anthropological speculations in a variety of modes. He imagines that some Indians originated in the northern Americas and others in the southern; northerners, or "Athabascans," are "a warlike race, possessed of no arts beyond those of the hunter state," whereas southerners, who "came from the ancient Mexican latitudes," are more intelligent, artistic, agricultural, and the like ("Indians 1" 7). Indians of the western United States are another matter altogether, and Ridge's judgment of them is similar to that of some contemporaneous white accounts, such as, famously, Mark Twain's *Roughing It* (1872), as several Ridge scholars have noted. Ridge writes understatedly that they "are not the best specimens of the race, if, indeed, they belong at all to the same stock" ("Indians 1" 7). The Cherokees, Ridge's own people, are singled out as the whitest of Indians. Unlike the typical "*brown*" Indian, "[they] have always had a lighter complexion than the adjoining Muscogee tribes, and travellers among them, a hundred years ago, saw young girls of the tribe who were nearly as fair as European females" ("Indians 1" 11). The darkening of the Cherokee is attributed, finally, to mixture with others over time.

Ridge, therefore, generates his own, singular anthropology of the Americas, one based on a phantasmagoric history of multiple Amerindian creations, of migrations and transmutations from one political-economic state to another, of white Indians turning browner after European contact. Enough boundaries and hierarchies are implied in the analysis to satisfy any nineteenth-century race theorist. This should give one pause, finally, about the political possibilities of history, even as, in our time, an analogous event is taking place in literary studies, with a return to history — to historicized cultural studies — said to be addressing the apolitical or fascistic tendencies of literary theory.

The remainder of this chapter takes up the problem of history and anthropology from several perspectives. I first read Ridge's anthropology in relation to craniology (Samuel Morton's work) and to legendary history (Longfellow). I then compare midnineteenth-century histories of individual figures in cultural contexts (histories that are anthropological through and through, entirely concerned with multiple others, border crossings, conquest and vengeance): William Hickling Prescott's *History of The Conquest of Mexico* (1843) and Ridge's *The Life and Adventures of Joaquín Murieta, the Celebrated California Bandit* (1854). Ridge's text, the first "novel" written by an Amerindian, describes relations among whites, Mexicans, and California (that is, "not the best specimen") Indians; Prescott's more famous work explores relations between Spaniards and Aztecs. History's relationship to anthropology will appear, under different guises, but the question at stake is one of judgments: what is the *status of judgments,* their terms and conditions, the rules for determination of a historical-anthropological judgment?

RIDGES OF ANTHROPOLOGY

It is not clear that Ridge, in writing about the work of "the ethnologist," is directing his attack at any particular craniological text ("Indians 1" 11), but all roads in midcentury lead back to Samuel Morton and *Crania Americana* (1839). Morton was seen as the "undisputed founder of a new science" by an anonymous writer in the *Boston Medical and Surgical Journal* of 1844, for example, and his death in 1851, while serving as president of the Academy of Natural Sciences of Philadelphia, produced an explosion of hagiographic lament (*Boston* 423).[4] Morton, a doctor of "descriptive anatomy," rapidly developed a secondary interest in geology, animal species, and, finally, the taxonomy of human beings (Bieder 55–58). *Crania Americana,* his best-known and first book-length work, is a far more peculiar volume than its reputation might suggest. A "full" reading of Morton's work would necessitate a great deal of space, but it would repay the effort because no major nineteenth-century anthropologist is more misread — or, perhaps, unread — than Morton.[5]

The book is divided in two, with only the second part devoted to the actual analysis of skulls. The book's introductory essay, nearly as long as the rest of the text, is a general account "On the Varieties of the Human Species." This compendium on race eccentrically summarizes the conclusions of an extraordinary number of texts, written over several centuries, on racial characteristics of all sorts. It is a crazy quilt or patchwork affair, with everything ever said about the "other" taken seriously, nothing taken for granted, everything scrupulously footnoted. Experience — virtually anyone's experience, or anyone's second-hand gossip concerning anyone else's experience — serves as the deep historical ground for Morton's skull work.

Morton links all of these forms of behaviors or cultures — "moral peculiarities" — to race. And unlike the monogenists, Morton believes that all physical characteristics date "from the beginning" of creation and are "independent of external causes" such as geography and climate (*Americana* 3). For Morton, therefore, no "history" has any meaning for reading "race." Morton, if not Ridge's actual disputant, is a prime candidate; Morton should be Ridge's bête noire. Nothing could be further from the case, however, since they broadly agree on many crucial points. Morton agrees with Ridge regarding, for example, the division of the Amerindian races into northern and southern races (as has already been suggested), with the southern peoples marked as superior:

> The most natural division of the American race is into two families, one of which, the Toltecan family, bears evidence of centuries of demi-civilisation, while the other, under the collective title of the American family, embraces all the barbarous nations of the new world excepting the Polar tribes or Mongol-Americans. (*Americana* 63)

More surprisingly, Morton singles out the Cherokee nation — Ridge's affiliation — for particular praise, a judgment that Ridge heartily endorses. The Cherokee, according to *Crania Americana,* are large, fair-skinned, and intelligent people who practice the arts of peace. Cherokee enslavement of Africans is a sign of their "true civilization," a remark that resonates with the Ridge family's slaveholding and Ridge's own lifelong paternalism toward Africans, with his support of Unionist politicians and membership in pro-slavery fringe groups, and with his inability to condemn slavery anywhere in his voluminous work as a journalist.[6]

When it comes to questions of strangely shaped skulls — surely a topic over which the craniologist and the auto-historian should quarrel — Morton is already in Ridge's camp: he says that it is the art of compression, not nature, that accounts for oddly shaped, seemingly nonhuman Indian skulls (66), and that overall skull size is not affected (98). In 1849 Morton clarified this position, arguing that "the various artificial modes of distorting the cranium, occasion no diminution of its internal capacity, and consequently do not affect the size of the brain" ("Observations" 224).

Morton and Ridge, then, seemingly at odds over the status of scientific racialisms and the importance of history, make strange bedfellows, but bedfellows they are on crucial matters of distinction (and nondistinction). One wonders whether, in the end, the "auto-anthropology of the other" presents any critical differences from the better-known "anthropology of the other." The Amerindian other says that he or she writes in order to mark or map out a space distinct from white anthropology — to set the record straight; to reverse certain forms of prejudices and racisms; to highlight the difference between running in the forest and sitting in armchairs, between abstract theorizing and historical knowledge — but do these gestures amount to differences, and do the differences make a difference?

Of Morton and Ridge, it is Morton who exhibits the greater caution with regard to conclusions about the Amerindian. Though in *Crania Americana*, in its pages on the Indian, Morton writes credulously about many things, as he progresses through the book he increasingly admits that skull size and type cannot be correlated with the logics of phrenology, that the relationship between intellect and head size cannot be demonstrated. In fact, according to Morton, the Incans — the "modern" Peruvians, whom Morton argues are genealogically related to the most highly civilized group of ancient Indians — have the smallest skulls of any living people, "not excepting the Hindoos"

(132).[7] And the Indians with the largest skulls are the Ottimagimies, or Fox, whom Morton grades off the scale of human development and attainment by comparing them to "insects" (184).

Crania Americana begins by positing a frankly racist thesis and then proceeds to mark the tentativeness or capriciousness of such presuppositions and the inadequacy of the thesis in relation to test results. *Crania Americana* consists of 300 pages in small type documenting the failure, on multiple levels, of emergent racial science. Morton himself ends his text by admitting that his work concludes nothing, that head size appears to be in inverse relation to the marks of civilization, that he may be studying the wrong facts (overall size as opposed to size of discrete cranial chambers), and that he has opened lines of inquiry that suggest eventual failure:

> Respecting the American Race I have nothing to add, excepting the striking fact that of all the American nations the Peruvians had the smallest heads, while those of the Mexicans were somewhat larger, and those of the barbarous [northern] tribes the largest of all.... An interesting question remains to be solved, viz: the relative proportion of the brain in the anterior and posterior chambers of the skull in the different races; an inquiry for which I have hitherto possessed neither sufficient leisure nor adequate materials. (261)

If there is something of interest to be learned from the study of skulls, *Crania Americana* notes that it has yet to find it.[8] The book then reads as the opening *and* the closing of the books on a science without history, or perhaps on the "hard" scientific method generally, with reference to anthropology.[9]

The gesture that Ridge makes in the second of his long pieces for *The Hesperian* provides an opportunity for further consideration of such problems. After demonstrating in his first piece that the game of resemblances between Indians and other premodern people is limitless and, finally, intellectually useless, Ridge sets out to prove in the second that "the Egyptian and Pythagorian doctrine of Metempsychosis, or of the transmigration of souls, was an important part of their [the Indians'] creed" ("Indians 2" 53). Ridge bases his arguments entirely on references to Henry Wadsworth Longfellow's *The Song of*

Hiawatha (1855), and half of Ridge's eight-page text consists of seven long excerpts from section 17 of the poem, "The Hunting of Pau-Puk-Keewis."

Thus, even though Ridge wrote several times of his desire to narrate the authentic story — that is, not the white version — of Indian life (for example, he wrote, "I want to write the history of the Cherokee nation as it should be written and not as white men will write it and as they will tell the tale, to screen and justify themselves"),[10] he did not have much to say apart from decidedly white interpretations of Indian history. His reliance upon Longfellow, whose *Hiawatha* has been regarded as little more than an armchair fantasist's romance of "real" Amerindian culture for most of the twentieth century (and, indeed, by many scholars and literati of his own time), stands as yet another of those curious moments in nineteenth-century identity formation — such as Copway's enthusiasm for Fenimore Cooper, noted in chapter 3 — in which the white/red line blurs beyond hope of being redrawn. Longfellow, famously, relied on a misreading of Schoolcraft for his legendary matter (as well as on incidents and organization from the Finnish epic the *Kalevala*), and Schoolcraft, in turn, explicitly rewrote his field notes in order to score moral points. The status of Schoolcraft's transcriptions were therefore already problematic, Longfellow redoubled the troubles, and Ridge reports Longfellow as accurate anthropology based upon Ridge's firsthand knowledge of Indian culture and thought. Ridge's biographer paraphrases an 1858 newspaper column in which Ridge answers contemporaneous attacks on Longfellow's poem: "The American poet has taken what is noteworthy and valuable in the early history of his native land and rendered it into romance" (Parins, *Ridge* 158).

The modern "Indian," then, is a complex of white and red narratives, with no secure ground — no authentic Indian histories and myths at bottom. Ridge's "Indians" are dialectically produced through two white intermediaries, and the result is "Indians," definitely, but marked in equal measure by both the white loving (Longfellow) and loathing (Schoolcraft) of premodern peoples.

The citing of Longfellow comes with other implications as well, including, perhaps, the endorsement of Longfellow's largest narrative shapes (Hiawatha's welcoming the whites to the New World, even as he acknowledges that he must pass into the mists of myth in order to make way for them) — a progressive-evolutionary tale that Ridge endorsed throughout his career.[11] And such citation reiterates, more tellingly, the exclusionary action of section 17 of the poem. Pau-Puk-Keewis, whom Hiawatha kills repeatedly, and eventually successfully, in section 17, is for Longfellow the figure of the dandy, the lady's man, the gambler, the idler, the near-vaudeville entertainer: "the merry mischief-maker," "dressed in shirt of doeskin, / White and soft, and fringed with ermine, / All inwrought with beads of wampum" (Longfellow 138).[12] At Hiawatha's wedding feast, for example, in section 12, Pau-Puk-Keewis performs the Beggar's Dance, which brings down the house, after which he "sat down laughing / There among the guests assembled, / Sat and fanned himself serenely / With his fan of turkey-feathers" (Longfellow 138). He is, then, the opposite of serious Hiawatha, who is the man's man and devoted husband, the bringer of corn and all things civilized, the builder of nations and ties between nations, and, most crucially, the inventor of writing — the first Indian historian of record.

All of this — all the implications of citing Longfellow — suggests a broad analogy between Ridge's reiteration of Longfellow and Ridge's own exclusionary practices regarding what he perceived as the enemies in his own life — the antitreaty, antiremoval Cherokee who murdered members of his family and who followed him halfway to California (in section 16 clever Pau-Puk-Keewis is revealed to be Hiawatha's secret nemesis, enslaving one of Hiawatha's friends, killing his raven, tearing up his lodge, slaughtering his mountain chickens). Hiawatha's vitriol inhabits Ridge's texts, whether directed at fellow Cherokee or at northern and western Indian peoples.

The creation or generation of Indian history — its writing — is thus, in Ridge/Hiawatha and more generally, a project of cultural formation and retention that is also, inevitably, a work of cultural exclusion. Hiawatha cannot lead Indians toward a proper Indian culture and destiny without eliminating some of the Indians — those annoying tricksters who stand out in the crowd and refuse to conform, who refuse to sign treaties and band with the rest. The history of culture is a history of "who" is written out of the culture, and thus a history of "who" must be violently removed (much like the antitreaty Cherokee party was removed from the eastern seaboard). To write history on behalf of the "Indians," then, is to banish those who are not quite Indian enough. Whatever racial science offers by way of exclusionary and hierarchical practices, historical determination more than keeps pace.

FROM ANTHROPOLOGY TO BIOGRAPHY

To put it most succinctly, Prescott's *Conquest of Mexico* and Ridge's *Joaquín Murieta* are moral meditations on murder's relationship to the history of border crossing, border violations, and conquest. As Prescott wrote in his notebook, in the middle of composing *Conquest of Mexico,* "I have still to write the 'improvement' of the narrative, — and *moralise* the story" (*Memoranda* 2:97).[13] These two texts are virtual analogues for one another, and perhaps they are completed as a trilogy by Américo Paredes's retrieval and evaluation of the *corridos* about Gregorio Cortez, ballads that tell the story of the turn-of-the-century Texas border "outlaw" — a figure through whom the symbologies of Hernando Cortés (by the surname and other markers) and Murieta are united.[14]

Both texts are both history and biography, and they are anthropological through and through. Prescott's celebrated book opens and closes with heavily footnoted sections of historical, archival ethnography (the concluding "Appendix, Part 1" is actually a portion of the introductory "View of the Aztec Civilization," which Prescott removed for reasons of length). Prescott's armchair anthropology is surprisingly supple and rich. His work stands out among texts by white anthropologists of midcentury in terms of the sheer number of categories of analysis and the fine gradation of distinctions. The sheer complexity of the first hundred pages of *Conquest of Mexico* makes his fieldworker colleagues — Schoolcraft, Morgan, and Stephens, for example — seem narrow and pinched by comparison. Morgan, as was noted in chapter 3, measures development in political economy, government, and religion, whereas Prescott also charts engineering and architecture, historical consciousness, property arrangements and embourgeoisement, aesthetics and representational conceits, the military, trade relations, and still other matters, all the while keeping Toltec, Aztec, and Tezcucan[15] societies distinct with reference to these categories.[16]

When Prescott is cited and discussed, his most sweeping and clear-cut formulations regarding the savage/civilized dichotomy and the progressive force of History are often the best remembered: "It was the conflict of the European with the American; of civilized man with the barbarian," and Cortés was "the instrument selected by Providence to scatter terror among the barbarian monarchs of the Western World, and lay their empires in the dust" (415, 143).[17] But it is very difficult to read Prescott's pages on the Aztec world and come away with these conclusions. This is of some large importance in nineteenth-century America, because narratives such as Prescott's could be read for implications regarding, and justifications (or not) for, imperial expansion in the Americas — particularly with reference to Mexico on the eve of all-out war (see McWilliams, *American Epic* 160–61). Some of Prescott's most devoted readers, then and now, have found the shaping of his remarks into a coherent whole a herculean challenge.

David Levin, for example, in his landmark and highly suggestive reading of the crucial early to midnineteenth-century U.S. historians, highlights Prescott's "confusion" and "self-contradiction" regarding the conquest (Levin 151). The generally high marks that Prescott grants the Aztecs in his opening pages generate moral problems for the later parts of the text and for the justification of conquest. Levin resolves the conflict by arguing that *Conquest of Mexico's* "turning point" is "Prescott's discussion of priests, sacrifices, and cannibal feasts," through which "the inescapable limits of Aztec civilization are clearly established" (Levin 164).[18] In other words, religion becomes the most important index of cultural development in *Conquest of Mexico,* and the Aztecs' other attainments are thereafter downgraded and diminished. This is an interesting reading, and it finds powerful support in parts of Prescott's text. But Prescott himself foregrounds such a thesis late in the introduction, only to dismiss it:

> That such [religious] usages should have existed with the degree of refinement they showed in other things is almost inconceivable. It can only be explained as the result of religious superstition; superstition which clouds the moral perception, and perverts even the natural senses, til man, civilized man, is reconciled to the very things which are the most revolting to humanity. *Habits and opinions founded on religion must not be taken as conclusive evidence of the actual refinement of a people.* (*Mexico* 91; emphasis added)

That is, religion, in this passage, is a semi- to fully autonomous realm or field that does not necessarily permit one to form opinions about other institutions or about a culture in general. At one point in the analysis, for example, Prescott produces a short list of key domains for measurement of attainment, and religion is not included: The Toltecs are said to have produced the "true fountains of the civilization" of Mexico through agriculture, engineering, metal work, and the "complex arrangement of time" (*Mexico* 14).

Conquest of Mexico's judgments, then, point toward multiple conclusions. As point of comparison, the rhetorical motifs highlighted in chapter 3's reading of Lewis Henry Morgan's work point toward a second, less obvious reading of the Iroquois — one that situates them as at least equal to Europeans in their development of polity. Prescott's text, on the other hand, is baldly polyvocal. On one page, *Conquest of Mexico* argues that "the Mexicans had many claims to the character of a civilized community" and that sixteenth-century European countries (and particularly those, such as Spain, that were involved in the Inquisition) could stake no greater one (50). But on the next page the book delivers one of its harshest judgments, and one that Levin surely noted: "It was beneficently ordered by Providence that the land should be delivered over to another race, who would rescue it from the brutish superstitions that daily extended wider and wider, with extent of empire" (51–52). Again, it states on the one hand, with reference to the Spaniards' destruction of Aztec libraries, that "we may well doubt which has the strongest claims to civilization, the victor, or the vanquished" (60), and on the other, that Aztec hieroglyphic records contained nothing but "the annals of barbarians" (58).

On the line in this regard are Prescott's frequent remarks about what he refers to as "anomalies" in his Mexican or Aztec researches. The Dresden Codex, unlike other surviving Aztec writings, "infers a much higher civilization than the Aztec" (61). Some Aztec prayers and maxims are "as sublime as any inculcated by the enlightened codes of ancient philosophy" (41). In the juridical sphere, "the provision for making the superior judges wholly independent of the crown was worthy of an enlightened people" (24). Tezcucan law "evinces a profound respect for the great principles of morality, and as clear a perception of these principles as is to be found in the most cultivated nations" (27). Descriptions of the Tezcucan "council of music," which "was devoted to the encouragement of science and art," "argue the existence of a taste in the nation, which relied for its gratification of pleasures of a purely intellectual character" (98).

Sometimes — in fact, several times — Prescott writes that these strange facts, added to all the negative characteristics Prescott can assemble, constitute a set of "marked peculiarities . . . as far removed from each other as the extremes of barbarism and refinement" (91). *Conquest of Mexico* says that in the precontact Mexican world the farthest limits of savagism and civilization were alternately "blended" (91) or "closely in contact" (48) or side by side in "incongruity" (37) or, finally, temporarily coexistent in a world "imperfectly civilized" (115).[19] Whatever the metaphor or model, Prescott contradictorily has been telling his reader all along that barbarism and civilization cannot co-exist, that neither can tolerate the presence of the other, that the latter must vi-olently displace the former when the two come in contact.[20]

This creates enormous problems for the bulk of the text, which regularly explains that history must be judged by the light of *mentality,* the spirit of the age, the "circumstances in the period" — by shared culture, belief, situation (6).[21] Unlike Morgan, who at least attempts to yoke together his fields of analy-sis into an overall sketch of the Iroquois' position on a scale of development (*League of the Iroquois* is always gesturing toward grand synthesis), Prescott generates endless categories and contradictions within categories until one is flirting with a culture of fragments — and therefore, making highly specific judgments about this or that particular part of an institution, aspect of law, book in a collection. In a strong nineteenth-century, evolutionary anthropo-logical reading of state-of-civilization, fields and institutions are determined by the level of development (that is, by the system as a whole). In a "weaker" reading, semiautonomy is possible among society's parts: law might begin to outstrip aesthetics for example, in terms of development, and the result would force the system to advance. In a maximally "weak" reading, there is complete autonomy: one law is civilized, another one in the same code is barbaric; one religious precept is sublime, and it coexists with the practice of human sacri-fice. This last is Prescott's reconstruction of the Aztec world, and Prescott's anthropology tends toward the collapse of synthesis into singularities. The center cannot hold, and overall judgment is impaired: "What was the actual amount of Tezcucan civilization, it is not easy to determine" (*Mexico* 115).

The overall shape of Prescott's book *should* lead one down a carefully pre-pared path: Aztec civilization is situated in the first book, and the subsequent recounting of the emperor Montezuma's actions should be contextualized within this anthropological frame. But the shift in the text from the group (Book 1) to the individual (basically, the remainder of the text) should already suggest certain things.[22] As Prescott's anthropology moves according to a logic of entropy, so does *Conquest of Mexico* as a whole: if groups of institutions cannot be classified, and individual institutions suffer the same fate, then the subjects who erect or who are supposedly conditioned by these institutions will not cohere under the logic of the group. This is to argue, broadly, that *Mexico* early on shifts from an analysis of the group to that of the multiply and selectively conditioned person.

This is *the limit of the culture concept,* and a broad analogy might be made to developments in anthropology in the late twentieth century: what was once called "culture" by one is determined to be merely the culture of men by another, or the culture of white men, or the culture of white heterosexual men, or the culture of white heterosexual men without disease or disability, or the culture of white heterosexual men without disease or disability who are neither juveniles nor senior citizens, and so on.[23] Multiple, perhaps infinitely many, cultures inhabit the same geographies and cut across and through each other. At the limit of such pressure, the group concept evaporates: each separate person is so complexly articulated that sharing or community dissolves. That is, the very idea of culture finds its destination in the counterconcept of the cultured individual; anthropology is locked into a relation with such individuation. One might go so far as to suggest that the bourgeois subject — filled with internal energies and choices — is anthropology's ultimate complex extension, as cultures are understood to be polyvalent, and the contours of personhood are read as the outcome of choices made within and upon a field of competing cultures. The implication of such for a text like *Conquest of Mexico* is that the determination of the relative cultural merits of the crucial players on Prescott's stage — Cortés and the Aztec emperor, Montezuma — is made difficult if not impossible. The practice of reading morals from the "spirit of the times" dissolves under the pressure of culture understood as multiple, contradictory, contingent.

By tracing this logic, Prescott's *Conquest of Mexico* implicitly takes up key thematics of the present book: the limits of anthropology and the recognition of the representational violence and silencing inherent in the concept of culture. But these problems are addressed by Prescott in a way that in the end does not exceed the conclusion of Deloria's *Custer,* which is that culture's problems need to be displaced by a respect for, or at least attention to, "individuals" (or something closely akin to them). This strategy, finally, amounts to critiquing

culture from the reverse of the direction urged by the present study—from
the perspective that anthropologists need to imagine the world as far *more* complex rather than less complex in order to resolve questions of justice and equality. Ultimately, the problem that is anthropology, if approached this way, is
not solved but multiplied, since the world then consists of as many unique,
hybridized "cultures" as there are bodies. If, under such conditions, judgment
is necessary (as it is for a moralizing historian such as Prescott, and indeed for
anyone concerned with theorizing the social), the terrain of judgment is necessarily exponentially expanded, and alternately, if one is to respect "cultures"
(as Prescott surely argues in his insistence on taking account of the terms and
limitations of tenor, spirit, or mind), the result is monadism and the breakdown
of judgment, since persons will necessarily be judged as meeting the conditions of their own existence—that is, as being equivalent to their accumulated
personhood. (The only conceivable counterargument would be the equivalent
of a diagnosis of madness: that a person literally is not him- or herself.)

Prescott attempts to advance both of these competing conceptions at the same
time. The resultant contradictions can begin to be specified with reference to
the main body of Prescott's book. *Conquest of Mexico* is clear on the technical
or particular "how" of conquest: Montezuma fails, and the empire falls, because of his lack of will, his passivity, his fatalism—what the text ascribes to
what one might call his feminine side. At the crucial moment, "he might be
said to forego his nature; and, as his subjects asserted, to change his sex and
become a woman" (438). Prescott paints a picture of two Montezumas inhabiting the same body, "exhibited . . . under two aspects, of the most opposite and
contradictory character" (437). One of these Montezumas might be said to be
fundamentally Aztec: "bold and warlike," "perfidious, the terror of his foes,
with a haughty bearing which made him feared even by his own people" (437).
In the anthropological chapters, at moments when Prescott describes Aztec
character, he invariably shows them as hypermasculine: ferocious, feuding, warlike, cruel, just like their leader (15, 16, 20, 30). (And this does not include the
descriptions of the "bloody" religious sacrifices.) But nothing in Prescott's
anthropological pages prepares one for the second Montezuma: "gentle even
to effeminacy in his deportment," "prey to the most dismal apprehensions"
and trembling like some dithering and neurotic girl, seeking counsel from his
"impotent deities" (437, 289, 279). Prescott's portrait of Montezuma thus floats

free from the determinations of culture. *Conquest of Mexico* suggests that Montezuma's double character—his double personality, his male and female sides—can only be explained "by the extraordinary circumstances of his position" (437). *Extraordinary circumstances:* Montezuma is complexly articulated—shot through with competing identities—because Montezuma is unlike other Aztecs. He is specially or even uniquely "positioned"—for example, by the early age at which he ascended to the throne, the special conditions and needs of the kingdom at that time, and, finally, the unprecedented rupture of the continuity of his situation and worldview that Cortés's arrival initiates (437–38).[24] Montezuma, then, is not "Aztec" in any meaningful way. Caste, age, situation, and the imposition of world-shattering events mold him into a *someone* unprecedented and "extraordinary."[25]

And yet, interestingly, there is no account in Prescott of why Montezuma's feminine side eclipsed the masculine at the crucial moment. *Both* were equally determining, and Montezuma's slide into passive acceptance of conquest is literally unreadable in terms of culture. Something happened to Montezuma, something that can be generally described but that is not a *determined* something. It can be read as happenstance or temperament or will, and it finally makes no difference to the main issues at stake here. Montezuma's successor, his brother Cuitlahua, was raised precisely as Montezuma was raised, in the same time, experiencing the same events. And yet Cuitlahua, "unlike his predecessor, . . . held the white man in detestation" and boldly organized counterattacks against Cortés (473). Cuitlahua operates, according to Prescott, "by the strength of his character" (472), which is to suggest that two Aztec brothers behaved completely differently because of their personhoods, and not because of culture.[26]

For the moralizing historian, judgment becomes increasingly complex and incoherent. Prescott's purpose is to avoid retrospective judgments that would separate Montezuma and Cortés from their respective cultures. He seeks to judge them against the standards of their own cultural moments, and yet such a project is no longer clearly sustainable. At times Prescott's judgments burst forth apart from historical context, as when he assesses Montezuma's lies to Cortés: "One cannot contemplate this pusillanimous conduct of Montezuma without mingled feelings of pity and contempt" (280). At times Cortés is granted a conscience about his actions—for example, about "whether it is right to ex-act personal service from the natives" (677)—which undermines the portrait of a man whose actions are determined and which situates at least some of his thoughts in near relation to the views of Bishop Bartolomé de las Casas, whom Prescott judges to be a kind of science-fictional time traveler, living in the wrong century.[27] Indeed, Prescott's reference to Cortés's frequent disagreements with Spanish authorities, including the king, over the issue of slavery positions Cortés as out of step with the tenor of the times (for example, 477, 628, 636).

Not surprisingly, Prescott's early reviewers were divided as to the moral of the tale. The London *Quarterly Review* found him too hard on Cortés, too soft on the "ignorant savages" (quoted in Cline, Gardiner, and Gibson 160–61), whereas the *United States Magazine and Democratic Review* chided Prescott for letting Cortés off the hook (quoted in Cline, Gardiner, and Gibson 164). The former attacked him as inattentive to the rigors of "mentality" critique, whereas the latter suggested that Prescott had carried the technique too far, that moral judgments should be universal and not historically based. Prescott's general *motion*, however, is toward neither pole but, rather, toward a reconstitution of anthropology as biography, toward an anthropology in which cultural judgment should be all but impaired, while, paradoxically, judgments of all sorts are invited from every temporal and cultural angle.

BORDERLINE PERSONALITY

Ridge's *Life and Adventures of Joaquín Murieta* tells the "true" story of a "respectable" Mexican immigrant to California, who, in the early 1850s, is stripped of his newfound mining wealth, forced to witness the rape of his "mistress," and publicly whipped for a crime he did not commit (Ridge, *Murieta* 8–12).[28] "Wanton cruelty and the tyranny of prejudice had reached their climax," and Murieta subsequently leads a life of crime to revenge himself upon "the whole American race" (12, 14). In a sense, Murieta is a version of Cooper's Magua in *The Last of the Mohicans:* The cathartic whipping is straight out of Cooper, as is the portrait of the damaged, racialized figure who can wreak nothing but havoc upon the "Anglo-Saxon" world (58).

But one can read Ridge's only full-length book as a kind of response to *Conquest of Mexico*—a modern version of the problems addressed therein—

and this means, in the first place, recognizing *Murieta*'s fundamental representational compression. Murieta, is, on the one hand, a latter-day embodiment of Cortés's spirit and that of the conquistadors, and he is described in precisely the same stereotypical ways: he has the "proud blood of the Castilians" and has "inherited the old chivalrous spirit of his Spanish ancestry" (9). He soon will evidence "indomitable and daring spirit" and has always been "full of the exhilarating spirit of adventure" (8).

On the other hand, he is Indian, too: Ridge describes him as a "partial descendant of the Mexiques," which accounts for his color, "neither very dark or very light" (9, 8). He is also *marked* as an other by "lawless" Americans (read: the dangerous and the working classes) in a manner that ties together the image of the Mexican and Indian:

> A feeling was prevalent among this class of contempt for any and all Mexicans, whom they looked upon as no better than conquered subjects of the United States, having no rights which could stand before a haughtier and superior race. (9)

This is Prescott's language (the language of Manifest Destiny in general), described here as a prejudice rather than as Providence. And one cannot help but read passages such as these without seeing in them a reflection on Ridge's own condition and situation (an Indian in white man's country),[29] as well as the irony that the sixteenth-century position of the American "Castilian" has been inverted in the nineteenth century. One might say that Cortés experiences conquest in *Joaquín Murieta*; Murieta himself at one point describes his situation as a continuation of the Mexican-American War (74–75).[30]

Ridge, it should be noted, more than once addressed the question of the Spanish annihilation of the worlds of Mexico and Peru. In "Poem" he celebrates southern Indian civilizations and condemns the anthropological justification of conquest: "Were peace and plenty but the Spaniard's right? / And Aztec *barbarous* because not *white*?" (quoted in Parins, *Ridge* 150). And yet, in his strictly anthropological texts, Ridge faulted the Aztecs in the following way:

> The capacity of his mind when directed in a certain channel, is evidenced in the indigenous antique civilization of the Mexique races, whose progress in agriculture, in architecture, in weaving, in painting, in general manufactures, and in vari-

ous of the arts of peace, was indeed wonderful. Yet the effect of this civilization seemed to be to diminish their physical courage and to abate their warlike spirit; and they fell an
easy prey to their Spanish conquerors. ("Indians 1" 13)

In other words, the Aztecs and other southern Indians were *too* mentally developed to fight off a less settled, or perhaps less-"civilized," people. Ridge's
reading is a near variant of Prescott's remarks concerning Aztec pomp, leisure,
and general self-satisfaction.[31]

Anthropologically, Murieta is positioned as both "Mexican" (in whatever
and all senses racial and colonial) and as fundamentally not Mexican. On the
one hand, Ridge claims to be writing about a "truly wonderful man" who

> was *nothing more than a natural production of the social
> and moral condition* of the country in which he lived, acting
> upon certain peculiar circumstances favorable to such a re-
> sult [that is, the production of social history], and, conse-
> quently, his individual history is part of the most valuable
> history of the State. (7; emphasis added)

"Nothing more than a natural production of the social and moral" — this is a
reading of personhood that is entirely given over to a cultural or situational
logic, to persons understood as representing "condition." Murieta is emblem-
atic of California history; his story stands for the confluence of forces that
have shaped the region and its identities. He is a "production," or index, of
such forces and conflicts — a constrained result of outside forces acting upon
the body. He is shaped into the Mexican bandit, as even he proclaims,[32] and as
in the work of other auto-anthropologists, he is the expression not of a singular culture but of a set of relations. He is a manifestation of "border-life" (34).

And yet in the volume's "Editor's Preface" (probably written by Ridge), the
subsequent text is said to be

> doing justice to a people who have so far degenerated as to
> have been called by many, "A Nation of Cowards," to hold
> up a *manifest contradiction, or at least an exception to so
> sweeping an opinion,* in the character of a man who, bad
> though he was, possessed a soul as full of unconquerable

courage as ever belonged to a human being. Although the Mexicans may be whipped by every other nation, in a battle of two or five to one, yet no man who speaks the truth can ever deny that *there lived one Mexican* whose nerves were of iron in the face of danger and death. (4; emphasis added)

The first sentence in this passage implies that Murieta may be an example of Mexican personhood that disproves racist and ethnocentrist conceptions of the "Mexican." Mexico is not, perhaps, "A Nation of Cowards." But the second sentence erases this reading, leaving only one possible interpretation: that Mexicans *are* cowards who cannot win a battle even when the odds are heavily in their favor. Murieta is a "one," a "manifest contradiction," an "exception." He has a "character" (a word that, perhaps inevitably, implies a personhood that belongs to and is possessed by an individuated being) rather than a culture or history. And Ridge goes on to argue that Mexicans are Murieta's "degenerate countrymen" (8), an argument in general that again situates Ridge as Prescott's mirror (and Stephens's, too), since Prescott also imagined the Mexico of his day to be home to a fallen people who had all but forgotten their heroic origins. Ridge further suggests the difference between Murieta and other emergent Chicanos when wealthy Mexican American ranchers assist Murieta out of "fear" or "in consideration of a share his plunders," but decidedly not out of a sense of solidarity with his race war (42).

Only one thing is clear in this text: that the bandit Murieta would not have been produced without the aid of border prejudices and border violence (158). Beyond that, Murieta's story is one of Fate (12), or not, "if we may call it Fate when it was born from his own extreme carelessness" (153); he is watched over by a supernatural "guardian fiend" (58, 139), or he is subject to the rule of California and is successful only because he appears at a time of relative lawlessness (158–59).

In addition, Murieta seems to suffer from Montezuma's problem of double character:[33] In a moment straight from Robin Hood and the bourgeois tradition of the good bandit, Murieta refuses to rob a poor Mexican because he "had yet a remnant of the noble spirit which had been his original nature" (65). That is, he once had a single, "original nature" to which a border personhood has been grafted, obliterating all but traces of the original man, which suggests that "culture," in the broadest sense, is not something one has but is a *historical imposition*—an interiorization, an internalization—of racism and its consequences. Murieta may finally be "an author who acted out his own tragedies," a curious, circular formulation that suggest both will *and* subjugation to some larger pattern at one and the same time (109). Murieta is a prisoner of the border's penetration of and merging with his character. An individual, then, *and* a border subject, "he leaves behind him the important lesson that there is nothing so dangerous in its consequences as *injustice to individuals*—whether it arise from prejudice of color or from any other source; that a wrong done to one man is a wrong to society and to the world" (158).

Ridge's text, therefore, risks leaving a certain domain of nineteenth-century anthropology altogether, because his historical ethnography—focused on contact and transformation—recognizes the analytics of race, color, and the like not as descriptions but as acts of violence. Ridge's border anthropology, in short, critiques group identities and insists on the primacy of the individual—in Murieta's case, his original nobility. Ridge insists on remarking Murieta's numerous acts of benevolence and "conscience," even in a case when "he regretted the necessity of killing so honest and hard-working a man" (33). Another murder, that of General Bean, was "only an act of self-preservation" (49), and during a pure murder for money Ridge at least permits Murieta to call them " 'poor fellows' " (132).

What is crucial for this history, as for nineteenth-century history in general, is the question of final judgment. What is one to make of Murieta in his totality? How should he be remembered? Ridge addresses the problem of moralizing the past early in *Joaquín Murieta*. Murieta and his fellow bandits have hidden themselves in the mountains near Mount Shasta, a California aesthetic-geographic landmark—a conventional object of "sublime" contemplation—and the subject of "Mount Shasta—Seen from a Distance," Ridge's most famous poem among his contemporaries.[34] Ridge interpolates his poem into *Joaquín Murieta*, and the verses end with this insight:

> And well this Golden State shall thrive, if, like
> Its own Mount Shasta, sovereign law shall lift
> Itself in purer atmosphere—so high
> That human feeling, human passion, at its base

Should lie subdued; e'en pity's tears shall on
Its summit freeze; to warm it, e'en the sunlight
Of deep sympathy shall fail —
Its pure administration shall be like
The snow, immaculate upon that mountain's brow!
    (*Murieta* 25)

With all the "tears" and "pity" that *Joaquín Murieta* marshals onto Murieta's side, one should expect, even demand, that the book end by peeling back such considerations and administering or rendering an objective and "pure" judgment of him.

And, in a surprising way, this may be the book's project. Murieta, it seems, is himself "perfectly sublime" and "super-human," precisely like the vision of justice in "Mount Shasta" (87).[35] He says that he lives for "higher purposes" than any of the people around him, and the text takes him seriously (105). And he himself moves beyond tears and pain when he is stripped and whipped by the Tejon Indians, and he laughs like a "jolly bandit" in response (40, 41).

It is "society," finally, that is judged in Ridge's book, and not Murieta. "Society has no right," Ridge says, in a rare moment of first-person, direct address to the reader ("it seems to me"), compared to the "right" of individuals to behave morally according to their own lights. "In such matters God is the only judge" — and, perhaps, Murieta by analogy, who sits on high and is dispassionately more than human (80). The latter is capable, with regard to his indeterminate physical appearance, of operating on both sides of the border, of walking the borderline of identity apart from either side's determinations.[36]

Murieta's final plans in the book are grandiose:

"I intend to arm and equip fifteen hundred or two thousand men and make a clean sweep of the southern counties. I intend to kill the Americans by 'wholesale,' burn their ranchos, and run off their property at one single swoop. . . . My brothers, we will then be revenged for our wrongs, and some little, too, for the wrongs of our poor, bleeding country." (75)

This, according to Ridge's reading, is Murieta's

crowning glory — a deed of daring and of power that would
redeem with its refulgent light the darkness of his previous
history and show him to aftertimes, not as a mere outlaw, but
as a *hero* who has revenged his country's wrongs and washed
out her disgrace in the blood of her enemies. (80)

Murieta will erase the white-imposed and white-dominated border, he will
erase border society and all of its wrongs, and Ridge heartily approves of these
plans, finding them worthy of a man with the vision of Mount Shasta.[37] But
things are not as simple as they seem: The plans themselves are at least in part
a product of his border identity — a clear "wrong" in Ridge's judgment, both
in terms of its imposition upon Murieta and the criminal rage that results.[38]
The border, then, and its injustice produce the temperament and mental acuity
necessary to annihilate the border.

One can only conclude that Ridge misses something fundamental in his
analysis, something that relates to his indecision with respect to the problem
of character and historical culture. Murieta, the man who at bottom has a
good and even remarkable character, will never be able to disentangle his
"original" self from its interpenetration with the border. Murieta's final plans
fail, but were they to succeed, one can only imagine the imposition of a new
form of the border: one in which California Indians are marked as dark, pa-
thetic, worm-eating, greedy, cowardly, and full of "superstitious dread" (36–
37, 130); perhaps one in which the California Indians are subjected to Ridge's
phrenological jokes: "so largely developed is the bump of caution on the head
of a California Indian. But cunning is equally developed" (38). In this new
border, Southerners are read as "chivalrous" with regard to Southern "honor,"
slavery, and such (111). And despite Ridge's protestations that his book is not
"ministering to any depraved taste for the dark and horrible" (7), he imagines
characters who can say, " 'I love to smell the blood of a Chinaman. Besides,
it's such easy work to kill them. It's a kind of luxury to cut their throats' "
(64).[39] In this new border, finally, whites are erased from the whole of Murieta's geography, in a "clean sweep" that would include former friends and enemies alike.[40]

The border, then, awaits another form of judgment: not one of mountains,
masquerades, and murder; not one in which anthropology's strategies are mul-

tiplied nor one in which anthropology's problems are displaced; not one in which individuals are complexly reconstructed or simply reified; and not one, finally, that would make the disciplines of science *or* history preeminent in the just or true resolution of identity disputes. Perhaps the border awaits judgment in which the political and epistemological invitation to withdraw from anthropology is heard and once heard, is forgotten, because the condition for all of this is an active forgetting, a willed dissolution of the will to knowledge and the subjects it constructs.

And here I would be willing to part, and leave the reader to wander
alone and at will through the labyrinth of mystery which hangs
over these ruined cities; but it would be craven to do so, without
turning for a moment to the important question, Who were the
people that built these cities?

—JOHN LLOYD STEPHENS,

INCIDENTS OF TRAVEL IN CENTRAL AMERICA,

CHIAPAS, AND YUCATAN (1841)

There are three questions which will very naturally occur to those of
my readers who have done me the honor to follow me through the
preceding details and statistics:—1st. By whom were these ruins
built?

—BENJAMIN MOORE NORMAN,

RAMBLES IN YUCATAN (1842)

American archaeology's "golden age," its celebrated origin, is the 1840s his-
torical-philosophical investigation into the Mayan ruins of Spanish America,
and anthropology's "who" question haunted all of the published accounts.[1]
The value of the works written by two crucial travelers to the Central American ruins—John Lloyd Stephens and Benjamin Moore Norman—is of a different order from the value of those examined in the previous five chapters.
Apparently there is no 1840s Amerindian countertext that one might put in
conversation with the founding documents of archaeology in the Americas.[2]
So here, in this coda to *The Limits of Multiculturalism,* multiple standpoints
will not be at issue.

But there is no more important body of midnineteenth-century anthropological literature for purposes of highlighting questions of social scientific
method—that is, for highlighting its empiricism and the problem of evidence,
and the equally thorny matter of marshaling facts into significant distinctions.
Indeed, more than that of any of the other figures analyzed in these pages,
Stephens's work (as well as that of his field partner, the renowned architec-

tural illustrator Frederick Catherwood) remains today celebrated as serious, "hard" scientific and social scientific investigation.[3] In a word, Stephens had "method." Stephen Williams, who otherwise looks long and casts a skeptical eye upon nineteenth-century archaeologists, excludes Stephens from his study of "fantastic archaeology" and simply refers to his work as "pioneering" (Williams 165). And famed Mayan code breaker Michael Coe, another doubter of many things archaeological and anthropological, says of Stephens and Catherwood, "These two will live forever in the hearts of Mayanists, for they founded and defined an entirely new field of study. We are still building on that foundation" (Coe 98).[4]

Schoolcraft may be honored today for discovering Amerindian expression or Morgan for kinship structures, but neither of them overtly elaborates an empirical method that links their smallest units of observation with overarching conclusions about "Indians." Morgan's evolutionary schema, for example, bears no necessary relationship to data he collected. The data are simply interpreted in light of known evolutionary steps, in the light of the fact that Indians are already, in the first place, among the lower orders of mankind. Hence Morgan's texts, and Prescott's, too, reveal the tensions between a set scheme and recalcitrant "facts." Their texts evidence a grudging respect for different sorts of empirical data collection, but both *League of the Iroquois* and *History of the Conquest of Mexico* are oddly unworried double narratives, with remarks on individual pieces of the data always threatening "from below" to overthrow their overarching historical developmental narratives. Still other figures in this same period, such as Morton, are vilified today for making a mockery of scientific method, even though Morton's work evidences a greater care and caution in this regard than his critics have permitted themselves to see.

So Stephens serves as the touchstone of method, the founder of properly disinterested Amerindian inquiry. And if Morgan, Prescott, Morton, and the like are open to dismissal from a late twentieth-century perspective — if the present moment can easily disentangle itself from them by simply speaking the names "scientific racism" and "evolutionism" — Stephens will prove more difficult to shrug off.

Stephens, though trying to concentrate his energies on rambles to ruined cities and archaeological investigations, was at least equally concerned — burdened, by choice — with a diplomatic mission to Central America, and he un-

wittingly found himself in the middle of a Central American "Indian" uprising, led by the spectacular figure of Rafael Carrera. One could devote many
pages to analyzing this "political" Stephens, who meets Carrera on more than
one occasion,[5] who makes many remarks about Indians and their character,
and whose ideas about present-day Central American Indians have obvious
implications for American race relations in general in Latin America and the
United States, including on matters of peonage, enslavement, removal, and
civil war. But this coda will instead focus almost entirely on Stephens as archaeologist, on Stephens as brooder and metacommentator on social scientific
knowledge claims in his two works of Incidents of Travel (1841 and 1843).
And later in the chapter Norman's two volumes of Rambles (1842–43 and 1845)
will serve as counterpoint to Stephens in this regard. Norman is a nearly unknown figure in American archaeology and American studies in general, but
that, perhaps, will need to change. Like a figure from the novels of H. Rider
Haggard or Sir Arthur Conan Doyle, Norman shadows Stephens to the Mayan
ruins, slavishly imitating his stories and strategies in his first volume and mercilessly parodying him in the second. Norman is Stephens's sycophant and
court jester. He is the aberrant humorist lodged at the formative moment for
American archaeological discourse, and even today his texts have the rhetorical capacity to unsettle received methodological wisdom.

ARCHAEO-LOGICALITY

The 1840s version of the "who" question most directly extended investigations into the earth formations left by the so-called Moundbuilders of the
Midwest, which had been examined and interpreted for half a century. At the
time that the ruins in Spanish America came to the attention of Stephens, Norman, and others, field-workers had spent decades "proving" that the Moundbuilders were an extinct race, entirely unrelated to North American Indians.
The mounds, then, were thought to be the remains of a relatively sophisticated
civilization that predated the Indians; America had been the site of a "higher"
civilization long before the coming of the Europeans.

John T. Irwin describes this early nineteenth-century trope of the "lost
race" and its unreadable artifacts as "disturbing" to the "concept of progressive human development" and the "plausibility of historical consciousness

per se" because "it suggests the possibility of radical discontinuity in history" (Irwin 179, 174). Yet the lost-race thesis proved soothing in other ways: as Williams argues, it rested upon and reinforced the "stereotype of the lazy and ignorant Indian"; there was a "virulent racism inherent in much of the argument against the American Indians as being the authors of these mounds, earthworks, and elaborate artifacts" (Williams 72). And one could argue that it served a psychic purpose to imagine America as a place of past greatness, and that perception further legitimated the conquest of the Americas for purposes of reestablishing civilization in this part of the world. The Indians could not be (that is, were not) narrated into the massively influential theory that history as such was composed of the rise and fall of great nations. The Indians, it was said, did not rise or fall; they merely squatted on a land destined for greater things.[6]

The vague but extravagant details about far more elaborate ruin sites in Spanish America, which filtered north via European accounts during the Jacksonian era, reenergized the hunt to discover a highly "civilized," primordial America. Stephens acknowledges, relatively late in his first set of accounts, that he traveled to the ruins with this assumption in mind: "Our feelings were in favour of going back to a high and venerable antiquity" (*Central America* 2:455).

It perhaps goes without saying that, as Williams reminds us, "perception plays a very important part in archeological interpretation." But Stephens's writings do not produce a concluding thesis that matches the preliminary one, and this is crucial to the power of his discourse, to its truth value, or "truth effect" (Williams 41). Indeed, in his work one senses the testing of theory through, and the modification of his theoretical model in line with, the results of empirical analysis of facts found in the field. He seems to know how to sift data and how to compare and contrast. And along the way Stephens constantly warns of the dangers of investigating with a foreordained thesis in mind, of jumping to hasty conclusions, of "speculating" without the support of further information. Summarizing the information gleaned from his visit to a first set of ruins, at Copan, Stephens notes:

> In regard to the age of this desolate city I shall not at present offer any conjecture. Some idea might perhaps be formed

from the accumulations of earth and the gigantic trees growing on the top of the ruined structures, but it would be uncertain and unsatisfactory. Nor shall I at this moment offer
any conjecture in regard to the people who built it, or to the
time when or the means by which it was depopulated, and became a desolation and ruin; whether it fell by the sword, or
famine, or pestilence. (*Central America* 1:159)

More than any of the proto-anthropologists working on the question of the
Moundbuilders, Stephens constantly meditates upon the very problem of interpretation, and he foregrounds seeing and what can be known from sight as
the crucial problem for anthropology. He and Catherwood travel twice between
1839 and 1841 to the ruins of Central America in order to see for themselves
what all the fuss is about—to decide for themselves what these ruins truly are
in a historical-anthropological sense. Stephens's investigative reports on these
expeditions are contained in two, two-volume works: *Incidents of Travel in
Central America, Chiapas, and Yucatan* (1841) and *Incidents of Travel in Yucatan* (1843). Stephens understands his project or purpose as one of making
judgments about the "who" question: "who" were the people who built the
ruins, and where did they stand within the grand, progressive continuum that
runs from absolute savagery to the heights of civilization? It is a nineteenth-
century evolutionary anthropological project through and through.

But the easiest way to see and comprehend the ruins, as Stephens several
times reminds us over the course of his four volumes of reminiscences and reports, is in the manner of the moral-aesthetical traveler on the hunt for the picturesque. The concept of the "picturesque" was a kind of catchall for everything that was not beautiful in a neoclassical sense—everything that was not
regularly ordered, symmetrical, properly proportioned—and though both nature and certain types or classes of human beings were viewed as picturesque,
human "ruins" were a favored topos for moral speculation on mutability and
death. Many nineteenth-century U.S. painters, poets, and occasional philosophers meditated upon the picturesque, but the linkage between ruins and picturesque vision had reached its fullest formulation in Comte de Volney's *Les
Ruines; ou, Méditation sur les révolutions des empires* (1791), translated into
English and published by Thomas Jefferson and Joel Barlow in 1802.[7]

The moral-aesthetical traveler who visited everything from abandoned pyramids and castles to decaying forest cabins was a deeply familiar figure to even occasional readers of travel literature in the eighteenth and nineteenth centuries. And Stephens's texts increasingly slip into a moral discourse upon ruins, the first time most clearly in the middle of his report on the ruins of Palenque:

> Here were the remains of a cultivated, polished, and peculiar people, who had passed through all stages incident to the rise and fall of nations; reached their golden age, and perished, entirely unknown. The links which connected them with the human family were severed and lost, and these were the only memorials of their footsteps upon earth. We lived in the ruined palace of their kings; we went up to their desolate temples and fallen altars. . . . In the romance of the world's history nothing ever impressed me more forcibly than the spectacle of this once great and lovely city, overturned, desolate, and lost; discovered by accident, overgrown with trees for miles around, and without even a name to distinguish it. Apart from everything else, it was a mourning witness to the world's mutations. (*Central America* 2:356–57)

Broken buildings overgrown with trees, a mysterious and dead people, the theme of the rise and fall of nations, the viewer's feeling of mourning — these elements add up to a kind of précis for Volneyesque moral vision.

There are several political implications of Stephens's picturesque moments and of picturesque travel writing in general: first, the mourning of mutability obscures a reading of history as a series of conquests. Civilizations fall naturally, under their own weight, typically due to their inevitable lassitude or decadence when mighty and prosperous (Edward Gibbon, for example, comes to mind as a proponent of this view). Second, the picturesque traveler typically has little time for consideration of the economic or political fate of peoples who occupy ruin sites in the present day. They may be oppressed, enslaved, or impoverished, but above all, in the first place, they are fallen, too, like the ruins, because of their ancestors' (and therefore their own) actions. Third, the concept of mutability serves as a morally conservative or reactionary call to arms for the writer's home nation. Picturesque travel writing functions, then, much like a jeremiad: the nation must redouble its efforts to be morally firm and righteous in order to stave off, if only for a while, a terrible fall. This last point is often racist in its extrapolation, highlighting the danger of the imperial nations of the West mixing with peoples from degraded stock.

But Stephens often opposes merely picturesque vision and its judgments to the type of seeing appropriate to his scientific project; he understands moral-aesthetical vision — the work of the bourgeois traveler — as the counterconcept and counterproject to real archaeology. "We were neither sentimental, nor philosophical, nor moralizing travellers," he warns his readers (*Central America* 2:235). Still later, at Palenque, he notes:

> I have omitted a series of views, exhibiting the most picturesque and striking subjects that ever presented themselves to the pencil of an artist. The ruins and the forest made the deep and abiding impression upon our minds; but our object is to present the buildings as restored, as subjects for speculation and comparison with the architecture of other lands and times. (2:338)[8]

Such an amoralizing, scientific project of representation and comparative analysis, however, is not as simple as it sounds. Upon arrival at their first set of ruins, at Copan, Stephens announces, "I am entering abruptly upon new ground. . . . The ground was entirely new; there were no guide-books or guides; the whole was a virgin soil" (1:96, 1:119). The ruins are so different from Stephens's and Catherwood's preconceptions of any sort of known human world — in part, they defy categorization because of the mass of daunting hieroglyphs inscribed upon them — that they at first, quite literally, cannot be represented. Stephens and Catherwood are metaphorically "in the dark"; the ruins are not visible:

> We resolved first to obtain drawings of the sculptured columns. Even in this there was great difficulty. The designs were very complicated, and so different from anything Mr. Catherwood had ever seen before as to be perfectly unintelligible. (1:117)

After much effort toward reproducing the designs, Stephens reports:

As we feared, the designs were so intricate and complicated, the subjects so entirely new and unintelligible, that he had great difficulty in drawing. He had made several attempts, both with the camera lucida and without, but failed to satisfy himself or even me, who was less severe in criticism. The "idol" seemed to defy his art; two monkeys on a tree on one side appeared to be laughing at him, and I felt discouraged and despondent. (1:120)

The monkeys, as an earlier passage makes clear, appear to be "the wandering spirits of the departed race guarding the ruins of their former habitations" (1:103). This trope of fallenness or devolution links the Volney thematic to the problem of scientific presentation and interpretation. Moral travelers can mourn the fall of the ancients, but Stephens attempts to swerve from such a reading, even as these same ancients seem to mock any other sort of meditation, including a scientific one, upon the ruins.

The result is a kind of impasse or block, and a confused and indeterminate feeling about the ancient structures:

Of the moral effect of the monuments themselves, standing as they do in the depths of a tropical forest, silent and solemn, strange in design, excellent in sculpture, rich in ornament, different from the works of any other people, their uses and purposes, their whole history so entirely unknown, with hieroglyphics explaining all but perfectly unintelligible, I shall not pretend to convey any idea. Often the imagination was pained in gazing at them. (1:158)

This is a breakdown of two types of vision at once: the scientific and the aesthetical gaze. The passage is Stephens's acknowledgement of the ruins' total alterity, and it implies that they were built by a people—that they belong to a people—absolutely other to West, East, Indians, and, probably, recorded world history. They are works, then, of some radically other time and human type. With no Western point of reference, neither architectural drawing nor (as a kind of backup strategy) moral reflection is possible. Archaeology cannot begin.[9]

But suddenly it does, and "Mr. Catherwood was much more successful in his drawings; indeed, at the beginning the light fell exactly as he wished, and he mastered the difficulty" (1:121). Finally, Catherwood produces "accurate and faithful representations" of the monuments at Copan (1:158). Catherwood's success coincides with Stephens's project to map the city — to create a city "plan" that would make the whole of Copan visible. "The plan was complicated, and the whole ground being overgrown with trees, difficult to make out" (1:139). But a detailed plan is formed, and Stephens publishes Catherwood's "Plan of Copan" before he presents any of Catherwood's drawings of the ruins (1:133, facing page). The map produces the possibility of seeing any of the ruined fragments of Copan.[10] The Stephens/Catherwood survey map of Copan accomplishes several things at once: first, it regulates the "boundaries" of what Stephens calls "this city," establishing it as something discrete and determined and as something with a definable purpose. One result of regulating the boundaries of the city is that some nearby ruins are ruled out of the city proper (1:133). Second, it subjects Copan to the defining measurements of a survey: straight lines, four compass points, scale. In short, Copan is made comprehensible according to the science of geography, the calculus of mapmaking. Third, the map determines not only the arrangement of the surviving structures but their purposes as well. "There are no remains of palaces or private buildings," Stephens determines (1:133); the "city" is uniformly religious in its significance — a series of altars, temples, sepulchres, and devotional statuary. The very ability to "restore" the structures of Copan through detailed drawing and description depends upon all of the preshaping strategies of the map, which, Stevens says, seems a kind of "black art" to the local Indians whom he hires to cut down trees and clear brush (1:145).

Such is the foundation of archaeology in the Americas. Stephens would have his readers believe that "we began our explorations without any theory to support," and this may indeed have been the case — but only at the point where the ruins are radically "unintelligible" to Stephens and Catherwood (2:455). Such a point, which is the temporal moment prior to mapping, is a bold one for archaeology; it is a moment in which everything is laid bare. It is, perhaps, archaeology's moment of truth, with the translation of the ruins, much less the interpretation of them, held in suspense. Copan is a mass of

points, a welter of possibilities, without line, form, or shadow, much less coherent buildings, builders, time schemes, or race theories.

Beyond this point, this moment, it is all downhill for archaeology. "Intu-
ition" intervenes. "Experience" is rewarded. Stephens and Catherwood achieve
line of sight, and with the strategy for representation of Copan secured, each
further city explored is increasingly easier to present. For example, at Palenque,
the second city Stephens and Catherwood visit, the former writes that, with
"six months' " effort, "the whole of these ruins could be laid bare" (*Central
America* 2:307). And Stephens and Catherwood plunge right in:

> As at Copan, it was my business to prepare the different ob-
> jects for Mr. Catherwood to draw. Many of the stones had to
> be scrubbed and cleaned; and as it was our object to have
> the utmost possible accuracy in the drawings, in many places
> scaffolds were to be erected on which to set up the camera
> lucida. (2:309)

Importantly, here and throughout Stephens's travel books the mechanics of vision are foregrounded. In this case, for example, the technics include the
preparation of the object, the use of scaffolding to gain a certain perspective
on it, and the technology of the "camera lucida"—a device that uses a prism
in order to project an image on paper, which then can be traced.

But Stephens's text cannot see all of this. Or, better, he cannot see the significance of his mechanics of vision so long as he wants to produce archaeological
knowledge. The maps, the clearing of the ground, the platforms, the camera that
supplies line, perspective, and shade—all of these are treated in the text as
value-free tools in the service of scientific investigation, as instruments that separate Stephens and Catherwood from picturesque travel writers and their senti-
ments. But archaeology is grounded by these instruments, these *strategies* for
representation and comprehension. Without them, there would be unintelligibility—that is, the experience of alterity or difference as such. With them, everything appears, from the shape of the door frames at Copan to a theory of racial
origin and development and the builder's place within such an evolution.

Archaeology is a complex structure built on top of such blank and incoherent spots. This is archaeology's "archaeo-logicality." Archaeology "rests" on a

swirling, confusing abyss ("complicated" and "unintelligible," Stephens and Catherwood keep asserting), but its grid of intelligibility makes the "complication" — the amorphous cloud of proto-matter, proto-data, possibilities — appear to be navigable, readable, comprehensible. In short, the grid gives the appearance that "unintelligibility" is being assembled into a structure. But archaeology does not touch anything, "really," and its knowledges "appear" as something akin to visions; they are castles in the air. Although 150 years of subsequent archaeology is quite capable of building upon these "foundations," the structures become no more stable over time. They simply become mass, multigenerational articles of faith, of sheer consensus, and they are always on the verge of disappearing again, once the conditions and parameters of the foundation are laid bare, are reexcavated. The Copan monkeys' laughter, then, points to such a judgment of archaeology; and at the very least, there is no disinterested gaze, no representation or interpretation of the ruins without their preassembly.

All of this is clear from Stephens's report of Catherwood's difficulties and from other anecdotes within the *Central America* text as well. For example, one of the large questions that hang over the whole of Stephens's volumes concerns the relationship between the ruins and the present-day Amerindians he encounters, hires as servants, and berates. At the start of Stephens's Copan adventures, the text foregrounds a radical undecidability concerning this question within the structure of one of his sentences, through a curious use of writerly mechanics. This is, interestingly, the first time in his writings that Stephens broaches the "who" question:

> Who were the people that built this city? In the ruined cities of Egypt, even in the long-lost Petra, the stranger knows the story of the people whose vestiges are around him. America, say historians, was peopled by savages; but savages never reared these structures, savages never carved these stones. We asked the Indians who made them, and their dull answer was "Quien sabe?" "who knows?" (*Central America* 1:104)

Two readings of the final sentence in this passage are possible, given the indeterminate status of the words "who made them." One can read these three words as a full sentence addressed to his Indian servants: "We asked the Indi-

ans, 'Who made them?' " In other words: "Who *were* the long-dead people of
this region?" Reading this way, Stephens imagines the people of Copan as
non-Indian — a lost race. But this reading depends upon interpolation of both
punctuation and quotation marks. A second reading interprets "who made
them" as a clause referring to the "Indians": "We asked the Indians who made
them." In other words: "We asked the living Indian descendants of the people
of Copan about the ruins, but they have forgotten everything about their own
past." Reading this way, Stephens imagines present-day Amerindians as a fallen
race who have drifted backward from "civilized" Copan to savagism.

The indeterminacy of this sentence is worth preserving for the sake of unearthing the terms of archaeo-logicality. It is another extremely bold moment
in proto-archaeology — a moment in which archaeological foundations tremble
even as they are being sketched, laid out, fortified, and in general determined.
Everything in Stephens's archaeology depends upon the answer to this question, and it is not a riddle that the ruins themselves can solve for him. The answer to this question is one of those matters that is preconditional for presentation, much less the representation, of the ruins; it is preconditional for seeing
in general.

The movement over the course of the 1,500 pages of Stephens's travels is a
gradual one from the first reading to the second — from the presumption of
the ruins' ancient construction to a far more modern dating. Beginning from
the hope that the ruins belong to "antiquity," he slowly decides that the structures are of recent date and were abandoned only at time of Spanish conquest.
Finally, Stephens determines that the present-day Indians of Central America
are essentially the same Indians who built Copan, Palenque, and all the rest.

At Palenque, Stephens begins his account by noting that one of the images
of the inhabitants "represents a different species from any now existing in that
region of country," and that in general the human images at Palenque "indicate a race of people now lost and unknown" (*Central America* 2:311). But he
soon observes that some of the images the builders made of themselves are at
least similar to the appearance of Central American Indians. "The nose and
eyes are strongly marked, but altogether the development is not so strange as
to indicate a race entirely different from those which are known" (2:353). And
still later:

Among the Indians who came out to escort us to the village was one whom we had not seen before, and whose face bore a striking resemblance to those delineated on the walls of the [Palenque] buildings. In general the faces of the Indians were of an entirely different character, but he might have been taken for a lineal descendant of the perished race. (2:358)

Perhaps the ancients amalgamated with the Indians. Perhaps at least some of the Indians bear the marks of descent from the lost race. Later still, in the report from Stephens's second round of travels, he relies on Samuel G. Morton's influential works on craniology, including *Crania Americana* (1839), in order to secure the link between the so-called ancients and present-day Indians. Skulls unearthed during a second visit to the ruins of Uxmal appear to be those of "full-blooded Indians," and Stephens concludes: "These are not the works of people who have passed away, and whose history is lost, but of the same great *race* which, changed, miserable, and degraded, still clings around their ruins" (*Yucatan* 1:143, 1:168).[11]

In, broadly, the first section of Stephens's first two volumes, the decision to imagine the ruins as the product of some "other" people results in one reading of the "evidence," just as, in the second section, the decision to think the Indians as the builders results in another. For example, in *Central America*, the first two volumes of travels, Stephens mostly does not doubt that everything he sees — including what he considers to be the "vastness" of the ruins, their "rich" and complex ornamentation, the use of "rare" and "costly" wooden lintels over the doors, and so on — points to "highly civilized" in answer to the "who" question (*Central America* 2:413). But even by the end of these volumes, the "highly civilized" reading is slowly changing. Uxmal, the last stop on Stephens's first trip, "presented a scene of barbaric magnificence" (2:427). These are important words: This is the first time that Stephens uses the term "barbaric" (that is, savage or near-savage, or at least not civilized) to describe the ruin builders, and his word choice has everything to do with his gradually unfolding belief that the ruin builders were little more than Indians after all. He immediately contradicts his reading that Uxmal is "barbaric" — arguing that at least one of the buildings demonstrates "no rudeness or barbarity in the design or proportions; on the contrary, the whole wears an air of architectural symmetry and grandeur" (2:429) — but the damage has been done.

On his second visit to Uxmal, Stephens finds "a rude circular mound" in which lies buried a stone cat: "The sculpture is rude" (*Yucatan* 1:104). Another set of monuments "had no beauty or fitness of design or proportion" (1:117), and even though Stephens continues to note examples of "taste" (1:106, 1:192), of the "purity and simplicity" of design of "aboriginal art" (1:108), he regularly finds himself full of "surprise" upon encountering something "graceful and pretty" (1:240), given the mass of objects that now appear to be otherwise. The volumes of travels to Yucatan increasingly use the terms "rude" and "magnificent" (the latter is an Orientalism for Stephens and is connected to a "barbaric" world) to describe what he finds in the region: "Of the rest there is nothing which stands out . . . and the whole, loaded as it is with ornament, conveys the idea of vastness and magnificence rather than that of taste and refinement" (*Yucatan* 1:183). At the ruins of Kabah, relatively late in Stephens's travels, the transformation of his vision of the ruins is clear:

> The cornice running over the doorways, tried by the severest rules of art recognised among us, would embellish the architecture of any known era, and, amid a mass of barbarism, of rude and uncouth conceptions, it stands as an offering by American builders worthy of the acceptance of a polished people. (1:237)

Overwhelmingly, the ruins are judged "barbaric" in design, dotted by isolated instances of "polish."

The interpretation of the lives of the builders proceeds apace. At Copan, for example, at the beginning of his archaeological work, he imagines various "highly civilized" sculptures as "deities" or as "the portrait of some king, chieftain, or sage," and he determines that the scenes presented in bas-relief are evidence that "the people were not warlike, but peaceable, and easily subdued" (*Central America* 1:136, 1:142). The builders' world, in sum, was wonderful, perhaps idyllic: arts were prized, not warfare. The builders valued spiritual contemplation and sagacity, not force.

As Stephens's text shifts ground, however, with respect to the builders' relationship to present-day Indians, so do his metaphoric resources. For example, the most often repeated association made in Stephens's volumes concerns the ruins' resemblance to Egyptian structures, sculptures, writings, and other motifs. Such an association recurs continuously in the first volume and occasionally in the second of *Central America* but only once in the first volume of *Yucatan*, and by the end of that volume Stephens is denying any possible "family" connection between Egyptian pyramid builders and their Central American counterparts: he claims "the utter impossibility of ascribing these ruins to Egyptian builders," either through theory of "common origin" or "international communication" (*Yucatan* 1:165, 1:277).

"Egypt," which is a trope that can function in any number of ways in the nineteenth-century anthropological imaginary,[12] is here deployed not as an early point in an evolutionary scheme of nations and cultures but as an independent, highly developed civilization from "extreme antiquity." Egyptians were a people of "skill, industry, and wealth," and Stephens concludes that neither they nor their descendants nor the people who learned from them could have constructed structures "so rude" as those found in Central America (*Yucatan* 1:165). The Central American builders are *like* Egyptians so long as Stephens's original theory of their non-Indianness is intact, but they are increasingly and then absolutely *unlike* them once their Indianness is posited.

As "Egypt" fades into the analogical background, other interpretive possibilities emerge, including what one might broadly identify as a more "primitive" thesis. Within this network of associations is a growing presumption in Stephens's text that the ruin builders' culture was religiously centered, that it was a world dominated by temples, public rituals, "vestal virgins," "sacred fires," and non-Christian fetishization of spurious gods. Every building seems to Stephens the scene of "grand religious ceremonies." There is no place in Stephens's account for a polis, the law, education, entertainment, or anything else, for that matter (*Yucatan* 1:150).

This judgment is bolstered by Stephens's "outside" reading: The more Stephens assumes the ruins to be the product of relatively recent Indians — that is, the more the work of a clearly "barbaric," colored people — the more Stephens relies upon the writings and the very vocabulary of Spanish conquistadors, friars, and historians (Antonio de Herrera and Bernal Díaz are prominent examples in the text), who reported that at least some of the ruins were inhabited in the fifteenth and early sixteenth centuries (see, for example, *Central America* 2:443–52). In *Incidents of Travel in Central America* Stephens warns his readers (and himself) about being transported by "the romantic and seemingly half-fabulous accounts of the chroniclers of the conquest" (2:302). But by the time he writes *Incidents of Travel in Yucatan,* Stephens is citing long sections from these same Spanish colonial records, either approvingly or without comment, in order to manifest an accurate picture of the ruins. The superbly artistic sculptures and reliefs of deities and sages are now "serpents" or "idols," signs of a "pagan" and "superstitious" people (see, for example, *Yucatan* 2:8, 2:207, 2:257). Stephens's own vocabulary is, finally, inflected in this direction; for example, he notes a pedestal at Chichen, "upon which probably once stood an idol" (*Yucatan* 2:200).

Most dramatically of all, in the *Yucatan* volumes Stephens becomes more interested in evidence that the ruins were used to conduct human sacrifices, reversing his earlier description of the builders as nonviolent. He cites a long passage from "the padre Cogolludo, the historian," which describes in gory detail how "the High Priest with wonderful dexterity ripped up the Breast [of the person to be sacrificed], tore out the Heart, reeking, with his Hands, and showed it to the Sun, offering him the Heart and Steam that came from it." Stephens comments:

> In all the long catalogue of superstitious rites that darkens the page of man's history, I cannot imagine a picture more horribly exciting than that of the Indian priest, with his white dress and long hair clotted with gore, performing his murderous sacrifices at this lofty height, in full view of the people throughout the whole extent of the city. (*Yucatan* 1:193)

It took Stephens approximately 1,100 pages of descriptions of ruins to reach this point, to "prove" the "horribly exciting" character of the builders, and this is the nadir of ruin interpretation in terms of its immediate, practical xenophobic implications. Present-day Central American Indians are a vanquished, colonized people, but rightly so: "It seemed a righteous award that the bloody altar was hurled down [by Spaniards], and the race of its ministers destroyed" (*Central America* 2:185).

Finally, in terms of Stephens's shifts in association, one might term *Central America* and *Yucatan* the "volcano" and "cave" books, respectively, in terms of their interest in topographic features — the climbing books versus the penetrating books. The volumes documenting the first expedition regularly note the region's many near-active volcanoes. Not only does this serve, quite obviously, as a metaphor for the region's ongoing civil war, but it also is a natural analogue for the builders' greatness and the sublimity of their works. Volcanoes equal pyramids. Big things happen here and have happened here before. Stephens takes joy in rising to the heights of seething activity and breathes in the energy of the region. The second expedition's volumes, on the other hand, place tremendous focus on the Yucatan's caverns and underground passageways. Stephens is looking for evidence of feats of engineering — massive, complex cisterns — or for richly appointed tombs and intact skeletons. Mostly Stephens is disappointed. He finds nothing much but some holes in the ground, and even the man-made ones do not thrill. Builders equal cave men.

But, finally, does it matter which way Stephens decides the matter, which version of his grid of intelligibility he chooses, this or that? Either way, there is a prize to be had — a discovery, a history, a confirmed knowledge. Either way, the game is rigged so that nineteenth-century hierarchies of distinction are preserved: white/colored, savage/civilized, and the like. Either way, those whom Stephens meets and identifies as Amerindians are written out of a narrative of American accomplishments. Either way, archaeology is constituted. One must look elsewhere in Stephens, and then in Norman, for a wholly other strategy that might undermine or subvert this double edge, this decision without consequence.

LAUGHING PHILOSOPHERS

In the opening of the first volume of *Travels in Yucatan* Stephens twice foregrounds the technology of vision, as he and Catherwood play at alternative careers as photographers and eye surgeons in the Mexican city of Merida. The descriptions of both of these experiences act in the text as metaphors for the difficulty of right seeing in general.

On their second trip to the region the two men bring a daguerreotype camera with them and enter the potentially lucrative trade of "ladies' ... portrait takers" (*Yucatan* 1:54). Producing an image of a "beautiful little head" proves as complex as representing Palenque; the two men must devote constant attention to the apparatus:

> Next it was necessary to get the young lady into focus —
> that is, to get her into the box, which, in short, means, to get
> a reflection of her face on the glass in the camera obscura at
> that one particular point of view which presented it better
> than any other. (*Yucatan* 1:55–56)

As at Palenque, Stephens does not question the "faithfully reflected" final result. "Point of view," in short, seems to pose no problem for the scientific
artist attempting to produce the "better" or best representation possible. But
the mere fact that Stephens must dwell on the procedure — the need to "get
her into the box" — is some indication that the problem of presentation is never
far from Stephens's mind. And later Stephens and Catherwood give up the
practice because during a particularly strenuous session of family portraiture,
"the stubborn instrument seemed bent upon confounding us":

> Suffice it to say that we tried plate after plate, sitting after sit-
> ting, varying light, time, and other points of the process; but
> it was all in vain. (*Yucatan* 1:57)

The problem of Copan has returned with a vengeance, albeit in a slightly different register because the photographic subjects are a different "species" of
ruin. The inhabitants of the country now present the problem of unrepresentabil-
ity due to light and angle as the issue shifts from the "what" of the buildings
to the "who" of bodies.

The two immediately thereafter become apprentice eye surgeons under the
supervision of their friend, Dr. Cabot. Stephens says that "there is no immediate connexion between taking Daguerreotype portraits and the practice of
surgery, but circumstances bring close together things entirely dissimilar in
themselves, and we went from one to the other" (1:58). The "connexion," however, is obvious: the problem of the production of right vision. Stephens notes
that Merida's citizens seem to suffer inordinately from "squinting eyes, or
biscos" (they are, from Stephens's perspective, cross-eyed), and Cabot is the
first doctor in the region to offer a "cure," which involves cutting through one
of the eye muscles. The first performances of the procedure go well enough
and seem to be successful. But Stephens's final case involves a "young lady,"
and the trauma of watching her undergo the procedure makes Stephens "worn

out" with "visions of bleeding and mutilated eyes," to the point where "I almost felt doubtful about my own" (1:64). Again, the production of right seeing is undercut by recognition of the technic needed to produce it. At the end of his time as a surgeon, Stephens no longer knows what constitutes proper vision. It may be, finally, that it is Stephens's *own* vision that is faulty and that his procedures produce nothing but "bleeding and mutilated" casualties. Both "incidents" — the stories concerning portrait photography and surgery — are cautionary tales concerning the presumption of unmediated presentation/representation.

Stephens's caution at times threatens to overwhelm his project, turning him into what Benjamin Moore Norman refers to as just one of a "formidable array of eminent names in the list of [archaeological and philosophical] doubters" — and "timid," "universal doubters" at that (*Land and Water* 202). In an extraordinary scene from *Incidents of Travel in Central America*, Stephens and Catherwood encounter the curate of Santa Cruz del Quiché, or as they finally refer to him, the "laughing philosopher" (*Central America* 2:182). This "cura" is both an antiquarian and a historian; of all the men they meet in their travels together, the "cura," or padre, is the most knowledgeable concerning the ruins. And yet, at the same time, all of the cura's disquisitions on the ruins are laced with reflexive laughter about his acquired knowledge. Each conversation among these three men is described as an "unbroken stream of knowledge, research, sagacity, and satire" (2:189): "He laughed at our coming to see the ruins, and said that he laughed prodigiously himself when he first saw them" (2:181).

In part, his laughter seems to be a reversal of Volneyesque brooding: the ruins are funny precisely because they are of a piece with history's endless round of conquest, revolution, and destruction (of which the curate claims to have seen more than his share). But the laughter also includes matters archaeological and historical — that is, scientific investigation into this black comedy of political history: "His own laugh was so rich and expressive that it was perfectly irresistible. . . . The world was our butt, and we laughed at it outrageously. Except the Church, there were few things which the cura did not laugh at." (2:181).

In general, "the more serious the subject, the louder was our cachinnation. And all the time the padre made continual reference to books and manuscripts, showing antiquarian studies and profound knowledge" (2:187). This master of scholarship about the ruins cannot help but inflect his readings in such a way that scholarly judgments themselves become subject to radical doubt. "A laugh was the comment upon everything, and in the evening we were deep in the mysteries of Indian history" (2:190). During their days and nights as the curate's guest, Stephens and Catherwood lose their sense that there is a Mayan "mystery" needing solution. The "who" question implodes upon itself, and the real mystery may now involve explaining the desire to produce solutions to the "who" question under the guise of scientific archaeology and ethnography. Until they move on in their travels, Stephens and Catherwood cannot examine ruins without hearing the cura, standing behind them, "laughing all the time" (2:182).

Perhaps only such a radically skeptical pause or caesura in Stephens's text can explain the ending to the first pair of volumes, *Incidents of Travel in Central America*. As Stephens and Catherwood prepare to return to the United States, the text slowly slips into the mode of the fantastic. Stephens's last thought on the "who" question foreshadows Haggard and involves imagining the existence of an unscathed and flourishing "lost city" of ruin builders, hidden deep in the jungle:

> And if, in consideration that I have not often indulged in speculative conjecture, the reader will allow one flight, I turn to that vast and unknown region, untraversed by a single road, wherein fancy pictures that mysterious city seen from the topmost range of the Cordilleras, of unconquered, unvisited, and unsought aboriginal inhabitants. (*Central America* 2:457)

"In conclusion," Stephens suggests that it may be more productive to search for such a city than to perform painstaking historical-archaeological research, which involves "wad[ing] through the accumulated manuscripts of three centuries in the libraries of the convents" (2:457).[13]

With this thought Stephens boards ship for Havana, and the final chapter of the book reads like a Coleridgean nightmare. The sea turns absolutely still 150 miles from Yucatan, "dead calm," and "the captain said we were incantado or enchanted"—a point that the text reiterates every page or so (2:461). The sun is burning hot, and the drinking water runs out. Several pages at the end of

Stephens's narrative read as delirious hallucination: giant sharks surround the boat and "everything that fell overboard was immediately snapped up" (2:462). Both the passengers and the captain imagine, for a time, that "enormous monsters" are moving toward them (2:464). Strangest of all, a magical whale is captured by the crew:

> [They] tore out his heart and entrails. They then chopped off about a foot of his tail and threw him overboard; what he did I will not mention, lest it should bring discredit upon other parts of these pages which the reader is disposed to think may be true; but the last we saw of him he seemed to be feeling for his tail. (2:463)

This Melvillean whale, which cannot be killed and which behaves, with its heart removed, in an unnameable, Lovecraftian manner that jeopardizes the truth claims of the preceding 900 pages, is the great beast upon which Stephens's book threatens to smash itself to pieces.

Stephens's ending of his account of his travels on this magical note is a moment of curious reflexivity for the newly professionalizing social scientific discourses. His "enchanted" discourse may reveal more about the status of the social sciences — about the proximity, finally, of the fantastic and the scientific — than about ancient civilizations. And other, related texts of the era necessarily foreground a similar problem. Prescott, for example, ends his *Conquest of Mexico:* "When the Europeans first touched the shores of America, it was as if they had alighted on another planet" (689). Travel literature always risks a close encounter with fantasy literature, and science with science fiction.

Benjamin Moore Norman's second account of his travels in Stephens's wake, *Rambles by Land and Water* (1845), is even more remarkable in this regard. Norman — a second-generation bookseller, publisher, printer, and binder from Hudson, New York — is truly the lost man among those who broached the "who" question in the 1840s. In the 1880s Lewis Henry Morgan treated Norman and Stephens as equally interesting (and problematic) explorers of the Mayan ruins, but few since that time have bothered to read all the way through Norman's two books, which admittedly seem to be quick-and-dirty knockoffs of Stephens's best-sellers.[14]

Particularly in his first volume, entitled *Rambles in Yucatan* (1842–43), Norman's work seems to be merely a self-conscious digest of Stephens. Stephens had been a conspicuous and prominent traveler; so much so that Norman is mistaken for Stephens at one point in Norman's wanderings (Norman, *Yucatan* 89). And Stephens's book, already published by the time Norman wrote his, looms so large in Norman's mind that he continually refers to it, sometimes simply by trying to imitate Stephens's strategies for managing relations with Amerindians (wearing a formal coat to dazzle them, producing an American half-dollar as a sign of power and influence, and so on). Norman imagines the people who built the ruins as having been both highly civilized and tyrannical in matters of government, just as Stephens does. Again, like Stephens, he resorts to comparisons to medieval and Egyptian life worlds and works. And his eventual conclusion is straight from Stephens: The builders were the ancestors of present-day Indians, and he bases this conclusion upon skull analyses by Morton.

The second volume, however, may be the single most peculiar archaeological text of the period, especially given Norman's rising importance in and contribution to archaeological studies.[15] *Rambles by Land and Water* satirizes both travel literature and archaeological investigation, and it is difficult to determine what truth claims, if any, Norman is making. The centerpiece of the book is the tenth chapter, which Norman describes as "treating banteringly" the problem of artifact interpretation, particularly ethnological comparison on the basis of "ten words in a thousand of a language" or "some slight analogies" in ceremonial practice (*Land and Water* 215, 155). In this chapter Norman uses "two very singular and grotesque looking [talismanic] images" to prove, in a single page of analysis, that ancient American men were Chinese and their wives were Japanese. Such is his version of a "triumphal philosophical disquisition": "I trust no one will presume to dispute it, after the pains I have taken, and the learning and research I have displayed in proving it" (160, 158).

The satire is clear, but its limit is not. Norman's obvious target is Stephens, but can one imagine a legitimate archaeology? Is archaeology nothing but a philosophy premised on nothing, or on small, incoherent fragments? Or does archaeology go wrong only when it begins the work of ethnology, of comparison? Norman saves direct critique for his final chapter, when he writes,

There are two errors, lying at the two extremes of the broad area of philosophical inquiry, into which men are liable to fall, in undertaking the discussion of questions of this nature. The one leads to hasty conclusions upon imperfect, ill-digested premises; the other shrinks from all conclusions, however well supported, and labors only to deepen the shadows of mystery which hang about its subject. (*Land and Water* 201)

The first error is the one satirized in Norman's tenth chapter. This occurs when "one forms a shallow theory of his own, suggested by the first object he meets with on entering the field" or when one enters the field already certain about the truth of some theory or other (201). Parts of Stephens's text—his strong and long-enduring presuppositions regarding the "who" question—are subject to this critique.

The second error is that of the laughing philosopher, the universal doubter, the skeptic. And yet Norman's text might lead one to just such skepticism because it suggests that the writing of archaeological history demands more than the field can possibly provide:

This chain is probably complete in its parts, though the links are separated, and cannot be brought together again. They are all there, but so scattered and confounded together, that he who attempts to assign them a place and date, or to build a theory upon their apparent relations to each other, will probably soon find himself "in wandering mazes lost," and rather amuse, than convince or instruct his readers. (*Land and Water* 184)[16]

The archaeologist's "facts" are few in number, then, and indeterminately disconnected from one another. The problem may be a geographically limited one, however, true only of archaeology in the Americas. Norman writes that the ruins and antiquities of Europe have been explained and their uncertainties resolved because they were "embalmed by a magical spiritual photography"; a light—albeit "the dim, uncertain twilight" of the present—still shines upon the past and records its people and monuments whole and intact (*Land and Water* 200). Is the corresponding American archaeological record too fragmented for such resolution? Or, for Norman, are the "Americans" too alterior for Europeans to grasp the picture? In that reading, Norman would be satirizing the way Stephens and Catherwood negotiate and thereby reduce and obliterate radical difference through the work of the Western "lens."

Such appears to be the case, given Norman's recurrent emphasis on the problem of the work of comparison. The "who" question as it pertains to the ruins of Europe is, finally, not a "who" question; the people who produced such ruins are continuous, in Norman's view, with those of modern Europe. The archaeologist abroad, however, is on different ground, on the ground of a different "who." The precontact American ruins, whatever "chain" of linkages they may share with Europe, are beyond intellectual reconstruction. The facts or the terrain of the case preclude the "who" question, and given such circumstances, given the perhaps maximum alterity of the Mayan ruins, Norman suggests that the American archaeologist's answer to the "who" question can be little else than the product of the social scientist's xenophobia. The traveling anthropologist takes as "a foregone conclusion, that every nation except their own is peopled with Ishmaelites, whose hands are ever raised against the rest of mankind" (*Yucatan* 14). Norman's lesson is that the comparatism that lies at the heart of the "who" question is only ever answered in an ethnochauvinist manner and is only ever founded as a kind of nonscience, or nonsense.

Apparently this is so because of what today would be called "hybridity," but this is not the sort of hybridization I explored in the prolegomenon — the sort historicized and forecast by critical multiculturalism. It is, instead, a vision of hybridity all the way down, the results of which disturb any possibility of categorization. Norman writes,

> In the early ages of the world's history, the families of men were far more unsettled, and migratory in their habits, than they are now. It was not an uncommon thing for whole nations to change their abode at once. (Norman, *Land and Water* 215)

Norman's answer to the "who" question, then, is an extreme re-elaboration and generalization of diasporic twelfth-tribe theories circulating in the nineteenth century. In the time of Moses, according to Norman,

there was an extensive interchange, and blending of nations
and races. Each melted into each, like the glacier of the mountain, and the lakes of the valley, blended and lost in the stream
that bears them both to the ocean. The same irruptions, the
same amalgamations of conquerors with conquered, took
place in earlier ages, in the far east. And there is no violent
improbability in supposing, that the overcharged fountain of
humanity, in the central regions, sometimes overleaped its
eastern boundaries, as well as its western, and, meeting with
no resistance, as in the south, spread itself quite to the shores
of the Pacific, and thence into the neighboring continent of
America. This may have been done at many different and
distant periods, even back to the dispersion of Babel. And
who shall say it was not so?... But we do know that it *might*
have furnished all the races that are known, or supposed, to
have existed there. (215)

Human history, then, was inaugurated by overflowing borders, powered with
all of the force and fecundity of an "overcharged fountain." Whatever differences constituted separations between human groups before, say, Babel were
swept away in the flood tide of intermingling. The builders of the American
ruins were always already a mixed race, "melted" and "blended" in the manner of nature, in the manner of waters. The present-day races of Mexico (and
Norman distinguishes at least eight [*Land and Water* 184–85]) are a product
of gradual historical separation, and the seeming clarity of the nineteenth century's race and blood and culture borders is of recent vintage, man-made and
fashioned from unbridled nature. *Distinction,* one might extrapolate, is a coun-
tercategory to nature: modern and political through and through, and potentially degrading and even deevolutionary (ruins of original magnificence, and
present-day wrecked races on separate shores). Distinction is detached from
original "irruptions"— the pre-amalgamated stream of memory and history.

"Whose" ruins? Everyone's and no one's. Norman's representational strategy is an act of possession followed by radical dispossession. A joke perhaps,
given his penchant for such. But "who" shall say?

INTRODUCTION

1. Hinsley provides the best single-volume account of the era.

2. These writers are the province of "Indian" specialists in the field of historical-biographical study, who tend either to characterize texts without the tools of close reading or not to characterize them at all and to focus, primarily, on life stories. I choose not to pursue such a course in this book for several reasons, and where appropriate, I refer to the strong biographical literature on Copway, Ridge, Parker, and Apess (far less work has been done on Jones, perhaps because he spent his entire life in Canada, and Cusick, about whom little has turned up to date).

3. The major exception to this characterization is American literature scholar Barry O'Connell, whose biographical and textual work on and edition of William Apess's texts, *On Our Own Ground* (1992), is a model for scholarly work in this area, including my own. As a further note, Apess's writings, perhaps because of O'Connell's book, and Ridge's novel *Joaquín Murieta* are the only Amerindian texts taken up in *The Limits of Multiculturalism* that have generated anything like an ongoing literary critical conversation.

4. I adopt the language of the "plural" here with some reservations. I want to imply that certain sensibilities and concepts within the Amerindian auto-anthropology of the nineteenth century would necessarily be excluded from any known formulation of multiculturalism, and I am here thinking, for example, of the manner in which Cusick positions his text *against* the idea of self-sufficient culture (see chapter 1).

5. Here, too quickly, one should refer to such things as Jean-François Lyotard's many commentaries on the sublime in Kant; to Rodolphe Gasché's forthcoming volume on Kant's aesthetics, which treats the problem of the beautiful in terms of singularity; and to the writings on community by Jean-Luc Nancy and Giorgio Agamben.

6. Though the details cannot be worked out here, one must insist that anthropology, through its network of presuppositions about identity, cannot take account of the

singular and that the possibility of "freeing" the alterity of singularity depends upon the removal of the covering debris of anthropology. The singular, to follow Nancy's texts on community, would not appear so much as *compear.*

7. See chapter 4.

8. Lott can demonstrate that African American intellectuals, such as Frederick Douglass and Martin R. Delany, reflected upon and even reimagined through satire the work of minstrelsy, and he can show that African American singing troupes performed music much related to the music of blackface minstrelsy.

9. These languages come from the examples that Kroeber and Kluckhohn assembled (Kroeber and Kluckhohn 81–83) and are drawn from, in order, M. C. Burkitt, R. B. Dixon, R. Benedict, and C. J. Kluckhohn and W. H. Kelly. Definitions in these same pages supplied by Boas, Malinowski, Lowie, and the like are very nearly the same.

10. Furthermore, it makes no difference what *modality* of cultural analysis is utilized, and here one might think of systemic or agential accounts, controlling or liberating ones, holistic or fragmentary approaches, structuralist, functionalist, structural-functionalist, and so on.

11. At times Lott calls similar arguments "bizarre" or at least "provisional," given the "confusing history of cultural intermixing," but he makes them nonetheless (94).

12. And there may be good reason to doubt some of these simple "facts" of appropriation. Dale Cockrell, for example, believes that the banjo of the 1820s "was a handmade, preindustrial instrument" that made "noise" rather than music and that minstrelsy invented an entirely different, commercial banjo, fit for respectable music, "with none of its original potential for noisemaking" (Cockrell 147–48).

13. William Apess's *A Son of the Forest* (1829) is judged to be Native American, whereas N. Scott Momaday's autobiographical texts are said to be fundamentally Western (see Krupat 201–31).

14. See chapter 3 for a full reading of Parker's rhetoric.

15. As one prominent example of this tendency, see Rosaldo, *Culture and Truth,* especially 204–7.

16. Which is not to say that Morton, Stephens, and others are not equally preoccupied in their anthropology with the dead, with deadening the Indian. There is every reason to believe that anthropology functions analogously to Michel de Certeau's definition of history, because, as Johannes Fabian writes in *Time and the Other,* anthropology is fundamentally a discourse about time and one's relationship to the past (1–35). De Certeau, in turn, suggests that the minimal condition of history — to make the dead speak — is that there must be a death (46).

17. Appiah's *In My Father's House,* for example, argues for an end to the use of the "race" concept, to be replaced by the more enlightened science of the "gene."

18. See Marcus and Fischer 95–108 for an elaboration of this trend.

19. See the related argument made in Johnson and Michaelsen 3ff.

20. Toni Morrison has written about this problem in the following way: "A writer's response to American Africanism often provides a subtext that either sabotages the surface text's expressed intentions or escapes them through a language that mystifies what it cannot bring itself to articulate but still attempts to register.... [Such responses] provide paradox, ambiguity; they strategize omissions, repetitions, disruptions, polarities, reifications, violence" (66).

PROLEGOMENON

1. See, as prominent examples, Johannes Fabian's *Time and the Other* (1983); Stephen A. Tyler's "Post-Modern Ethnography" (1986) and *The Unspeakable* (1987); Lila Abu-Lughod's "Writing against Culture" (1991).

2. As a first example: Deloria's early work has profoundly influenced well-known anthropologist Thomas Biolsi, who ends a recent article, "The Anthropological Construction of 'Indians,'" by focusing on anthropology's determining power rather than its analytic truth: "It remains an open question as to whether or not we and the Lakotas have *humanly* survived the consequences of the anthropological division of Indians and whites into 'clearly different cultures, histories, traditions, societies, even races.' Whatever the consequences, anthropological cultural relativism and its intellectual construction of the primitive and of authentic and inauthentic Indians had a great deal to do with that division. Anthropology needs to come to terms with the consequences" (Biolsi and Zimmerman 150). One notes in these lines, in Biolsi's use of "open question" and "whatever," a certain equivocation. Such equivocation is foreign to Deloria's *Custer* but not to his later texts, including texts written in the immediate aftermath of *Custer*'s reception.

3. Yet Deloria does name something, "tribalism," which he says "is one single cause which has importance today for Indian people" (*Custer* 88). He sees it as potentially analogous to "black power" and he is careful to distinguish it from nostalgia for precontact identity formations.

4. The shift, in fact, is immediately apparent. In the wake of *Custer*'s publication, when Deloria was invited to participate in the American Anthropological Association (AAA) symposium in November 1970—where he spoke alongside Margaret Mead, Bea Medicine, and Alfonso Ortiz, among others—he altered considerably the substance of his critique. During his talk, he noted that he only wanted to "half-way" make the arguments that had been read into "Anthropologists and Other Friends": "If I were really mad at you [anthropologists] I would *not* have done it in a satirical way or put a chapter on humor into what others think is an Indian manifesto" ("Criticisms" 88). Deloria, at the AAA, rehabilitates precisely those cornerstones of anthropological method that he had evacuated in *Custer,* particularly experience and friendship ("Criticisms" 97, 95). Indians and anthropologists, jointly, through time and ties, can produce infor-

mation whose use value, and perhaps truth value, can be acknowledged and affirmed. Some such work already exists "unpublished," is currently being done, and can in the future be extended (95–96). "And this is what I would say: that it is time for Indian organizations and the American Anthropological Association to sit down and discuss what issues are relevant to the Indian community; what studies you have that are relevant to the things we are doing; what needs we have that would be relevant to future research that you might want to undertake on a professional basis" (97–98). This is a newly "liberal" Deloria, with faith restored in the positivist science of man.

5. And again: "Information is lacking because our scholars and scientists are wedded to an outmoded framework of interpretation and spend their time arranging facts and evidence to fit these old ideas" (Deloria, *Red Earth* 251).

6. Deloria further argues: "I have a rule when quoting elders and traditional leaders in a book. Basically the stories belong to them and so I do not want to be the first person to put a story in print. I therefore try to find a published account that confirms what an elder has told me and use that version instead of the tradition as related to me by the elder" (Deloria, *Red Earth* 11).

7. Churchill has issued two recent collections of cultural essays, *Fantasies of the Master Race* (1992) and *Indians Are Us?* (1994), which are entirely concerned with patrolling the same white/red border, unmasking the naivetés and racisms of white scholars, novelists, and filmmakers who attempt to incorporate an Indian voice into their work, and vigorously critiquing the work of cultural-structuralist scholars interested in problematizing perseverance narratives of Indian culture. The implications of Churchill's work are spelled out by Annette Jaimes Guerrero, his sometime editor and colleague at the Center for Studies of Ethnicity and Race in America at the University of Colorado–Boulder. She joins her argument with his in describing the difference between Indian and white knowledges: "Within Churchill's schema, the 'linear conceptual model' marking European culture dominates modern U.S. academic life, extracting conformity to its structures and conclusions as the price of intellectual legitimacy. American Indian intellectualism, which he defines as being structured in a 'circulinear' fashion and belonging to the tradition of 'the relational indigenous worldview,' is thus excluded by institutional mandate.... Nowhere is this more evident than in the epistemologies of Western philosophy that permeate most academic disciplines and define our conventional notions of truth. Significant in this regard are the time/space/place constructions as human-derived. By contrast, indigenous knowledge and traditional practice emphasize natural and seasonal rhythms" (Jaimes Guerrero 57). As in the cases of Deloria's *Red Earth* and Sioui's *For an Amerindian Autohistory,* the argument is multicultural-epistemological: "Not all people 'know' the same way," and Western reasoning has become a form of neocolonialism (Guerrero 58). The West has a great deal to learn from Amerindian "holistic totalism."

8. Kroeber and Kluckhohn remind one that Boas himself did not attempt a definition of the word "culture" until 1930, although Clark Wissler, one of his students, de-

fined it along Tylor's lines as early as 1916. There are, curiously, no strictly anthropological definitions of culture between that of Tylor in 1871 and Wissler's, although a handful of sociologists and chemists began to use "culture" as a term of art in the intervening years. The modern "culture" concept, therefore, is primarily a product of the 1920s and beyond (Kroeber and Kluckhohn 291–97).

9. It is not clear from the text whether Gunew finally approves of this formulation. And perhaps it is worth noting that Gunew is misreading Jean Baudrillard in this passage.

10. Another interesting piece for purposes of distinguishing multiculturalisms is McLaren.

11. Sioui writes: "AmerIndians always say that to attain reason, one must first treat the emotions with honour and respect. To gain someone's trust or cooperation, or to comfort others so as to have them participate in a shared objective, 'it is necessary to deal in the first place with the emotions (of people), to lift up the spirits so as to sit down (together) and think clearly.' . . . For five centuries, Amerindians and Whites have dealt with their emotions only very sporadically and superficially. . . . Division was the rule, so that it was essential to produce and maintain emotional confusion by instilling feelings of guilt or superiority, prophesying, and so forth" (5).

12. Phrase citations from Golderg, "Introduction" 7, 10.

13. Dennis Tedlock's and Barbara Tedlock's anthology *Teachings from the American Earth* (1975) stakes out a position entirely consonant with Deloria's later thought: that white thinking is object- rather than subject-oriented, that "the possibility of learning directly from the Indian" is of utmost importance for our cultural moment (xiii). Here, a certain cultural relativism is already implicitly and necessarily linked to the kinds of universal judgments advocated by Tzvetan Todorov's "well-tempered humanism," described later in the text.

14. This point is made, among other places, in Newfield and Gordon 108–9 and Nelson 55.

15. Ernesto Laclau agrees that all multicultural negotiations involve original exclusions: "As the demands of various groups will necessarily clash with one another, we have to appeal to some more general principles — if not some kind of preestablished harmony — in order to regulate such clashes. In actual fact, there is no particularism that does not appeal to such principles in the construction of its own identity" (87).

16. See, for example, Scheper-Hughes, which argues for the political importance of acknowledging emotional difference, in the study of world cultures. See, also, two collections — edited, respectively, by Lutz and Abu-Lughod and by Samuels — whose contributors often address the neocolonial, exclusionary consequences of foreclosing difference at the level of affect.

17. See Dunn for a similar argument with respect to the multicultural theorist Charles Taylor.

18. Churchill is a thornier matter: it is not clear that he has ever found a white scholar who could speak Indian truth.

19. Todorov, *Diversity* 390, 399, 391, 361. In general, see Todorov, *Diversity* 353–99.

20. See also Appadurai 297, where much the same argument is made.

21. Sometimes versions of these critiques are referred to as "critical multicultural-ism," which I will not do here in order to avoid confusion. It is, however, important to note that "critical multiculturalism" is a term used to describe very different forms of multicultural argument.

22. See also Davis, "Gender" 45. Davis is interested primarily in the gender aspect of this problem.

23. See Hall 16 on hegemony as consent rather than coercion.

24. See also Poster 572, which presents Lyotard's related critique of Habermas.

25. This logic is repeated in any number of texts emphasizing relational identity. A similar, final affirmation of hybridity in the name of human essence and human poten-tial is found in Turner 423.

26. See also Gordon and Newfield, "Introduction" 5. Gordon and Newfield argue that concepts of "borderlands, biraciality, and intersectionality" are "boundary-shatter-ing." See the introduction to Michaelsen and Johnson's *Border Theory* for a recent reading of problems in Anzaldúa and Hicks.

27. This may be the more common stereotype of Marxism in general, and one might look at the brief text by Eric Hobsbawm listed in the works cited for an exam-ple. It may, however, be more common for left scholars, at least since Antonio Gram-sci, to take cultural politics very seriously. Roseberry, in fact, is an example of this, as are Mouffe and Hall. Mouffe writes, "We must move beyond the sterile dichotomy op-posing the working class to the social movements" (98). And Hall writes that Marxist ambitions can only be reached indirectly—that is, through struggle at the level of the political and cultural (19). Often, it should be said, such Marxist accounts of cultural power and value are quite similar to Goldberg's critical multiculturalist formulations.

28. Here one might want to review Marx's *Ethnological Notebooks,* an enormous body of notes that he made late in life on anthropologists such as Lewis Henry Mor-gan, as well as Engels's book on the family, which picks up these threads and thema-tizes them.

29. See Goldberg's *Racist Culture* for an example of the argument that seeks to read the premodern world as fundamentally less difference-bound and "racist."

30. More specifically, as to the value of multiculturalism for purposes of progres-sive politics: both Wallerstein and Jameson refer in their texts briefly and negatively to multiculturalism's value. Jameson suggests that the recovery/discovery and "affirma-tion of such nonhegemonic cultural voices remains ineffective if it is limited to the merely 'sociological' perspective of the pluralistic rediscovery of other isolated social groups" (*Unconscious* 86). More dramatically, multiculturalism is "disintegrating into

the more obscene consumerist pluralisms of late capitalism" (*Postmodernism* 323). And Wallerstein finds literary multiculturalism oddly complicit with defenders of the canon of great works in that "one arrives, it seems to be argued by both sides, at the universal via the particular (though they differ as to which particular)" (197).

31. See Wallerstein 198, for example, and 230, where he writes that an acknowledgment of "multiple civilizations" may lead to a recognition of alternative "wisdom" or important "experiential variation" as well as variable "interests"—all of which will "increase...the likelihood of discovering correct paths" toward a more equalitarian society (230). This paradoxical gesture—critiquing multiculturalism to its political-economic foundations and then reiterating its logic—is repeated in other Marxist critiques of multiculturalism. For example, John Cruz's work argues that multiculturalism is "*symptomatic*" of and very useful to late capitalism, and yet he affirms multiculturalism, in part because "it is the height of arrogance to dismiss [cultural identities] as socially constructed moral fictions" (19, 34).

32. Jameson elsewhere (and later) identifies this as modernist differentiation—the expression of a break between "the West and the rest, between the modern and the traditional" (*Postmodernism* 344).

33. Some Marxist interpretations of culture cohere around this argument. Richard Applebaum argues that we are witnessing the "ethnicization of capitalism" and that the production of ethnic identities is useful for creating class along lines of culture (309, 312–13). Paul Smith makes a similar point ("Capital" 347, 360). Also see Appadurai, which describes in more detail the manner in which ethnicity is marketed in late capitalism (302).

34. Jameson's comments on feminism in *The Political Unconscious* may be useful for partially situating his folk thoughts. The battle against "sexism and the patriarchal" is contextualized as taking place in relation to "the sedimentation and the virulent survival of forms of alienation specific to the oldest mode of production of human history" (99–100). Thus, feminism is legitimized in Jameson only because of the "survival" or imbrication of older modes of production: it is a project that does not relate to the essence of capitalism (capitalism could dispose of sexism and retain all of its power). Folkways, too, might be explained similarly, had Jameson devoted pages to the significance of their "subversive strategies."

35. See, for example, Jameson, "Progress."

36. And he has, for example, in *Postmodernism* 306.

37. See also Laclau 88.

38. As Rorty notes, "The implicit cultural essentialism of a good deal of celebratory multiculturalism disguises the powerful intracultural politics of determining the right of authoritative description" (156).

39. The very image on the jacket of *Red Earth* has a tale to tell in this regard. The title of the book is printed over a 1995 photograph taken by Lee Crum that invokes Ed-

ward Curtis–style, turn-of-the-century traditions in Indian portraiture: the gaze of the noble savage, the feathered headdress and fringed leather jacket, even the sepia tone of the print.

1. POSITIONS, EX-POSITIONS, DIS-POSITIONS

1. See, for example, Christopher Bracken, who tracks the colonial invention of the category of potlatch; and Vincent Pecora, who reads the entire trajectory of the "gift" as elite, trickle-down economics. Close reading of Mauss's work, *Essai sur le don* (1924, translated as *The Gift*), has also subjected the category of the "gift" to question — here, see Sahlins 149–83; and Gasché.

2. Such banal, "self"-motivated moralizing is at least part of the historical work of anthropology, as Marcus and Fischer argue (157–64). I would go further than Marcus and Fischer and suggest that it saturates the field.

3. The presumption of the "oral tradition" means that Amerindians informants' materials, from whatever period of anthropological research, need not be subjected to shockingly obvious questions: does the collected folklore reflect how Amerindians *want* to be remembered (that is, is it fantasy)? Does it reflect *present* consciousness rather than past (that is, is folklore in general always about the here and now)? Is the informant simply telling the folklorist what he or she wants to hear (that is, are they answers to "Tell me about your wonderful past")? Are various informants ideologically positioned *within* Amerindian thought (for example, male, or elite, or senior, or Indianist)? The presumption of the "oral tradition" understands "people" as mere recording mechanisms — without interests or contexts. It presumes, in short, culture as a prisonhouse of memory.

4. Some of this is quite explicit in Richter's text. "International relations," for example, are part of a "mundane" world, and of relatively little consequence for Iroquois identity (41).

5. See Lyons 32, 33, 34, 38, 39, 40.

6. On the connection between the bourgeoisie and health, see Foucault 122–27.

7. Here I would explicitly like to separate my argument from that in Mary Louise Pratt's otherwise interesting *Imperial Eyes: Travel Writing and Transculturation* (1992). In her introduction she talks usefully about "contact zones," that is, "social spaces where disparate cultures meet, clash, and grapple with each other, often in highly asymmetrical relations of domination and subordination" (4). For her, though the contact zone is a place where cultures meet and even mix, they are not fundamentally problematized. This makes her identity politics somewhat more conservatively essentialist than Richard White's. For example, Pratt argues that "transculturation" occurs in contact zones: "Subordinated or marginal groups select and invent from materials transmitted to them by a dominant or metropolitan culture" (6). Sometimes such transculturation takes the form of "autoethnography," in which colonized subjects act in "partial collab-

oration with and appropriation of the idioms of the conqueror" (7). All of her metaphors suggest that cultures can be crossed—that people can live biculturally—but that fundamental cultural positions remain unchanged. Her descriptions, then, of the "autoethnographies" of both Felipe Guaman Poma de Ayala and Garcilaso de la Vega is at some distance from the way I here contextualize David Cusick's *Sketches*.

8. It should be noted that although Schoolcraft grants that Indians have a "history" (a gesture that Eric R. Wolf found it necessary to repeat 140 years later), it is not one in which very much *happens*. Indian history in Schoolcraft's terms is perhaps best understood as a mostly static difference from everything European.

9. See White, *Metahistory*, and, more particularly, McGrane 93–100, which discusses historicism in relation to nineteenth-century anthropology.

10. Another remnant of Columbian discourse is Schoolcraft's figuring of Amerindians as Oriental (*Indian Legends* 22). Also, see Said for his famous reading of the politics of such "Orientalism"; this key topic within "postcolonial theory" has generated a massive secondary literature—too large to do more than acknowledge here.

11. See Schoolcraft, *Indian Legends* 10, for an example. McGrane understands the savage/civilized polarity as part of the heritage of the "Enlightenment" (ix). The classic study of the concepts savage/civilized in American writing is Pearce, whose discussion of Schoolcraft's work (120–28) locates it as "the culmination of a tradition, the culminating episode in the history of a mode of belief" (128).

12. See Jordan 240, n. 49, where he says that the first narratives to suggest that Amerindians constituted a separate race are dated 1775 and 1778. See, more recently, the essays collected by Henry Louis Gates Jr.

13. Bieder's chapter on Schoolcraft makes it clear that Henry Schoolcraft considered himself an opponent of "polygenism," or separate racial creations (Bieder 179–82). In *Notes on the Iroquois*, Schoolcraft succinctly declares that Indians "are a branch of the original Adamic stock" (58). And it is this belief, perhaps, that permits Schoolcraft to predict that Amerindians would reclaim their Christian heritage. But the term "branch" means that, somewhere in early biblical history, the Indians branched off and became a subspecies of "man" that calcified at a relatively low position on the scale of human development. "The early migrations must have been necessarily confined to portions of the old world peopled by the *red race*—by a race, not only of red skins, black hair and eyes, and high cheek bones, who would reproduce these fixed characteristics, *ad infinitum*, but whose whole mental as well as physiological developement assimilates it, as a distinct unity of species" (*Notes* 60). In a passage like this one, the difference between polygenism and monogenism is nearly meaningless, since Schoolcraft suggests that the inferiority of Amerindians is physiologically based.

14. Later a more pessimistic and monological Schoolcraft would argue that even the Iroquois were in the "absolute barbaric state" at the time of contact and that all Indians were in the "hunter state": "We are in want of all evidence to show that there ever was in America, a pastoral state" (*Notes* 11, 16).

15. "Evidence" of human evolution is also furnished by Schoolcraft's evolutionary model of language—from simple to complex words—which is explained in some detail on pages 18–21 of *Indian Legends*.

16. See McGrane ix–x for a summary statement.

17. Permitting Schoolcraft his complications, we should note where he writes that "superstition has engrafted upon the original stock" of Indian lore, meaning that even his stories are partly contaminated by spiritual ideas of more recent date. Finally, Schoolcraft also readily acknowledges that a "moral point" has been added to some of his texts, although the "original" texts always "justify it."

18. Philip P. Mason, who edited a collection of *Literary Voyager* issues, believes that this text was orally transmitted by Jane's mother to Jane. This may or may not be true, but even if true, it would not alter the dynamics I am noting (Schoolcraft, *Voyager* 171, n. 39). Henry Schoolcraft treated the character "Leelinau" as a stand-in for his wife.

19. The Ojibwa are a "tribe" constructed at a relatively late date out of refugees from the Iroquois wars; see Richard White 19; Wolf 171. See also Fried on the very idea of "tribe."

20. The story of Jane's father, John, is told in brief by Tomaszewski.

21. Thomas McKenney, a friend of the Schoolcrafts who was respected and admired in his own right as a scholar on Amerindian matters (for example, by George Copway), described Johnston as more European than Chippewa: "She dresses with great taste, and in all respects in the costume of our fashionables, but wears leggins of black silk, drawn and ruffled around the ankles, resembling those worn by our little girls. I think them ornamental. You would never judge, either from her complexion, or language, or from any other circumstance, that her mother was a Chippeway, except that her moderately high cheek bones, her dark and fine eye, and breadth of the jaw, slightly indicate it—and you would never believe it, except on her own confession, or upon some equally responsible testimony, were you to hear her converse, or see her beautiful, and some of them highly finished compositions, in both prose and poetry. . . . Mrs. S. is indebted, mainly, to her father, who is doatingly fond of her, for her handsome and polished acquirements" (quoted in Tomaszewski 19–20).

22. Compare *Voyager* 71 to *Indian Legends* 168.

23. The only place in Schoolcraft's published writings where he discusses his wife's work directly locates her within this corpus: "The writer, who from early years was a member of the church, had made a translation of the Lords prayer, and, occasionally, as delicate and declining health permitted, some other select pieces from the sacred writings, and hymns" (*Wigwam* 409). Schoolcraft does not mention any of her ethnographic work.

24. In the first place, one might wonder what is going on when Schoolcraft drops a letter from Cusick's name between the time of his references to him in *Notes on the Iroquois* and in *Historical and Statistical Information*. In the former text Schoolcraft

writes about "Cusick" whereas in the latter it is always "Cusic." This may be a small enough matter, a simple proofreading oversight, but it is more interesting in the light of Schoolcraft's temporary transformation of his own name during the 1840s from "Schoolcraft" to "Colcraft"—dropping the letters "s," "h," and an "o" from his surname. Were one so inclined, one could tease cabalistic significances out of these shortenings. On another level, Bieder reports that at least one scholar believes the shift to "Colcraft" was a "symbolic act of suicide" during a desperate time of "debt and ravenous insecurity" (Bieder 173). And even less dramatically, one could suggest that *both* name changes are diminutions, that is, subtractions from the authority of the signature. The more Schoolcraft reflected upon "Cusick," the smaller became the worth of the "Cusic" project.

25. Curiously, Schoolcraft appears to be making Amerindians entirely Ostic in this passage, as if he has forgotten his previous distinction between Algic and Ostic sociopolitics.

26. Schoolcraft perhaps understood the text in this manner. In a paragraph from *Notes on the Iroquois* that includes a discussion of Cusick's book, he notes that Iroquois folklore is produced with "the intent, perhaps, that they might put forth an undisputed title to the country they occupied" (*Notes* 48).

27. See Rogin for a useful intellectual history of the removal debates.

28. Cusick's text was highly marginalized within the Anglo cultural marketplace. Although three editions of Cusick's book had been published by 1848, all were by western New York local or regional presses (Beauchamp 41). Even the Beauchamp reprint, which is the most readily available edition today, was self-published at the turn of the century. Cusick's cultural force has been small indeed compared to that of Cooper or even Schoolcraft.

29. Michael Taussig's most recent book, *Mimesis and Alterity* (1993), is entirely about this sort of strange relation to the seemingly "other" within a postcolonial world—where the "reaction" to the other "tears at identity and proliferates associations of a self bound magically to an Other, too close to that Other to be but dimly recognizable, too much the self to allow for satisfying alterity" (253).

30. I put to one side the difficult problem of the "reality" of Cooper's Indians, a question of related concern to the issues raised in this paper. It is relatively easy to suggest that Cooper produced stereotypes of Amerindian identity, both in *The Last of the Mohicans* and in the 1831 introduction to the book. But what does one do with the fact that George Copway, perhaps the best-known Amerindian writer of Cooper's time, praised Cooper's depiction of Indian life? And what does one do with the fact that Russell Means, the merry prankster of the American Indian Movement, was willing to appear as Chingachgook in the recent film version of *Mohicans*? Who are Cooper's Indians?

31. Johnson cites Jacques Derrida's *Of Grammatology:* It is "remorse that produces anthropology" ("*Contando*" 12, n. 8).

32. See Judkins, for example, who celebrates Cusick's anthropological achievement.

33. I am explicitly considering the relationship between Cusick's work and anthropology as *unlike* what Prakash sees as a dialectical relationship between colonizer and colonized historiography in India.

34. Stephen A. Tyler, for example, says of postmodern ethnography that "it does not describe, for there is nothing it could describe. . . . It begins and ends in concepts" (137).

35. An interesting counteraccount from a humanist perspective is Todorov, even though he is equally critical of recent work on "othering" that ends up erasing the other, "refusing these Others any specificity at all" ("Race" 374).

36. See Mohawk, "Discovering Columbus." And in Mohawk's "Indians and Democracy," from the Lyons and Mohawk volume discussed at the beginning of this chapter, which focuses on the transmission of democratic values from the Iroquois to the British, the narrative of colonialism again refers almost entirely to the "Spanish" (47–51).

37. The reverse gesture is not deployed in the earliest or even the latest indigenous accounts of conquest from Mexican, Central American, or South American perspectives — and here one might specifically cite the texts produced by the Florentine Codex informants, Felipe Guaman Poma de Ayala, and Garcilaso de la Vega.

2. DESTRUCTURING WHITENESS

1. In chronological order, major publications include David Roediger's *The Wages of Whiteness* (1991), Toni Morrison's *Playing in the Dark* (1992), Ruth Frankenberg's *White Women, Race Matters* (1993), Roediger's *Towards the Abolition of Whiteness* (1994), Theodore W. Allen's *The Invention of the White Race* (1994), Noel Ignatiev's *How the Irish Became White* (1995), Fred Pfeil's *White Guys* (1995), and Ian F. Haney López's *White by Law* (1996).

2. A selection of texts from the journal's early numbers has recently been published by Routledge.

3. I explore this question in a review essay of Pfeil and López, "What's 'White,' and Whither?"

4. Pfeil's book is a good example of this.

5. Another useful work is that by F. James Davis, but unfortunately he does not disentangle color from race.

6. See Piedra, who argues that "black" and "white" were real but mutable categories at the time of conquest, when, he states, a language of racial difference was not yet in place. "Whiteness" was available to any individual through proof of literacy in Castilian Spanish and the receipt of a kind of "certificate" of "literary whiteness."

7. The other is Cherokee newspaper editor Elias Boudinot.

8. All of this has been assembled, edited, and annotated in Barry O'Connell's extraordinary edition of Apess, *On Our Own Ground.* O'Connell's introduction to the volume (xiii–lxxxi) includes an astonishing amount of information about Apess's hith-

erto unknown life, and I have relied on O'Connell for details about Apess, in this paragraph and others.

9. Murray 60 inquires into the text's status relative to the rest of the book in which it appears.

10. O'Connell situates Apess in relation to both Walker and Boudinot, and "militant consciousness" is his formulation as well (Apess xv).

11. As David Murray points out, Arnold Krupat has sometimes held to the latter position, arguing that the text's "voice" is one of white "salvationism" (quoted in Murray 58). On the other hand, a later Krupat work describes "An Indian's Looking-Glass" as "a brilliant and violent attack on racism" (Krupat 225). Gary Ashwill, on the other hand, reads the text as a radical act of strategic appropriation and resistance (Ashwill 220–26). Murray himself believes that Apess's "ruling out of bounds . . . of a natural or unmediated Indianness" is his most interesting feature as a writer (Murray 58).

12. Ralph Venning, from *Orthodoxe Paradoxes,* and Matthew Henry, from his biblical *Commentaries* on Genesis.

13. Which one, he does not know; nor does he see that his critique of Buffon — based on lack of evidence and less than "sound reasoning" — applies equally well to his own *Notes.*

14. One should read the totality of Apess's writings for more on this score. For example, in the *Eulogy* text Apess draws comparisons between King Philip and George Washington — both great men and comparable in many ways but operating on totally different levels, the natural and the civil, respectively (see Apess 277–78, 297). To *Son of the Forest* Apess appends a long anthropological text, filled with citations from white anthropology; it is sometimes unclear where the citations end and Apess begins, but some passages lead one to the conclusion that Amerindians begin life in an inferior intellectual position compared to whites (see, for example, Apess 68).

Also, in his autobiography, Apess makes clear his view that Indians are really the lost tribe of Israel. Apess's view of Indian history combines notions of Christian and secular time and suggests that the Jews migrated to America, where they lived for a time as a natural and happy people; "fell" during the era of white colonization and entered a degraded state; and will rise again according to a logic of white civilization.

15. Forbes dates this tradition to the "late medieval period" (99–100).

16. Cooper's *The Wept of Wish-ton-Wish* (1829) makes this quite clear, with its multiple captivities and cultural transformations and its satire on racist anatomy and craniology.

17. Dennis W. Allen comes close to this position when he argues that "the reader, presumably identifying with the hapless Duncan, feels a tremendous push toward the semiotic viewpoint of the Indian" (165).

18. Compare, in mideighteenth-century Spanish America, the texts of Baltasar de Esquivel. Piedra reads his work as "the visionary expression of blackness as an important element *within* the Hispanic culture" (326).

19. Slotkin's analysis of Cooper is exceptional in this regard. He says, "There is a hint that a portion of his [Hawk-eye's] spirit is bequeathed to the Indian and white heroes,... suggesting that through him there is ground for a kind of reconciliation between the two worlds" (Slotkin, *Regeneraton* 495).

20. Shirley Samuels's "Generation through Violence," which suggests that in *Mohicans* there is an "emphatically uncertain relation between human and nonhuman," is pathbreaking in this regard (96). Samuels argues that characters' "taking on of animal identities... involves both imitation and a kind of transformation" (107).

21. I want to thank Hugh C. MacDougall for suggesting Paulding's novel as relevant to my work.

22. See Trautmann 18–35 for a full discussion of Morgan's understanding of the relationship between animals, Indians, and Europeans. Bieder 234–42 also usefully discusses Morgan's views on progressive evolution.

3. AMERINDIAN VOICE(S) IN ETHNOGRAPHY

1. Service calls the book "perhaps the first full-length ethnological monograph written about an American Indian society... to be based on firsthand 'field' experience" (16). Bieder says, "When Morgan began his study of the Iroquois, there were no systematic descriptions of a tribal culture. Most ethnological accounts surveyed Indians in general from the perspective of philology, religion, or physical traits" (205).

2. The two most important archives for Parker's materials are the American Philosophical Library in Philadelphia and the Rush Rhees Library at the University of Rochester. The Parker materials in the latter collection are contained within the library's exhaustive Lewis Henry Morgan collection. Another large collection of Parker papers is housed at the Huntington Library in San Marino, California, but these materials are less relevant for my project.

3. Cooper's daughter, Susan Fenimore Cooper, noted that "his own opportunities of intercourse with the red man had been few" and that he had studied "Heckwelder [*sic*], Charlevoix, Penn, Smith, Elliott, Colden" as well as the journals of Lewis and Clark, among others, in order to produce *Mohicans* (Cooper, *Pages* 149).

4. Copway's long, "official" statement on this matter appeared in his weekly newspaper *Copway's American Indian* in the form of a "pre-obituary." It has never been reprinted and bears full citation: "Gratitude is one of the peculiar traits in the composition of the Indian character; and we would dishonor that attribute as an Indian, if we did not express our anxiety for the safety of one whom, for the few days past we have seen paragraphs in the papers, that our friend Cooper is seriously and dangerously ill. We sometimes doubted of the correctness of the report, for it is not long since we heard from him by letter, yet when we know the uncertainty of life, we could but feel anxious for his safety; yet the paragraph in last Friday's Tribune relieved us from our suspense for a while, and still we hope for his speedy recovery, and that such a man may be spared to the world and see many years of prosperity.

"It has been our good fortune to know him personally for several years, and we have thought often when we read his life-like descriptions of Indian character, when it was in our power to do him justice we should endeavor to do so, for the exhalted manner he has plead, of the wild and noble genius of the American Indians.

"No living writer, nor historian, has done so much justice to the noble traits of our people. The whole American feeling takes pride in such a man, as the author of 'The Last of the Mohicans,' and if the American can but be proud of such a literary man, what must the man of the forest feel, when he reads of heroes (possessing all the noble traits of an exalted character) as soon as he is brought to read, and find in the pages of history pencilled his forefather's features — yes! with us one word of commendation from the white man, either by his pen or in history, learns us to forget outrageous usages — and the sweet morsel of approbation outweighs all other wrongs, which have been inflicted on our races, in this country. It throws a rainbow of light around our heads and wins our hearts, when we hear one word of commendation, from a race who have been watching the gradual downfall of our ancestors.

"We attribute this carelessness on the part of the Americans, for the salvation of the Red Man on the ground, that no feasible means have been used for the recovery of the first owners of American soil; and not on the ground that they have no feeling for his good. In mentioning the name of our worthy and honored friend, we will here repeat what we have often said in our association with the learned sages of the old world last summer — 'that Mr. Cooper's writings give a better idea of Indian character, than any man living or dead.' For many questions of this nature were propounded to me, 'Does Mr. Cooper give a true picture to the Indian character?' and our knowledge of his writings compelled us to answer, that 'he did.'

"There may be many others in America who ought to receive the appellation as friends of the Indian with Cooper, we have not had the pleasure of knowing them personally, with the exception, perhaps, of Col. T. L. McKenney, whose writings, and whole life and means, have been expended in promulgating the great and feasible doctrine that the Indian is reclaimable, and can be made a worthy associate when polished by the refined influence of high-toned education. These men we adore for their love of our race — and may their lives be long spared to us for our special gratification, and if the prayers of the whole civilized race can be answered, they will" ("Cooper").

5. Sam Gill's *Mother Earth* (1987) is one such account. It is also possible that Copway's letter does not necessarily represent his own views. Donald Smith believes that this letter was written by the hand of Elizabeth Copway, George Copway's white wife (Smith, "Life" 36, n. 103). Other evidence, however, points strongly to the conclusion that the letter does represent Copway's attitudes.

6. See Morgan, Letter to Ely S. Parker, 29 December 1848, and Morgan, Letter to Ely S. Parker, 29 January 1850.

7. See Arthur C. Parker 86–87. Ely Parker's other biographer, William H. Armstrong, agrees with Arthur Parker: "Not only was Ely providing him with information,

but Morgan was using some of Ely's work almost verbatim in the book" (45). Trautmann too concludes that "much of the text-making that went into the *League* occurred among the bilingual and bicultural Parker children — above all the eloquent Ely" (46).

Morgan's two biographers, Carl Resek and Bernhard J. Stern, tend to de-emphasize Parker's role, although Resek twice notes Parker's significance as an oral informant (36, 38).

8. Trautmann, however, argues that technically "[Morgan's] position cannot properly be called racist for want of two essential ingredients of that view: the permanence of intellectual differences among the races and their physiological cause" (30).

9. See Clifford's remarks on the contours of what he calls "ethnographic liberalism" (*Predicament* 78–80).

10. This is the first part of the subtitle of Drinnon's *Facing West*.

11. I describe anti-anthropology in the opening pages of the prolegomenon.

12. I use the term "trickster" not as an Indianism but as a figure and an attitude that appears in popular literatures across all so-called cultural divides.

13. See, for example, his letter to Morgan, 13 February 1847.

14. I want to exercise caution in making this paragraph's remarks, which tend to essentialize birth or blood identities. I want to underline here that identity politics is never a matter of the blood; rather, it is a matter of self-perception. Ely Parker's own perception of his "race" was quite complex, to say the least, and it is not certain that he considered himself "red" to begin with. Arthur Parker makes a strong claim in this regard, emphasizing on the first page of his biography that Ely's lineage could be traced "back for generations to the Stone Age and to the days of Hiawatha" (*Life* 7). "He was a red man, a native product of the soil," and "of pure Indian lineage on both sides" (8).

But Ely Parker's grandmother on his father's side "had been a white woman who was taken captive and adopted as a Seneca. Ely and his brothers and sisters were therefore one-fourth white" (Armstrong 10). We do not know how Ely understood this fact, but it may account for his easy manipulation of his race identity in his texts. Biology talk, finally, matters less to me than the identity politics that Ely adopts.

15. Morgan's request for adoption was lent additional force because he and the other members of the Grand Order had, in 1846, been actively engaged in assisting the Seneca in their land dispute with the Ogden Land Company — preparing petitions and even, in Morgan's case, journeying to Washington, D.C., to make their voices heard (Resek 33–34).

16. The term often refers to white, self-styled Indians who claim knowledge of Indian spirituality. See Churchill's critique in *Fantasies* 215–28.

17. A substantial portion of this text is cited in Stern 11–12.

18. See, for example, Parker's "Notes."

19. See, for example and in order, *League* 48, 8, 106, 123. The word "race," it might be added, was variously deployed in the nineteenth century. So-called polygenists used the term in this period to describe separately created human species, whereas

monogenists often used the term with reference to what happened to different human groups once the monogene of creation dispersed across the globe and hardened into different life or environmental experiences (see, for example, Stocking 50, 63–64). Morgan never seems to have made a decision as to which way he wished to be understood. As late as *Ancient Society* (1877) Morgan writes: "Whether the gens originated spontaneously in a given condition of society, and would thus repeat itself in disconnected areas; or whether it had a single origin, and was propagated from an original center, through successive migrations, over the earth's surface, are fair questions for speculative consideration" (quoted in Terray 18). Trautmann and Bieder, however, believe that Morgan primarily was monogenist in outlook (Trautmann 78–79; Bieder 195).

The question of color predates that of race, and racialisms emerge out of hundreds of years of thinking about the significance of color. As Stocking notes of another famed social evolutionist anthropologist of the nineteenth century, E. B. Tylor, "color became an indicator of culture. Tylor's arrangement of 'races' in order of their culture — Australian, Tahitian, Aztec, Chinese, Italian — was also an arrangement in terms of color saturation" (Stocking 235).

20. Curtis M. Hinsley writes: "Morgan's schema of human development, further elaborated in *Ancient Society*, did embrace notions of change and progress, but these were, like Schoolcraft's visions, strongly teleological and bound to a system of unfolding ideas rather than to the immediate historical experiences of peoples. Morgan's legacy to the next generation — [John Wesley] Powell and the Bureau of American Ethnology — was the subordination of historical probings to the greater explanatory power and aesthetic satisfaction of ordering man in value-laden stages" (29). Morgan's work also is part of a larger midnineteenth-century international trend in the study of " 'the natural history of man,' which had been interpreted primarily in terms of movement in space, [and] was now to be understood in terms of development in time" (Stocking 76).

21. Morgan defines both "system" and "structure" (recurrent terms in his work) as a set of beliefs, laws, or rituals "internally consistent with each other" for which one can "deduce the general principles" (*League* 224, 61). As others have noted, this is all part of Morgan's anthropological and, in general, intellectual modernity — that is, his primary interest in demonstrating synchronic coherence within Indian social organization rather than producing Indian history (Trautmann 37; Terray 37).

22. In the articles Morgan had published earlier, upon which he drew heavily (often verbatim) in creating the final text for *League of the Iroquois*, he qualified the similarities by noting that "this Indian constellation paled only before the greater constellation of the American Confederacy" ("Letters" 179). Morgan did not include this qualification in the final text.

23. Two recent collections of essays discuss this claim: José Barreiro's *Indian Roots of American Democracy* (1992) and Oren Lyons's and John Mohawk's *Exiled in the Land of the Free* (1992).

24. The language of the "gift" or talent again should remind one of Cooper, because Natty Bumppo's Indian discourse increasingly focuses on "gifts" in the 1840s, particularly in *The Pathfinder* (1840), which I discuss briefly in chapter 4.

25. In these materials one can clearly see the shaping hand of Parker. The Johnson/ Handsome Lake speech as it appears in *League* is an extensively rewritten and reedited compound drawn from Parker's transcriptions of speeches Jemmy Johnson made in October 1845 and October 1848. For example, in Parker's notes there is no passage decrying interracial marriage, although the final version includes such a remark; Parker seems to have invented this material. And even this original note on living like whites is far less pointed than the version in the *League* (which is quoted later in the text): "The Great Spirit made the Indians to live by the chase. But he foresaw the day when the Indians would be deprived of their hunting grounds; therefore He has said it was not a criminal wrong to follow the example of the whites in some respects. He said that it was not wrong to build houses after the manner of the whites, to work your farms and raise domestic animals. But an Indian could not live and be happy when he exceeded these bounds" (quoted in Parker, *Life* 261). Parker shifts the original note's focus on "happiness" to the matter of sinning, which makes the final version far more dramatic in its exclusionist implications. The 1845 Parker notes are in Arthur Parker, *Life* 251–61. The 1848 Parker notes are in Fenton 306–9.

26. "As far as my personal observation has extended among the American Indian nations, the half-blood is inferior, both physically and mentally, to the pure Indian; but the second cross, giving three-quarters Indian, is an advance upon the native; and giving three-fourths white is a still greater advance, approximating to equality with the white ancestor. With the white carried still further, full equality is reached, tending to show that Indian blood can be taken up without physical or intellectual detriment" (quoted in Stern 72).

27. I analyze this tendency in my "Toward a Critique of Sentimentalisms in Cultural Studies."

28. Misidentified, I think, by Fenton as a draft from the 1848 council; see Fenton 303.

29. These are my best guesses as to dates. Fenton, who has studied the matter closely, appears to be uncertain as to whether the version Arthur Parker published as notes from 1845 actually dates from that year; and see note 25. What is clear is that the shorthand notes are clearly dated "1848" and the *Batavia Times* article is from 1847.

30. Basically verbatim in "Indian Council of the Six Nations at Tonawanda," with the exception of omission of the word "grossly."

31. The language is identical in both Parker's "Indian Council" (page 2) and his "Indian Council of the Six Nations of Tonawanda," both listed in the works cited.

32. Indeed, in *League of the Iroquois* Morgan writes that the Johnson speech is copied "from copious notes taken by him [Parker] at the time of its last delivery in Oc-

tober, 1848" (*League* 233, n. 1). This is undeniably misleading, based on comparison of Parker's shorthand notes and the *League* text. Morgan further suggests, in the same note, that Johnson's speech each year is *always the same:* "He [Parker] has listened to its delivery on several occasions, and is perfectly familiar with the subject."

33. Sentimentalism, premised on a biological-moral injunction that each and all "feel right," most typically involves an exclusion, finally, of a difficult other's body color, symbology, emotionality, and so on; see the essays collected by Shirley Samuels in *The Culture of Sentiment.* And one might say, even more generally, that the very idea of community is always secured by positing a contaminating other.

34. See, for example, Morgan, *League* 82, 92.

35. I borrow the term "beyond anthropology" from Bernard McGrane's Foucauldian reading of anthropological epistemes from the early modern period to the present.

4. METHODISTS AND METHOD

1. Their closeness is indicated by the fact that Jones also presided at Copway's marriage in 1840. See Smith, "The Life of George Copway," for what is known of the details of the relationship. Smith's *Sacred Feathers* includes additional material.

2. Smith tells us one or two things about Sunday. His Ojibwa name before conversion was Shawundais, and he was a close ministerial colleague to Jones, sometimes traveling with him on the missionary circuit. Sunday was a recovering alcoholic, a veteran of the War of 1812, a man who had his face painted red, wore feathers in his hair, and carried a rifle, tomahawk, and scalping knife (*Sacred* 92). He spoke little English, and Jones translated his speech to the whites at the Indian land rights council in 1828 (98). He preached fire and brimstone when it came to alcohol and conversion (120), but he also publicly acknowledged his struggle with "wicked thoughts and bad spirits" (232).

3. See, for example, Leach 505.

4. Smith, to date, has written a full-length biography of Jones (*Sacred Feathers*) and a long journal article on Copway's life ("The Life of George Copway"). He will soon publish a new text on Copway, a coedited edition of Copway's own autobiographical work. The decision of Smith's that I am sketching is latent and nascent in his work; it is not clear that Smith understands that he is making it. One must read both of his published texts in order to detect it.

5. The text is *The Ojibway Conquest* (1850).

6. Smith does say that this was simply "the practice of the time," but the remark comes in the context of generally discrediting the book.

7. "He had turned his back on his own people in Upper Canada and the American Northwest" ("Life" 23).

8. Smith, *Sacred* 156 seems to make the same point: Jones, under the influence of his wife, lost faith in the dream of "communal property" and converted to the Anglo

notion of "private property." In midlife he claimed as his own a portion of land set aside for the Ojibwa by the Canadian government.

9. His case for Copway's "outside helper" depends upon a single line of Copway's text: "These young rulers are apt to be more cautious in the exercise of their governing power than those who possess more mature age with its more mature vanities" (quoted in "Life" 22). It is a fine sentence, and it sets off a warning bell. Smith calls it a "sophisticated statement" beyond Copway's reach. (How could Copway, after all, understand the ideas of "vanity" and "cautious governing power"?) Smith implicitly may also be arguing that it is a non-Indian statement, that it contradicts the long-enduring mythos of Indian life that seniors are respected by juniors in matters cultural, social, and political.

10. James Treat notes: "We know that conventional wisdom...suggests that 'native' and 'Christian' are mutually exclusive identities: a native who has become wholeheartedly Christian has lost some measure of native authenticity" ("Introduction" 6).

11. Is Donald B. Smith's method Methodist-inflected? Does he understand Jones's conversion as providing objective perspective on the Ojibwa world (as providing, perhaps, Western tools for representation and evaluation), while seeing Copway's knowledge-strategies and life-turns (including his dismissal from the church) as invalidating his project? Or is Smith's position merely a matter of dismissing Copway as a crook and thus probably a fraud as well?

12. The published sermons and lectures of Samson Occum and Elias Boudinot are useful examples of this latter tendency.

13. The cite is from Southern Cheyenne writer James L. West. See West 33.

14. There are moments when Jones readjusts this discourse — for example, in a report of an address to a British governor-general, where Jones says that Amerindians were "free and happy" before the coming of the whites and that Amerindians "have been made" "poor" by liquor (Jones, *History* 123). Here, "savage cruelty" is a European imposition, and Amerindians bear no responsibility for it.

15. In a recent example, Steve Charleston (Choctaw), makes explicit what one finds in nascent form in Peter Jones's work: "Today I feel comfortable talking about Christianity as a faith that emerges from Native America....I believe with all my heart that God's revelation to Native People is second to none....[A] living Christ...arises from the Native covenant and speaks with the authority and authenticity of Native America" (Charleston 69). This is precisely the implication of Jones's text.

16. Copway eventually does present a "fall" story, set deep in precontact times, in which the disobedience of one of the Ojibwa results in a short breach with the creator and the beginnings of "disease and death" among Amerindians (*Indian Life* 163–69).

17. Bernd Peyer notes, for example, that they share the framework of "American ethnological methodology," proven by the fact that they both compartmentalize data in the manner of Bureau of Indian Affairs questionnaires distributed in the 1820s (269–71).

18. Jones's posthumous *History*, too, is framed by an introduction that relates his conversion.

19. "One has to be completely taken in by this internal ruse of confession in order to attribute a fundamental role to censorship, to taboos regarding speaking and thinking: one has to have an inverted image of power in order to believe that all these voices which have spoken so long in our civilization — repeating the formidable injunction to tell what one is and what one does, what one recollects and what one has forgotten, what one is thinking and what one thinks he is not thinking — are speaking to us of freedom. An immense labor to which the West has submitted generations in order to produce — while other forms of work ensured the accumulation of capital — men's subjection: their constitution as subjects in both senses of the word" (Foucault 60).

20. Both texts, Foucault would agree, identify and put pressure upon "mobile and transitory points of resistance, producing cleavages in a society that shift about, fracturing unities and effecting regroupings, furrowing across individuals themselves, cutting them up and remolding them" (Foucault 96).

21. Little of consequence has been written about *The Oak Openings* and its characterization of the Ojibwa; invective and curt dismissal have been the order of the day, mostly because of the positively inflected theme of conversion that runs through the text. The most dangerous Amerindian in the novel, Onoah, or Scalping Peter, is turned humbly Christian over the course of the book, prompting Richard Drinnon to characterize Peter as "one of the most egregious Uncle Tomahawks ever" (Drinnon 163). Drinnon goes on to suggest that with this book Cooper "exterminated his own white-Indian tendencies" and that the book serves as "a valuable indication of the power and pervasiveness of American Indian-hating" (Drinnon 164). The relationship between Peter's discourse and Uncle Tom was originally formulated by Leslie Fiedler, and many, including Drinnon, have followed him. Geoffrey Rans notes that "the treatment of Scalping Peter... has struck several critics from [John] McWilliams to [Heinz] Ickstadt as a shocking abandonment of the problem [of racism]" (260, n. 28). George Dekker, for example, says that Cooper's late work is "morally callous," the work of a "zealous and bigoted Christian missionary" (247).

22. I use eight as a conservative estimate. The eight are *The Pioneers* (1823), *The Last of the Mohicans* (1826), *The Prairie* (1827), *The Wept of Wish-ton-Wish* (1829), *The Pathfinder* (1840), *The Deerslayer* (1841), *Wyandotté* (1843), and *The Oak Openings* (1848). Relatively significant Indian and pseudo-Indian figures also appear in the Littlepage Trilogy — *Satanstoe* (1845), *The Chainbearer* (1845), and *The Redskins* (1846) — and Cooper writes about Indians in the nonfiction text, *Notions of the Americans* (1828). But at least as much Indian writing takes place in the last decade of Cooper's career as in the first one.

As a first step in the transformation of Cooper's thought, *The Wept of Wish-ton-Wish* (1829) includes an elaborate spoof of phrenology and craniology — suggesting the specious foundation of these two allied sciences that were, perhaps, the most respected racial discourses of the antebellum years. Even Henry Schoolcraft, a firm opponent of crania-based polygenism, or separate creationism, felt the need to solicit a new review piece about craniology by Samuel Morton, the "dean" of such studies, for his *Historical and Statistical Information.*

23. *Pathfinder* 78 is quite clear on this point, although Natty reiterates versions of same too many times to cite.

24. A particularly blunt example of the latter tendency: When Richard H. Kern, Morton's chief illustrator for *Crania Ægyptiaca,* died in an encounter with the Utah Indians while performing railroad survey work, Dr. Henry S. Patterson, a colleague of Morton's in the Medical Department of Pennsylvania College, wrote in an introduction to Josiah Nott's and George Glidden's *Types of Mankind* (1854) that "we have had too much of sentimentalism about the Red-man. It is time that cant was stopped now. Not all the cinnamon-colored vermin west of the Mississippi are worth one drop of that noble heart's-blood. The busy brain, the artist's eye, the fine taste, the hand so ready with either pen or pencil, — could these be restored to us again, they would be cheaply purchased back if it cost the extermination of every miserable Pah-Utah under heaven!" (Nott and Glidden xxxviii). Nott and Glidden's edited collection, *Types of Mankind,* was dedicated to Morton's memory and was one of the most popular textbooks of scientific polygenism in the mid- to late nineteenth century. It was reprinted many times.

25. In another metacommentary, Cooper's text spells out in greater detail how judgments are typically made. Again, it is the narrator who notes: "The virtues and qualities that are proclaimed near the centre of power, as incense and policy, get to be part of political faith, with the credulous and ignorant at a distance. . . . It is a consequence of this mental dependence, that public opinion is so much placed at the mercy of the designing, and the world, in the midst of its idle boasts of knowledge and improvement, is left to receive its truth, on all such points as touch the interests of the powerful and managing, through such a medium, and such a medium only, as may serve the particular view of those who pull the wires" (*Pathfinder* 212). A theory of power, interests, and belief: This is a purely statist account of ideological formation. Reading *The Pathfinder* through this paragraph, the book becomes tragicomic. Natty, Cap, and Serjeant Dunham operate far from the "centre of power." They are, undoubtedly, among the "credulous and ignorant" — breathing in and living on "incense," carrying out "policy" that is justified, in their minds, by a network of received ideas that the text exposes as ludicrous. Natty, in a rare moment of self-reflection, notes that "such consaits [judgments and preferences] will come over men, from long habit, and prejudyce is perhaps the commonest failing of human natur' " (97).

26. A caveat: Morgan crosses the line in his late works, and most particularly in *Systems of Consanguinity and Affinity of the Human Family* (1871). Furthermore, to the extent that the following network of Cooper strategies might be marshaled onto the

side of a universal humanism, it is important to follow Marc Shell's arguments regarding the implicit exclusions of such an approach; see Shell, *Kinship* and *Children.*

27. Cooper writes "Ojebway"; Jones and Copway write "Ojibway." As is evident, I use "Ojibwa" throughout this chapter.

28. Versions of the thesis exist today. For example, elaborate annotated and illustrated twentieth-century editions of the Book of Mormon continue to work this territory. Relatedly, a group of historians today are attempting to prove that the Spanish conquerors of the present-day U.S. southwest were Jews, using many of Father Amen's procedures. To listen to one of their presentations is to be transported back to nineteenth-century logics.

29. Even more so given that modern renderings of Gen. 49.21 say nothing of a deer or good words. The New English Bible's rendering, for example, is "Naphtali is a spreading terebinth putting forth lovely boughs."

30. For different versions of the argument, see Goldberg, *Racist*; Young; and Bhabha. In Bhabha, see particularly 34, where he argues for "the need to think the limit of culture as a problem of the enunciation of cultural difference."

31. This is a familiar narrative of color, proposed, among other places, in the Book of Mormon.

32. Elias Boudinot, a congressman from New Jersey and a founder of the American Bible Society, did have his Amerindian supporters, including the Cherokee newspaper editor Elias Boudinot (who was sponsored by the elder Boudinot and who took his English name from him) and William Apess, whom I discussed in an earlier chapter. Barry O'Connell, as part of his editing of Apess's texts, has studied and noted Apess's intellectual indebtedness to Boudinot (see Apess, *Ground* xli–xlii, n. 35).

33. Copway accepts at least some version of a migratory thesis: "My own belief is, that they [Amerindians] came to this country, and fought with the original inhabitants" (*Indian Life* 43). The Ojibwa, for example, are broadly shown to have migrated from north to south (*Indian Life* 45).

34. Cooper, *Letters* 5:245, 5:251ff. Cooper's journals note no more than the biblical book emphasized each day.

35. I find it useful here to treat *The Sea Lions,* but Cooper says a version of the same thing in *The Oak Openings:* "Nothing can be simpler than the two great dogmas of Christianity, which are so plain that all can both comprehend them and feel their truth. They teach us to love God, the surest way to obey him, and to love our neighbor as ourselves" (250).

36. The narrator of *The Oak Openings* had praised the Methodist missionaries for their "submission" to "personal privations" in order to carry out their labors (160).

37. The most vexsome character in *The Sea Lions* is Deacon Pratt, about whom the narrator writes, "It was not the love of God that was active in his soul, but the love of self" (4:28).

38. For example, Cooper clearly distinguishes "love of self" from "individuality," which he defines as competitive spirit and which he calls the "most powerful auxiliary in advancing civilization" (4:82). Self-love, then, is defined on one level as "the minimum of exertion," and Cooper suggests that cooperative labor (and here he is thinking of everything from corporate joint ventures to Brook Farm) is a prime example of loving the self (4:82).

39. Cooper acknowledges that this is the probable result (262).

40. After writing this passage, I found that Kay Seymour House has reached similar conclusions, although she finds them unwelcome. She writes, "The annihilation of Peter's character may well be the result . . . of a movement, on Cooper's part, away from Aquinas' theocentric humanism toward a more Lutheran emphasis on death and annihilation of the self as vital doctrine." She then mourns Peter's conversion as "a loss to Cooper's fictional world," a loss of "that marvelous sense of richness and complexity of human interdependence," a development "not true to his [Cooper's] world as a whole" (260). In short, it is a bad ending, given the achievement of the Leatherstocking series, which is the complex depiction of white/red conflict. House therefore comprehends the book in a way that Richard Drinnon and most other scholars cannot, but she nonetheless finds a way to partition it off and dismiss it from the Cooper canon.

5. Borders of Anthropology, History, and Science

1. Geoffrey Rans's study of dialogism in Cooper is extremely useful on this point.

2. See Parins, *Ridge,* as well as Dale and Litton's excellent collection of Ridge family letters.

3. I cite the original magazine texts throughout, but I have subsequently found them reprinted in Farmer and Strickland's San Francisco Book Club collection of Ridge's writings, entitled *A Trumpet of Our Own.*

4. "Morton won his reputation as the great data-gatherer and objectivist of American science, the man who would raise an immature enterprise from the mires of fanciful speculation" (Gould 51).

5. Gould's reading of Morton, for example, basically avoids an encounter with Morton's text, focusing instead on *Crania Americana*'s charts and the phrenological conclusion of the book, written by George Combe (Gould 50–69). I plan a rereading of Morton's corpus in the context of recent developments in hybridity theory, in a manuscript tentatively entitled *"Anthropology's Wake"* and cowritten with David E. Johnson. I might briefly note here that a careful reading of Morton and his milieu will be useful for several reasons, including an assessment of the return of "hard science" in certain cultural studies contexts, such as in Appiah's celebrated *In My Father's House* (1992), which replaces craniology with genetic science; see Appiah 35–39.

6. *Americana* 171–72; Parins, *Ridge* 160–65, 180–81. Dale and Litton's volume includes one letter from Ridge, written in 1849 to his uncle, on matters directly relating to his family's slaves, in which he attempts to calculate the relative values of several African men, women, and children—trading bodies for mortgages (Dale and Litton 71–72).

7. See also *Americana* 101, regarding Morton's discovery of very small skulls from the extinct pre-Incan civilization; and 115, on Incan skulls.

8. Bieder reports the phrenologist George Combe's later responses, in a review and personal letters, to Morton's text: "The phrenologist Combe was also distressed by these findings while writing his review of *Crania Americana* for the *Journal of Arts and Science*, and he urged Morton to rethink his position on the Peruvian skull. Morton's response was to admit that his findings might be erroneous. This upset Combe and he cautioned Morton against making such an admission, for he would lose the trust of his readers and the book's scientific reputation would suffer. Morton never fully resolved this contradictory evidence, which he felt threatened to nullify his thesis in *Crania Americana*" (Bieder 76–77).

9. Historically, of course, nothing could be further from the case. Morton did not stop producing readings of the essence of Indians and their brains (see his 1842 *Inquiry* for the former and his 1850 "Observations" for the latter). Morton went on to produce a second full-length work, *Crania Ægyptiaca*, which duplicates the strategies of *Crania Americana* on Egyptian terrain, in order to prove that the Egyptians were white. Finally, Morton's presuppositions and a general distortion of his views were promoted by George Glidden and Josiah Nott in their enormously successful *Types of Mankind* (1854), which went through numerous editions. The literature of the 1850s on these issues is enormous, but to grasp the other side of the problem—that is, the work of Morton's opponents—succinctly, consult John Bachman's *Unity of the Human Race*.

10. Letter to Stand Watie, Ridge's uncle, 9 October 1854 (quoted in Parins, *Ridge* 113). The full letter appears in Dale and Litton 81–84. Ridge's plan, it appears, was to "establish a newspaper somewhere in Arkansas, or some place where it will be safe from the commotion of Cherokee affairs, and devote it to the interest of the Indian race" (Dale and Litton 82). This plan, which much resembles Copway's, never came to fruition.

In a letter to his mother (5 October 1855) he argued much the same thing, saying that his future work would involve "handing down to posterity the great names of Indian history, and doing justice to a deeply wronged and injured people by impressing upon the records of the country a true and impartial account of the treatment they have received at the hands of a civilized and Christian race!" (quoted in Parins, *Ridge* 115).

11. See, for example, Parins, *Ridge* 125–27.

12. According to Parins, Ridge conceptualized himself as a "cavalier and a gentleman" in a California filled with ignorant and uncivilized Indians—which brings his

self-identity closer to the vain loner Pau-Puk-Keewis than to Hiawatha (Parins, *Ridge* 222). It is also true that Ridge conceives of his "hero" Murieta as a cultured bandit dressed in "finery" (Ridge, *Murieta* 150). Longfellow himself rendered relatively late judgment on George Copway, whose auto-anthropology is considered in chapter 4, in the following terms: "I fear he is developing the Pau-Puk-Keewis element rather strongly" (quoted in Peyer 258).

13. Kenney believes it was the norm in the nineteenth century for readers to use the early discoverers and conquerors, such as Columbus, to "cherish in themselves the virtues...ascribed to...[them]" (64).

14. See Paredes's *Pistol,* a text understood by recent scholars to have inaugurated modern Chicano Studies.

15. I should note here that I have preserved throughout Prescott's Indian analytics and spellings (including those of "tribes" and individuals, such as Montezuma). No attempt is made here to address the problem of colonial naming that Prescott would pose for the modern anthropologist and historian.

16. He considers the Toltecs a separate race, and the Aztecs and Tezcucans part of the Chichemec race. Prescott's text, later on, also goes into great detail describing Tlascalan society and culture (221ff.), yet another subgroup of the Chichemec.

17. And again: "That they should have triumphed against such odds furnishes an inference of the same kind as that established by the victories of the European over the semi-civilized hordes of Asia" (Prescott, *Conquest* 465).

18. McWilliams arrives at similar, albeit more complex, conclusions: "Prescott hoped to resolve the paradox of Tenochtitlán's high civilization and the Aztecs' barbarism by first insisting on the paradox and then presenting the Spaniard as a higher alternative. Sculpted gold and cannibalism, aqueducts and illiteracy, aviaries and human sacrifice, were contrasting parts of one culture that had combined the brutalities of the heroic age with quasi-Catholic refinement and priestcraft" (McWilliams 178).

19. Prescott's diaries and correspondence highlight his difficulties with the introduction, "the toughest part" of the book to write (*Correspondence* 99); see *Correspondence* 115; *Memoranda* 2:48, 2:51, 2:53, 2:62. "My *Introduction* for example — occupying half a volume, will have no doubt, now, — have cost more time in preparation and writing — viz: 2-½ years — than all the rest of the work — of 2-½ vols." (*Memoranda* 2:91–92).

20. See 83, for another example.

21. See also 149, 248, 275–76, 278, 349, 350–51, 367, 685.

22. Prescott calls the introduction "*philosophic*" because it is concerned with the "antiquities and origins of a nation," and he calls the rest "*historical*" and then "*biographical*" — thus already marking the distinction I am tracing (6).

23. Paredes's work, for example, has been subjected to this sort of critique, with reference to gender.

24. Levin suggests that Montezuma's "oriental" pomp and luxury—his over-refinement—and his superstitious nature (for example, his reliance on ministers who interpret signs and portents) account for his passivity and effeminacy (Levin 151). Both of these characteristics, one also might argue, position him uniquely within the Aztec world.

25. Although I will not devote the pages to it, the same can be demonstrated about Cortés. As Levin notes, Prescott in *History of the Reign of Ferdinand and Isabella the Catholic* (1837) positions Queen Isabella as a perfect product of her age, a representative "man," a model person (Levin 56–57). The portrait of Cortés is at some distance from this. Prescott wrote in his letters, "I don't like my hero [Cortés] however half so well as the good queen Isabel of pious memory" (*Correspondence* 79). And *Conquest of Mexico* is, at the very least, torn between situating Cortés as representative, or *more* or *less* than representative. One example: in summing up Cortés's character, Prescott notes, "Of all the band of adventurous cavaliers, whom Spain, in the sixteenth century, sent forth on the career of discovery and conquest, there was none more deeply filled with the spirit of romantic enterprise than Hernando Cortés" (681). "None more deeply filled": Cortés's "spirit" is both truly the spirit of the age and, paradoxically, more spirited than that of any other persons (which, it could be argued, is precisely Prescott's moral problem with Cortés—his excessiveness, his "too-spiritedness"). In other words, Prescott's confused moralisms turn on a question he cannot answer: are Cortés's actions justified by recourse to the spirit of the age, or condemnable or praiseworthy because of his unique and unequaled "genius" and "constancy"?

26. The portrayal of the final Aztec leader, Guatemozin, Montezuma's nephew, presents still further difficulties, as commentators have pointed out; see, for example, McWilliams 180.

27. John Ernest, in "Reading the Romantic Past," has investigated the textual gymnastics to which *Conquest of Mexico* resorts in situating las Casas's contemporaneous antislavery views within Prescott's conception of the spirit of the age of the conquistadors (Ernest 241–43; and see Prescott *Mexico* 203–9 for his biography of las Casas).

28. It appears that Ridge was writing history, not fiction, even though his book reminds many readers, both of his own time and later, of dime novel melodramas. He notes in the text the "reliability of the ground-work on which it stands" and states that the story is "strictly true" (4). And after the book was attacked for historical license and outright fabrication, Ridge wrote a response that highlighted his research methods, "arguing he travelled over the state, searched newspaper files, and talked to those who knew the bandit" (Parins, *Ridge* 105). Ridge firmly believed in the documentary character of the work.

29. Christensen 63 notes problems with this conflation.

30. At one point in the book another character compares Murieta to Padre Jurata, a Mexican patriot during the war (96).

31. Combe, in Morton's book, addresses precisely the same problem from a slightly different angle: racial superiority, or racial brain power, can be measured by a people's response to invasion, by the strength of its will for "independence," along a three-tiered scale: successful self-defense, self-annihilation, and eventual acceptance of subjection (the will to defend, interestingly, plays no part in this schema) (Morton, *Americana* 282). This without doubt suggests a reading of the Mexican Indians as at the bottom of the scale of racial abilities, since "success" eluded them and they did not commit mass suicide.

32. "I was once as noble a man as ever breathed, and if I am not so now, it is because men would not allow me to be as I wished" (*Murieta* 106).

33. Strangely, I think, Karl Kroeber reads Ridge's writings as "not necessarily afflicted with that 'double-consciousness' so famously formulated by W. E. B. DuBois" (Kroeber 9). He imagines Ridge as affirming or at least embodying "the interplay of conflictive reinforcements" (10).

34. The monument at Ridge's grave reads: "John Rollin Ridge. California Poet. Author of 'Mount Shasta' and other poems" (Foreman 309).

35. See Lowe 113, who agrees.

36. Murieta is said to be most disguised when showing his real features (30–31). "He spoke very good English and they could scarcely make out whether he was Mexican or an American" (85).

37. Maria Mondragón goes too far in her interesting reading of the text (useful as well for its summation of a number of readings of Ridge). She imagines Ridge/Murieta as a trickster figure, coming down on neither side of the border and "holding history" in general and "historical narratives accountable for their crimes" (Mondragón 185).

38. John Lowe, like Mondragón, overreads Murieta, at least from Ridge's accumulated perspective. Lowe, too, sees him as a trickster, whose "very exteriority and marginality ironically locate him in the magical realm of spatial and imaginative freedom, and he thus personifies the dream that was felt but rarely experienced by actual miners" (Lowe 121).

39. This last is said by Three-Fingered Jack, one of Murieta's band, a man whose excesses are criticized by the text but who was "as brave a man as this world ever produced" (154). The text's recurrent expression of anti-Chinese sentiment is, at best, equivocally rendered.

40. Peter Christensen's piece nicely reads the book's many racial/ethnic exclusions.

CODA

1. See also Prescott, *Mexico* 459 for another reiteration of the same theme, which still haunts anthropology. Linda Schele's and David Freidel's prominent *A Forest of Kings: The Untold Story of the Ancient Maya* (1990) begins with the same question;

Schele writes, "I had to understand how, why, when, and who had made these things" (Schele and Freidel 14).

2. This is not to deny the importance of Stephens's writing for the region's population. Quetzil Castañeda notes that "Stephens's *Incidents of Travel* was incorporated into the agenda of Yucatan intellectuals, which sought the reformulation of the (Spanish-speaking world's) vision of the Maya in order to establish a cultural heritage or patrimony that would legitimize the goal of a politically independent Yucatán" (Castañeda 5).

3. Victor Wolfgang Von Hagen is author of the best existing biographies of Stephens (1947) and of Catherwood (1950). They are listed in the works cited, but I do not otherwise cite these sources. Like most scholarship on Stephens, they come to praise, not explain. Von Hagen, in short, is at no remove from his subjects.

4. Perhaps this is because Stephens is widely understood today to have gotten things right, or at least to have oriented American archaeology toward the truth. The British Honduran–sponsored Walker-Caddy expedition of 1839–40, which barely predated Stephens's trip, was forgotten for more than a century, partly because of Stephens's book and the lack of a major, published countertext by either Patrick Walker or John Caddy, and partly because of Captain Caddy's belief that the ruins were of "Egypto-Indian origin" (Pendergast 193).

Coe's judgment of Stephens has been repeated many times in the literature. Robert Brunhouse says, "It is impossible to write about Stephens without using superlatives" because of his accuracy and careful reasoning (84). And David Adamson, as weary of fantastic archaeology as is Williams, nevertheless concludes that Stephens's second trip produced documents that "are still the most detailed guides there are on Maya remains in the Yucatán. One is continually impressed by Stephens' clarity, the lawyer's skill with which he dismisses the arguments of exotic origins" (Adamson 160).

5. At one point, situating Stephens in terms of Carrera seemed like a possible framework for this chapter. But during the period of his military insurgency Carrera left only a handful of words behind as auto-testament. Indeed, his opponents claimed he was illiterate and suggested that the occasional Carrera manifestos were penned by others. Hazel Marylyn Bennett Ingersoll's detailed study of the rebellion notes that there are only one or two very short military texts—a couple of notes from the field in the middle of the war—extant that can be attributed to Carrera.

Stephens's Carrera, it might be noted in passing, bears a rather strong resemblance to Mexican accounts of Subcomandante "Marcos" in the 1990s.

6. At the same time, however, the mounds were sometimes seen to be merely piles of dirt, and at least one midnineteenth-century account of the Moundbuilders—Samuel F. Haven's *Sketches, Historical and Bibliographical, of the Progress of Information and Opinion Respecting Vestiges of Antiquity in the United States* (1856), published under the auspices of the Smithsonian—argued that "the Moundbuilders were the ancestors of the contemporary American Indians" (Williams 49).

7. See Ringe 129 on the importance of Volney for American travel writers, although Szwed usefully reminds us that Volney's essay was severely edited in the 1802 edition in such a way that "all references to the Negro origins of civilization had been eliminated" (Szwed 68). Szwed characterizes the endpoint of Volney's argument as "a 'New Age' in which all people would shed their religious and class differences and be one together in self-knowledge" (67). A useful translated edition, which uses and expands the Jefferson/Barlow version, is Volney. See also Michaelsen,"*Roughing*" 106–9 for a brief look at some titles and strategies of classist deployment in the history of the literature of the picturesque.

8. Stephens, however, occasionally prints a picturesque image anyway. For a decidedly picturesque Catherwood illustration of the ruins at Palenque, see *Central America* 2:338, facing page.

9. See also Johnson, "Writing" for a related argument concerning Stephens. It is Johnson's work on Stephens that first drew me to Stephens's texts.

10. Castañeda's book, which only briefly considers Stephens, is entirely concerned with similar matters — the invention of the Mayan ruins through technologies of mapping and the arts of memory.

11. Stephens elaborates the theme of the fallen Indian throughout the Yucatan volumes. For example, when he witnesses the whipping of an Indian on the hacienda of Xcanchakan, he comments, "His whole bearing showed the subdued character of the present Indians, and with the last stripe the expression of his face seemed that of thankfulness for not getting more. Without uttering a word, he crept to the major domo, took his hand, kissed it, and walked away. No sense of degradation crossed his mind. Indeed, so humbled is this once fierce people, that they have a proverb of their own, 'Los Indios no oigan si no por las nalgas' — 'The Indians cannot hear except through their backs,' and the cura related to us a fact which indicates an abasement of character perhaps not found in any other people" (2:82). Stephens consistently reads scenes of near-enslavement and asymmetrical power relations between whites and Indians as evidence of Indians' meek acceptance of their "degradation."

12. Stephens himself was an Egyptologist. His earlier major publication was the well-regarded *Incidents of Travel in Egypt, Arabia, Petraea, and the Holy Land* (1837). John T. Irwin's *American Hieroglyphics* is an attempt to unlock the philosophical significance of Egypt — and in particular the decipherment of the Rosetta stone — for American Renaissance literati.

13. Brunhouse examines the early 1850s hoax, perpetrated by P. T. Barnum, that played on these pages of Stephens (109–12). Barnum arranged for the publication of a travel narrative that documented the discovery of Stephens's city and presented two live inhabitants from this metropolis for public consumption. Prominent figures such as Horace Greeley and Charles Dickens weighed in on the facts of the case.

14. See Morgan, *Houses* 281–310. The well-read historian and theorist of Mayan archaeology Michael D. Coe concludes that Norman's first book is "on the whole worth-

less," and Coe does not seem to have bothered to track down Norman's second volume (Coe 96). Neither Brunhouse nor Adamson mentions Norman.

15. On the basis of the first volume, for example, he was elected a member of the Royal Antiquarian Society of Copenhagen, and he was a key donor to the material culture collection of the New York Historical Society.

16. One might compare this to the aesthetic positivism of Norman's first volume, in which the ruins themselves seem to ask for an interpretation: "Carved stone and hieroglyphics...seemed as though they were striving to make me understand the story of their wonderful beginning," and the ruins as a whole produce a sense of awe or sublimity that "established a sort of parenthetic connexion between myself and elder ages" (*Yucatan* 106, 80).

Abu-Lughod, Lila. "Writing against Culture." In *Recapturing Anthropology: Working in the Present,* ed. Richard G. Fox, 137–62. Santa Fe, N.M.: School of Social Research Press, 1991.

Adamson, David Grant. *The Ruins of Time: Four and a Half Centuries of Conquest and Discovery among the Maya.* New York: Praeger, 1975.

Agamben, Giorgio. "Beyond Human Rights." In *Radical Thought in Italy: A Potential Politics,* ed. Paolo Virno and Michael Hardt 158–64. Minneapolis: University of Minnesota Press, 1996.

Ahmad, Aijaz. *In Theory: Classes, Nations, Literatures.* London: Verso, 1992.

Allen, Dennis W. " 'By All the Truth of Signs': James Fenimore Cooper's *The Last of the Mohicans." Studies in American Fiction* 9, no. 2 (1981): 159–79.

Allen, Theodore W. *The Invention of the White Race.* Vol. 1, *Racial Oppression and Social Control.* London: Verso, 1994.

Apess, William. *On Our Own Ground: The Complete Writings of William Apess, a Pequot.* Ed. Barry O'Connell. Amherst: University of Massachusetts Press, 1992.

Appadurai, Arjun. "Disjuncture and Difference in the Global Cultural Economy." *Theory, Culture, and Society* 7 (1990): 295- 310.

Appiah, Kwame Anthony. *In My Father's House: Africa in the Philosophy of Culture.* New York: Oxford University Press, 1992.

Applebaum, Richard P. "Multiculturalism and Flexibility: Some New Directions in Global Capitalism." In *Mapping Multiculturalism,* ed. Avery F. Gordon and Christopher Newfield, 297–316. Minneapolis: University of Minnesota Press, 1996.

Armstrong, William H. *Warrior in Two Camps: Ely S. Parker, Union General and Seneca Chief.* Syracuse, N.Y.: Syracuse University Press, 1978.

Asad, Talal, ed. *Anthropology and the Colonial Encounter.* New York: Humanities Press, 1973.

———. *Genealogies of Religion: Discipline and Reasons of Power in Christianity and Islam.* Baltimore: Johns Hopkins University Press, 1993.

Ashwill, Gary. "Savagism and Its Discontents: James Fenimore Cooper and His Native American Contemporaries." *American Transcendental Quarterly,* new series, 8, no. 3 (September 1994): 211–27.

Bachman, John. *Unity of the Human Race: A Refutation of the Theory of Dr. Morton, Professor Agassiz, and Dr. Nott, on the Characteristics of Genera and Species.* Nashville, Tenn.: Southern Methodist, 1880.

Barreiro, José, ed. *Indian Roots of American Democracy.* Ithaca, N.Y.: Akwe:kon, 1992.

Basso, Keith H. *Portraits of "The Whiteman": Linguistic Play and Cultural Symbols among the Western Apache.* New York: Cambridge University Press, 1979.

Beauchamp, W. M. *The Iroquois Trail, or Footprints of the Six Nations, in Customs, Traditions, and History, by W. M. Beauchamp, S. T. D., in Which Are Included David Cusick's Sketches of Ancient History of the Six Nations.* Fayetteville, NY: Beauchamp, 1892.

Behar, Ruth. *The Vulnerable Observer: Anthropology That Breaks Your Heart.* Boston: Beacon, 1996.

Bhabha, Homi K. *The Location of Culture.* London and New York: Routledge, 1994.

Bieder, Robert E. *Science Encounters the Indian, 1820–1880: The Early Years of American Ethnology.* Norman: University of Oklahoma Press, 1986.

Biolsi, Thomas, and Larry J. Zimmerman, eds. *Indians and Anthropologists: Vine Deloria, Jr., and the Critique of Anthropology.* Tucson: University Arizona Press, 1997.

The Boston Medical and Surgical Journal 31 (25 December 1844): 422–23.

Boudinot, Elias. *A Star in the West; or, A Humble Attempt to Discover the Long Lost Ten Tribes of Israel, Preparatory to Their Return to Their Beloved City, Jerusalem.* Trenton, N.J.: Fenton, Hutchinson, and Dunham, 1816.

Bourdieu, Pierre. *Language and Symbolic Power.* Ed. John B. Thompson. Trans. Gino Raymond and Matthew Adamson, 220–28. Cambridge, Mass.: Harvard University Press, 1991.

Bourne, Randolph S. "Trans-National America." 1916. In *Theories of Ethnicity: A Classical Reader,* ed. Werner Sollers, 93–108. New York: New York University Press, 1996.

Bracken, Christopher. *The Potlatch Papers: A Colonial Case History.* Chicago: University of Chicago Press, 1997.

Brown, Gillian. *Domestic Individualism: Imagining Self in Nineteenth-Century America.* Berkeley: University of California Press, 1990.

Brunhouse, Robert L. *In Search of the Maya: The First Archaeologists.* Albuquerque: University of New Mexico Press, 1973.

Burnham, Clint. *The Jamesonian Unconscious: The Aesthetics of Marxist Theory.* Durham, N.C.: Duke University Press, 1995.

Cabeza de Vaca, Alvar Núñez. *Adventures in the Unknown Interior of America.* Ed. and trans. Cyclone Covey. Albuquerque: University of New Mexico Press, 1983.

Castañeda, Quetzil E. *In the Museum of Maya Culture: Touring Chichén Itzá.* Minneapolis: University of Minnesota Press, 1996.

Charleston, Steve. "The Old Testament of Native America." *Native and Christian: Indigenous Voices on Religious Identity in the United States and Canada,* ed. James Treat, 68–80. New York: Routledge, 1996.

Christensen, Peter G. "Minority Interaction in John Rollin Ridge's *The Life and Adventures of Joaquin Murieta.*" *MELUS* 17, no. 2 (summer 1991–92): 61–72.

Churchill, Ward. *Fantasies of the Master Race: Literature, Cinema, and the Colonization of American Indians.* Ed. M. Annette Jaimes. Monroe, Maine: Common Courage, 1992.

——. *Indians Are Us? Culture and Genocide in Native North America.* Monroe, Maine: Common Courage, 1994.

——, ed. *Marxism and Native Americans.* Boston: South End Press, 1983.

Clifford, James. *The Predicament of Culture: Twentieth-Century Ethnography, Literature, and Art.* Cambridge, Mass.: Harvard University Press, 1988.

——. "Travelling Cultures." In *Cultural Studies,* ed. Lawrence Grossberg, Cary Nelson, and Paula A. Treichler, 96–112. New York: Routledge, 1992.

Clifford, James, and George E. Marcus. *Writing Culture: The Poetics and Politics of Ethnography.* Berkeley: University of California Press, 1986.

Cline, Howard F., C. Harvey Gardiner, and Charles Gibson. *William Hickling Prescott: A Memorial.* Durham, N.C.: Duke University Press, 1959.

Coates, D. B. "A Narrative, &c." *Memoirs of the Historical Society of Pennsylvania* 2 (1827): 63–74.

Cockrell, Dale. *Demons of Disorder: Early Blackface Minstrels and Their World.* New York: Cambridge University Press, 1997.

Coe, Michael D. *Breaking the Maya Code.* New York: Thames and Hudson, 1993.

Columbus, Christopher. *The Four Voyages.* Ed. and trans. J. M. Cohen. New York: Penguin, 1969.

Connor, Peter. *Theory and Cultural Value.* Oxford: Blackwell, 1992.

Cooper, James Fenimore. *The Last of the Mohicans.* Ed. John McWilliams. New York: Oxford University Press, 1990.

——. *The Letters and Journals of James Fenimore Cooper.* Vol. 5. Ed. James Franklin Beard. Cambridge, Mass.: Belknap-Harvard University Press, 1968.

——. *The Letters and Journals of James Fenimore Cooper.* Vol. 6. Ed. James Franklin Beard. Cambridge, Mass.: Belknap-Harvard University Press, 1968.

——. *The Oak Openings.* Iroquois edition. New York: Knickerbocker-Putnam's, n.d.

——. *Pages and Pictures, from the Writings of James Fenimore Cooper.* Ed. Susan Fenimore Cooper. Secaucus, N.J.: Castle, 1980.

——. *The Pathfinder.* Ed. Richard Dilworth Rust and William P. Kelly. Oxford and New York: Oxford University Press, 1992.

———. *Works of J. Fenimore Cooper.* 10 vols. New York: Collier, 1893.

Copway, George [Kah-ge-ga-gah-bowh]. "Causes Not Always Apparent; Or, Horse Radish and Religion." *Copway's American Indian* 1, no. 3 (26 July 1851): 2, col. 4.

———. *Indian Life and Indian History, by an Indian Author: Embracing the Traditions of the North American Indians Regarding Themselves, Particularly of That Most Important of All the Tribes, the Ojibways* [orig.: *The Traditional History and Characteristic Sketches of the Ojibway Nation* (1850)]. 1860. Reprint, New York: AMS, 1978.

———. "Cooper." *Copway's American Indian* 1, no. 2 (July 1851): 2.

———. *The Life, Letters, and Speeches of Kah-ge-ga-gah-bowh; or, G. Copway* [orig., in a shorter edition: *The Life, History, and Travels, of Kah-ge-ga-gah-bowh (George Copway), a Young Indian Chief of the Ojibwa Nation, a Convert to the Christian Faith, and a Missionary to His People for Twelve Years* (1847)]. New York: Benedict, 1850.

———. *Organization of a New Indian Territory East of the Missouri River: Reasons Submitted to the Honorable Members of the Senate and House of Representatives to the Thirty-First Congress of the United States; by the Indian Chief Kah-ge-ga-gah-bouh, or Geo. Copway.* New York: Benedict, 1850.

Cruz, John. "From Farce to Tragedy: Reflections on the Reification of Race at Century's End." In *Mapping Multiculturalism,* ed. Avery F. Gordon and Christopher Newfield, 19–39. Minneapolis: University of Minnesota Press, 1996.

Dale, Edward Everett, and Gaston Litton. *Cherokee Cavaliers: Forty Years of Cherokee History as Told in the Correspondence of the Ridge-Watie-Boudinot Family.* Norman: University of Oklahoma Press, 1939.

Davis, Angela Y. "Gender, Class, and Multiculturalism: Rethinking 'Race' Politics." In *Mapping Multiculturalism,* ed. Avery F. Gordon and Christopher Newfield, 40–48. Minneapolis: University of Minnesota Press, 1996.

Davis, F. James. *Who Is Black? One Nation's Definition.* University Park: Pennsylvania State University Press, 1991.

de Certeau, Michel. *The Writing of History.* Trans. Tom Conley. New York: Columbia University Press, 1988.

Dekker, George. *James Fenimore Cooper: The Novelist.* London: Routledge and Kegan Paul, 1967.

Deloria, Vine Jr. *Custer Died for Your Sins: An Indian Manifesto.* 1969. New York: Avon, 1970.

———. *God Is Red: A Native View of Religion.* New York: Grosset and Dunlap, 1973.

———. *The Metaphysics of Modern Existence.* New York: Harper and Row, 1979.

———. *Red Earth, White Lies: Native Americans and the Myth of Scientific Fact.* New York: Scribners, 1995.

————. "Some Criticisms and a Number of Suggestions." 1970. In *Anthropology and the American Indian: A Symposium,* ed. James Officer, et al. San Francisco: Indian Historian Press, 1973.

Derrida, Jacques. *Writing and Difference.* Trans. Alan Bass. Chicago: University of Chicago Press, 1978.

Drinnon, Richard. *Facing West: The Metaphysics of Indian Hating and Empire Building.* 1980. New York: Schocken, 1990.

Dunn, Thomas L. "Strangers and Liberals." *Political Theory* 22, no. 1 (February 1994): 167–75.

Ernest, John. "Reading the Romantic Past: William H. Prescott's *History of the Conquest of Mexico.*" *American Literary History* 5, no. 2 (summer 1993): 231–49.

Fabian, Johannes. "Presence and Representation: The Other and Anthropological Writing." *Critical Inquiry* 16, no. 4 (summer 1990): 753–72.

————. *Time and the Other: How Anthropology Makes Its Object.* New York: Columbia University Press, 1983.

Fenton, William N. "Iroquois Studies at Mid-Century." *Proceedings of the American Philosophical Society* 95, no. 3 (June 1951): 296–310.

Forbes, Jack D. *Africans and Native Americans: The Language of Race and the Evolution of Black-Red Peoples.* 2nd ed. Urbana: University of Illinois Press, 1993.

Foreman, Carolyn Thomas. "Edward W. Bushyhead and John Rollin Ridge, Cherokee Editors in California." *Chronicles of Oklahoma* 14 (September 1936): 295–311.

Foucault, Michel. *The History of Sexuality.* Vol. 1, *An Introduction.* Trans. Robert Hurley. New York: Vintage, 1980.

Fox, Richard G., ed. *Recapturing Anthropology: Working in the Present.* Santa Fe, N.M.: School of Social Research Press, 1991.

Frankenberg, Ruth. *White Women, Race Matters: The Social Construction of Whiteness.* Minneapolis: University of Minnesota Press, 1993.

Fried, Morton H. "On the Concepts of 'Tribe' and 'Tribal Society.' " *Transactions of the New York Academy of Sciences,* series 2, 28 (1966): 527–40.

Gardiner, C. Harvey. *William Hickling Prescott: A Biography.* Austin: University of Texas Press, 1969.

Gasché, Rodolphe. "Heliocentric Exchange." In *The Logic of the Gift: Toward an Ethic of Generosity,* ed. Alan D. Schrift, 100–17. New York: Routledge, 1997.

Gates, Henry Louis Jr., ed. *"Race," Writing, and Difference.* Chicago: University of Chicago Press, 1986.

Gill, Sam D. *Mother Earth: An American Story.* Chicago: University of Chicago Press, 1987.

Goldberg, David Theo. "Introduction: Multicultural Conditions." In *Multiculturalism: A Critical Reader,* ed. David Theo Goldberg, 1–41. Oxford: Blackwell, 1994.

————. *Racist Culture: Philosophy and the Politics of Meaning.* Oxford: Blackwell, 1993.

————, ed. *Multiculturalism: A Critical Reader.* Oxford: Blackwell, 1994.

Gordon, Avery F., and Christopher Newfield. "Introduction." In *Mapping Multiculturalism,* ed. Avery F. Gordon and Christopher Newfield, 1–16. Minneapolis: University of Minnesota Press, 1996.

————, eds. *Mapping Multiculturalism.* Minneapolis: University of Minnesota Press, 1996.

Gossett, Thomas F. *Race: The History of an Idea in America.* 1963. New ed., New York: Oxford University Press, 1997.

Gould, Stephen Jay. *The Mismeasure of Man.* New York: Norton, 1981.

Gunew, Sneja. "PostModern Tensions: Reading for (Multi)Cultural Difference." *Meanjin* 49, no. 1 (1990): 21–33.

Hall, Stuart. "Gramsci's Relevance for the Study of Race and Ethnicity." *Journal of Communication Inquiry* 10 (summer 1986): 5–27.

Handy, Jim. *Gift of the Devil: A History of Guatemala.* Boston: South End, 1984.

Heckewelder, John. *History, Manners, and Customs of the Indian Nations Who Once Inhabited Pennsylvania and the Neighboring States.* 1818. Reprint, Salem: Ayer, 1991.

Hinsley, Curtis M. *The Smithsonian and the American Indian Making a Moral Anthropology in Victorian America* [orig.: *Savages and Scientists*]. 1981. Reprint, Washington, D.C.: Smithsonian, 1994.

Hobsbawm, Eric. "Identity Politics and the Left." *New Left Review* 217 (May/June 1996): 38–47.

Horsman, Reginald. *Race and Manifest Destiny: The Origins of American Racial Anglo-Saxonism.* Cambridge, Mass.: Harvard University Press, 1981.

Horton, James Africanus. *West African Countries and Peoples.* 1868. Reprint, Edinburgh: Edinburgh University Press, 1969.

House, Kay Seymour. *Cooper's Americans.* Kent: Ohio State University Press, 1965.

Hymes, Dell, ed. *Reinventing Anthropology.* 1972. Reprint, New York: Vintage-Random House, 1974.

Ignatiev, Noel. *How the Irish Became White.* New York: Routledge, 1995.

Ingersoll, Hazel Marylyn Bennett. "The War of the Mountain: A Study of Reactionary Peasant Insurgency in Guatemala, 1837–1873." Ph.D. diss., George Washington University, 1972.

Irwin, John T. *American Hieroglyphics: The Symbol of the Egyptian Hieroglyphics in the American Renaissance.* Baltimore: Johns Hopkins University Press, 1980.

James Guerrero, M. Annette. "Academic Apartheid: American Indian Studies and 'Multiculturalism.'" In *Mapping Multiculturalism,* ed. Avery F. Gordon and Christopher Newfield, 49–63. Minneapolis: University of Minnesota Press, 1996.

Jameson, Fredric. *The Political Unconscious: Narrative as a Socially Symbolic Act.*
Ithaca, N.Y.: Cornell University Press, 1981.
———. *Postmodernism; or, the Cultural Logic of Late Capitalism.* Durham, N.C.: Duke
University Press, 1991.
———. "Progress versus Utopia; or, Can We Imagine the Future?" *Science-Fiction
Studies* 9, no. 2 (July 1982): 147–58.
———. "Third-World Literature in the Era of Multinational Capitalism." *Social Text*
5, 3 (fall 1986): 65–88.
Jefferson, Thomas. *Writings.* Ed. Merrill D. Peterson. New York: Library of America,
1984.
Johnson, David E. "Accounting for Culture." Manuscript.
———. "*Contando Cuentas:* The Economies of Conquest." Paper presented at Narra-
tive: An International Conference, Albany, New York, 1 April 1993.
———. "The Time of Translation: The Border of American Literature." In *Border
Theory: The Limits of Cultural Politics,* ed. Scott Michaelsen and David E. John-
son, 129–65. Minneapolis: University of Minnesota Press, 1997.
———. " 'Writing in the Dark': The Political Fictions of American Travel Writing."
American Literary History 7, no. 1 (spring 1995): 1–27.
Johnson, David E., and Scott Michaelsen. "Border Secrets: An Introduction." In *Bor-
der Theory: The Limits of Cultural Politics,* ed. Scott Michaelsen and David E.
Johnson, 1–39. Minneapolis: University of Minnesota Press, 1997.
Jones, Peter [Kahkewaquonaby]. *History of the Ojibway Indians; with Especial Reference
to their Conversion to Christianity.* 1861. Reprint, Toronto: Canadiana House, 1973.
———. *Life and Journals of Kahkewaquonaby (Rev. Peter Jones).* Toronto: Anson
Green, 1860.
Jordan, Winthrop. *White over Black: American Attitudes toward the Negro, 1550–
1812.* 1968. Reprint, Baltimore: Penguin, 1969.
Judkins, Russell A. "David Cusick's *Ancient History of the Six Nations:* A Neglected
Classic." In *Iroquois Studies: A Guide to Documentary and Ethnographic Resources
from Western New York and the Genesee Valley,* ed. Russell A. Judkins, 26–40. Gene-
seo: Department of Anthropology, State University of New York, Geneseo, 1987.
Kenney, Alice P. "America Discovers Columbus: Biography as Epic, Drama, History."
Biography 4, no. 1 (winter 1981): 45–65.
Knobel, Dale. "Know-Nothings and Indians: Strange Bedfellows?" *The Western His-
torical Quarterly* 15, no. 2 (April 1984): 175–98.
Kroeber, A. L., and Clyde Kluckhohn. *Culture: A Critical Review of Concepts and Def-
initions.* 1952. Reprint, New York: Vintage, 1963.
Kroeber, Karl. "American Indian Persistence and Resurgence." *boundary 2* 19, no. 3
(fall 1992): 1–25.

Krupat, Arnold. *Ethnocriticism: Ethnography, History, Literature.* Berkeley: University of California Press, 1992.

Kuper, Adam. *The Invention of Primitive Society: Transformations of an Illusion.* New York: Routledge, 1988.

Laclau, Ernesto. "Universalism, Particularism, and the Question of Identity." *October* 61 (summer 1992): 83–90.

Lasch, Christopher. *The True and Only Heaven: Progress and Its Critics.* New York: Norton, 1991.

Lauter, Paul, ed. *The Heath Anthology of American Literature.* Vol. 1. Lexington, Mass.: D. C. Heath, 1990.

Leach, Maria, ed. *Funk and Wagnalls Standard Dictionary of Folklore, Mythology, and Legend.* San Francisco: Harper and Row, 1984.

Levin, David. *History as Romantic Art: Bancroft, Prescott, Motley, and Parkman.* Stanford, Calif.: Stanford University Press, 1959.

Longfellow, Henry Wadsworth. *The Complete Poetical Works of Henry Wadsworth Longfellow.* Cambridge edition. Cambridge, Mass.: Riverside–Houghton Mifflin, 1893.

López, Ian F. Haney. *White by Law: The Legal Construction of Race.* New York: New York University Press, 1996.

Lott, Eric. *Love and Theft: Blackface Minstrelsy and the American Working Class.* New York: Oxford University Press, 1995.

Lowe, John. "Space and Freedom in the Golden Republic: Yellow Bird's *The Life and Adventures of Joaquin Murieta, the Celebrated California Bandit.*" *Studies in American Indian Literatures* 4, nos. 2–3 (summer–fall 1992): 106–22.

Lugo, Alejandro. "The Problem of Color in Mexico and the U.S.-Mexican Border: A Critique of Mestizje in the Context of Postcoloniality." Chapter in "Fragmented Lives, Assembled Goods: A Study in Maquilas, Culture, and History at the Mexican Borderlands." Ph.D. diss., Department of Anthropology, Stanford University, 1995.

———. "Reflections on Border Theory, Culture, and the Nation." In *Border Theory: The Limits of Cultural Politics,* ed. Scott Michaelsen and David E. Johnson, 43–67. Minneapolis: University of Minnesota Press, 1997.

Lutz, Catherine A., and Lila Abu-Lughod, eds. *Language and the Politics of Emotion.* Cambridge: Cambridge University Press, 1990.

Lyons, Oren. "The American Indian in the Past." In *Exiled in the Land of the Free: Democracy, Indian Nations, and the U.S. Constitution,* ed. Oren Lyons and John Mohawk, 13–42, 338–39. Santa Fe, N.M.: Clear Light, 1992.

Lyons, Oren, and John Mohawk, eds. *Exiled in the Land of the Free: Democracy, Indian Nations, and the U.S. Constitution.* Santa Fe, N.M.: Clear Light, 1992.

Marcus, George E., and Michael M. J. Fischer. *Anthropology as Cultural Critique: An Experimental Moment in the Human Sciences.* Chicago: University Chicago Press, 1986.

Marx, Karl. *The Ethnological Notebooks of Karl Marx.* Ed. Lawrence Krader. Assen, Netherlands: Van Gorcum, 1972.

Maungwudaus [George Henry]. *Remarks Concerning the Ojibway Indians, by One of Themselves Called Maungwudaus, Who Has Been Travelling in England, France, Belgium, Ireland, and Scotland.* Leeds, Eng.: C. A. Wilson, 1847.

McGrane, Bernard. *Beyond Anthropology: Society and the Other.* New York: Columbia University Press, 1989.

McLaren, Peter. "White Terror and Oppositional Agency: Towards a Critical Multiculturalism." In *Multiculturalism: A Critical Reader,* ed. David Theo Goldberg, 45–74. Oxford: Blackwell, 1994.

McWilliams, John P. Jr. *The American Epic: Transforming a Genre, 1770–1860.* Cambridge: Cambridge University Press, 1989.

———. "The Historical Contexts of *The Last of the Mohicans.*" In James Fenimore Cooper, *The Last of the Mohicans,* 355–63. New York: Oxford University Press, 1990.

———. *Political Justice in a Republic: James Fenimore Cooper's America.* Berkeley: University of California Press, 1972.

Michaelsen, Scott. "*Roughing It* under the Shadow of the Corporation." *Canadian Review of American Studies* 25, no. 3 (fall 1995): 101–28.

———. "Toward a Critique of Sentimentalisms in Cultural Studies." *Aztlán: A Journal of Chicano Studies* 23, no. 2 (fall 1998): 47–80.

———. "What's 'White,' and Whither?" *Minnesota Review* 47 (May 1997): 73–80.

Michaelsen, Scott, and David E. Johnson, eds. *Border Theory: The Limits of Cultural Politics.* Minneapolis: University of Minnesota Press, 1997.

Mohawk, John. "Discovering Columbus: The Way Here." In *Confronting Columbus: An Anthology,* ed. John Yewell, Chris Dodge, and Jan DeSirey, 15–29. Jefferson, N.C.: McFarland, 1992.

———. "Indians and Democracy: No One Ever Told Us." In *Exiled in the Land of the Free: Democracy, Indian Nations, and the U.S. Constitution,* ed. Oren Lyons and John Mohawk, 43–71, 339–43. Santa Fe, N.M.: Clear Light, 1992.

———. "Looking for Columbus: Thoughts on the Past, Present, and Future of Humanity." In *The State of Native America: Genocide, Colonization, and Resistance,* ed. M. Annette Jaimes, 439–44. Boston: South End Press, 1992.

Mondragón, Maria. " 'The Safe White Side of the Line': History and Disguise in John Rollin Ridge's *The Life and Adventures of Joaquin Murieta: The Celebrated California Bandit.*" *American Transcendental Quarterly,* new series, 8, no. 3 (September 1994): 173–87.

Morgan, Lewis Henry. *The American Beaver and His Works*. 1868. Reprint, New York: Burt Franklin, 1970.

———. *Ancient Society; or, Researchers in the Lines of Human Progress from Savagery through Barbarism to Civilization*. New York: Henry Holt, 1877.

———. "Form of the Initiation of the G. O. I." [adopted 9 August 1844]. Ms. Lewis Henry Morgan Papers. University of Rochester Library.

———. *Houses and House-Life of the American Aborigines*. 1881. Ed. Paul Bohannan. Reprint, Chicago: University of Chicago Press, 1965.

———. "Laws of Descent of the Iroquois." *Proceedings: American Association for the Advancement of Science* 11 (1858): 132–48.

———. *League of the Iroquois* [orig.: *League of the Ho-de'-no-sau-nee, Iroquois*]. 1851. Reprint, New York: Citadel, 1962.

———. Letter to Ely S. Parker. 29 December 1848. Ms. Lewis Henry Morgan Papers. University of Rochester Library.

———. Letter to Ely S. Parker. 29 January 1850. Ms. Lewis Henry Morgan Papers. University of Rochester Library.

——— [Skenandoah, pseud.]. "Letters on the Iroquois, by Skenandoah: Addressed to Albert Gallatin, LL.D., President New York Historical Society." Letters 1–3. *American Whig Review* 5 (February 1847): 177–90.

———. *Systems of Consanguinity and Affinity of the Human Family*. Vol. 17 of *Smithsonian Contributions to Knowledge*. Washington, D.C.: Smithsonian, 1871.

Morrison, Toni. *Playing in the Dark: Whiteness and the Literary Imagination*. Cambridge, Mass.: Harvard University Press, 1992.

Morton, Samuel George. *Crania Ægyptiaca; or, Observations on Egyptian Ethnography, Derived from Anatomy, History, and the Monuments*. Philadelphia and London: John Penington-Madden and Co., 1844.

———. *Crania Americana; or, A Comparative View of the Skulls of Various Aboriginal Nations of North and South America: To Which Is Prefixed an Essay on the Varieties of the Human Species*. Philadelphia: J. Dobson, 1839.

———. *An Inquiry in the Distinctive Characteristics of the Aboriginal Race in America. Read at the Annual Meeting of the Boston Society of Natural History, Wednesday, Apr 27, 1842*. Boston: Tuttle and Dennett, 1842.

———. "Observations on the Size of the Brain in Various Races and Families of Man." *Proceedings of the Academy of Natural Sciences of Philadelphia* 4 (1850): 221–24.

Mouffe, Chantal. "Hegemony and New Political Subjects: Toward a New Concept of Democracy." Trans. Stanley Gray. In *Marxism and the Interpretation of Culture*, ed. Cary Nelson and Lawrence Grossberg. 89–104. Urbana: University of Illinois Press, 1988.

Mudimbe, V. Y. *The Invention of Africa*. Indianapolis: Indiana University Press, 1988.

Murray, David. *Forked Tongues: Speech, Writing, and Representation in North American Indian Texts.* Bloomington and Indianapolis: Indiana University Press, 1991.

Nancy, Jean-Luc. *The Inoperative Community.* Trans. and ed. Peter Connor. Minneapolis: University of Minnesota Press, 1991.

———. *The Sense of the World.* Trans. Jeffrey S. Librett. Minneapolis: University of Minnesota Press, 1997.

Nelson, Cary. "Multiculturalism without Guarantees: From Anthologies to the Social Text." *The Journal of the Midwest Modern Language Association* 26, no. 1 (spring 1993): 47–57.

Newfield, Christopher, and Avery F. Gordon. "Multiculturalism's Unfinished Business." In *Mapping Multiculturalism,* ed. Avery F. Gordon and Christopher Newfield, 76–116. Minneapolis: University of Minnesota Press, 1996.

Newman, Louise M. "Coming of Age, But Not in Samoa: Reflections on Margaret Mead's Legacy for Western Liberal Feminism." *American Quarterly* 48, no. 2 (June 1996): 233–72.

Norman, B[enjamin]. M[oore]. *Rambles by Land and Water, or, Notes of Travel in Cuba and Mexico; Including a Canoe Trip up the River Panuco, and Researches among the Ruins of Tamaulipas, &c.* New York and New Orleans: Paine and Burgess/ B. M. Norman, 1845.

———. *Rambles in Yucatan; or, Notes of Travel through the Peninsula, Including a Visit to the Remarkable Ruins of Chi-Chen, Kabah, Zayi, and Uxmal.* 1842–43. 4th ed., New York: Henry G. Langley, 1844.

Nott, J. C., and Geo. R. Glidden. *Types of Mankind; or, Ethnological Researches, Based upon the Ancient Monuments, Paintings, Sculptures, and Crania of Races, and upon Their Natural, Geographical, Philological, and Biblical History: Illustrated by Selections from the Inedited Papers of Samuel George Morton, M.D.* . . . 1854. 9th ed., Philadelphia: Lippincott, 1868.

Paredes, Américo. *Folklore and Culture on the Texas-Mexican Border.* Ed. Richard Bauman. Austin: Center for Mexican American Studies, University of Texas at Austin, 1993.

———. *"With His Pistol in His Hand": A Border Ballad and Its Hero.* Austin: University of Texas Press, 1958.

Parins, James W. "David Cusick (Tuscarora), ?–1840." In *The Heath Anthology of American Literature,* vol. 1, ed. Paul Lauter, et al., 1225–26. Lexington, Mass.: Heath, 1990.

———. "Jane Johnston Schoolcraft (Ojibwa), 1800–1841." In *The Heath Anthology of American Literature,* vol. 1, ed. Paul Lauter, et al., 1216–17. Lexington, Mass.: Heath, 1990.

———. *John Rollin Ridge: His Life and Works.* Lincoln: University of Nebraska Press, 1991.

Parker, Arthur C. *The Life of General Ely S. Parker.* 1919. Reprint, New York: AMS, n.d.

Parker, Ely S. [Address.] [1847?]. Ms. 3541. American Philosophical Society Library, Philadelphia.

———. "A Composition Read by Ely S[.] Parker at Cayuga Academy November 18 1845." Ms. 3545. American Philosophical Society Library, Philadelphia.

———. [Essay on "the study of man."] Appears verso on 31 March 1845 account of expenses. Ms. 3536. American Philosophical Society Library, Philadelphia.

———. "History of the Government, Manners, Customs, Religion, and Literature of the Iroquois Confederacy, or the Nations of Indians." Undated. Ms. 1764. American Philosophical Society Library, Philadelphia.

———. "Indian Council." Undated. Ms. 1653. American Philosophical Society Library, Philadelphia.

———. "Indian Council of the Six Nations at Tonawanda." *Batavia Times* [October?] 1847. Clipping. Lewis Henry Morgan Papers. University of Rochester Library.

———. "Iroquois or Confederacy of Five Nations." In *The Heath Anthology of American Literature,* vol. 1, ed. Paul Lauter, et al., 56–59. Lexington, Mass.: D. C. Heath, 1990.

———. Letter to Lewis Henry Morgan. 13 February 1847. Ms. Lewis Henry Morgan Papers. University of Rochester Library.

———. "New Initiation of the Wolf Tribe of the Cayuga Nation, One of the Confederate Nations of the Grand Confederacy of Iroquois." [June?] 1847. Ms. 1854. American Philosophical Society Library, Philadelphia.

———. "Notes." [May?] 1848. Ms. 3270. American Philosophical Society Library, Philadelphia.

———. "A Report on the Adventures of L. H. Morgan, C. T. Porter, and T. Darling at Tonawanda on Saturday the 31st of October/46." Ms. Lewis Henry Morgan Papers. University of Rochester Library.

Parkman, Francis. *The Oregon Trail: The Conspiracy of Pontiac.* New York: Library of America, 1991.

Paulding, James Kirk. *Koningsmarke; or, Old Times in the New World.* New York: AMS, 1971.

Pearce, Roy Harvey. *Savagism and Civilization: A Study of the Indian and the American Mind.* 1953. Reprint, Berkeley: University of California Press, 1988.

Pecora, Vincent P. *Households of the Soul.* Baltimore: Johns Hopkins University Press, 1997.

Pendergast, David M., ed. *Palenque: The Walker-Caddy Expedition to the Ancient Maya City, 1839–1840.* Norman: University of Oklahoma Press, 1967.

Peyer, Bernd C. *The Tutor'd Mind: Indian Missionary-Writers in Antebellum America.* Amherst: University of Massachusetts Press, 1997.

Pfeil, Fred. *White Guys: Studies in Postmodern Domination and Difference.* London: Verso, 1995.

Piedra, Jose. "Literary Whiteness and the Afro-Hispanic Difference." *New Literary History* 18, no. 2 (1987): 303–32.

Poster, Mark. "Postmodernity and the Politics of Multiculturalism: The Lyotard-Habermas Debate over Social Theory." *Modern Fiction Studies* 38, no. 3 (autumn 1992): 567–80.

Prakash, Gyan. "Writing Post-Orientalist Histories of the Third World: Perspectives from Indian Historiography." *Comparative Studies in Society and History* 32, no. 2 (April 1990): 383–408.

Pratt, Mary Louise. *Imperial Eyes: Travel Writing and Transculturation.* New York: Routledge, 1992.

Prescott, William H. *The Correspondence of William Hickling Prescott, 1833–1847.* Ed. Roger Wolcott. New York: Da Capo, 1970.

———. *History of the Conquest of Mexico and History of the Conquest of Peru.* 1843; 1847. Reprint, New York: Modern Library–Random House, n.d.

———. *The Literary Memoranda of William Hickling Prescott.* 2 vols. Ed. C. Harvey Gardiner. Norman: University of Oklahoma Press, 1961.

———. *The Papers of William Hickling Prescott.* Ed. C. Harvey Gardiner. Urbana: University of Illinois Press, 1964.

Rafael, Vicente L. *Contracting Colonialism: Translation and Christian Conversion in Tagalog Society under Early Spanish Rule.* Ithaca, New York: Cornell University Press, 1988.

Rans, Goeffrey. *Cooper's Leatherstocking Novels: A Secular Reading.* Chapel Hill: University of North Carolina Press, 1991.

Resek, Carl. *Lewis Henry Morgan: American Scholar.* Chicago: University of Chicago Press, 1960.

Richter, Daniel K. *The Ordeal of the Longhouse: The Peoples of the Iroquois League in the Era of European Colonization.* Chapel Hill: Institute of Early American History and Culture, University of North Carolina Press, 1992.

Ridge, John Rollin [Yellow Bird]. *The Life and Adventures of Joaquín Murieta, the Celebrated California Bandit.* 1854. Reprint, Norman: University of Oklahoma Press, 1955.

———. "The North American Indians: Article No. 1." *The Hesperian* 8, no. 1 (March 1862): 5–18.

———. "The North American Indians: Article No. 2." *The Hesperian* 8, no. 2 (April 1862): 51–60.

———. "The North American Indians: Article No. 3." *The Hesperian* 8, no. 3 (May 1862): 99–109.

————. *A Trumpet of Our Own: Yellow Bird's Essays on the North American Indian. Selections from the Writings of the Noted Cherokee Author John Rollin Ridge.* Ed. David Farmer and Rennard Strickland. San Francisco: Book Club of California, 1981.

Ringe, Donald A. *The Pictorial Mode: Space and Time in the Art of Bryant, Irving, and Cooper.* Lexington: University Press of Kentucky, 1971.

Robertson, William. *The History of the Discovery and Settlement of America.* 1777. Reprint, New York: Harper, 1829.

Roediger, David R. *Towards the Abolition of Whiteness.* London: Verso, 1994.

————. *The Wages of Whiteness: Race and the Making of the American Working Class.* London: Verso, 1991.

Rogin, Michael Paul. *Fathers and Children: Andrew Jackson and the Subjugation of the American Indian.* 1975. Reprint, New York: Vintage, 1976.

Rorty, Amelie Oskenberg. "The Hidden Politics of Cultural Identification." *Political Theory* 22, no. 1 (February 1994): 152–66.

Rosaldo, Michelle. *Knowledge and Passion: Ilongot Notions of Self and Social Life.* New York: Cambridge University Press, 1980.

Rosaldo, Renato. *Culture and Truth: The Remaking of Social Analysis.* New ed. Boston: Beacon, 1993.

————. "Foreword." In Néstor García Canclini, *Hybrid Cultures: Strategies for Entering and Leaving Modernity,* trans. Christopher L. Chiappari and Silvia L. López, xi–xvii. Minneapolis: University of Minnesota Press, 1995.

Roseberry, William. "Multiculturalism and the Challenge of Anthropology." *Social Research* 59, no. 4 (winter 1992): 841–58.

Ross, John. *Rebellion from the Roots: Indian Uprising in Chiapas.* Monroe, Minn.: Common Courage, 1995.

Sahlins, Marshall. *Stone Age Economics.* Chicago: Aldine-Atherton, 1972.

Said, Edward. *Orientalism.* New York: Vintage, 1979.

Samuels, Shirley, ed. *The Culture of Sentiment: Race, Gender, and Sentimentality in Nineteenth-Century America.* New York: Oxford University Press, 1992.

————. "Generation through Violence: Cooper and the Making of Americans." In *New Essays on* The Last of the Mohicans, ed. H. Daniel Peck, 87–114. Cambridge: Cambridge University Press, 1992.

Schele, Linda, and David Freidel. *A Forest of Kings: The Untold Story of the Ancient Maya.* New York: Morrow, 1990.

Scheper-Hughes, Nancy. *Death without Weeping: The Violence of Everyday Life in Brazil.* Berkeley: University of California Press, 1992.

Schoolcraft, Henry Rowe. *The Hiawatha Legends: North American Indian Lore* [orig.: *The Myth of Hiawatha and other Oral Legends, Mythologic and Allegoric, of the North American Indians*]. 1856. Ed. Larry B. Massie. Reprint, Au Train, Mich.: Avery Color Studios, 1984.

————. *The Indian in His Wigwam; or, Characteristics of the Red Race of America. From Original Notes and Manuscripts.* 1848. Reprint, New York: AMS, 1978.

————. *The Literary Voyager or Muzzeniegun.* Ed. Philip P. Mason. Lansing: Michigan State University Press, 1962.

————. *Notes on the Iroquois; or Contributions to American History, Antiquities, and General Ethnology.* 1847. Reprint, New York: AMS, 1975.

————. *Schoolcraft's Indian Legends* [orig: *Algic Researches, Comprising Inquiries Respecting the Mental Characteristics of the North American Indians*]. 1839. Ed. Mentor L. Williams. Reprint, East Lansing: Michigan State University Press, 1991.

————, ed. *Historical and Statistical Information Respecting the History, Condition, and Prospects of the Indian Tribes in the United States.* 6 vols. Philadelphia: Lippincott, Grambo, 1851–57.

Service, Elman R. *A Century of Controversy: Ethnological Issues from 1860 to 1960.* Orlando, Fla.: Academic, 1985.

Shell, Marc. *Children of the Earth: Literature, Politics, and Nationhood.* New York: Oxford University Press, 1993.

————. *The End of Kinship: "Measure for Measure," Incest, and the Ideal of Universal Siblinghood.* Stanford, Calif.: Stanford University Press, 1988.

Sioui, Georges E. *For an AmerIndian Autohistory: An Essay on the Foundations of a Social Ethic.* Trans. Sheila Fischman. Montreal: McGill-Queen's University Press, 1992.

Slotkin, Richard. *The Fatal Environment: The Myth of the Frontier in the Age of Industrialization, 1800–1890.* Middletown, Conn.: Wesleyan University Press, 1986.

————. *Regeneration through Violence: The Mythology of the American Frontier, 1600–1860.* Middletown, Conn.: Wesleyan University Press, 1973.

Smith, Donald B. "The Life of George Copway or Kah-ge-ga-gah- bowh (1818–1869) — and a Review of His Writings." *Journal of Canadian Studies* 23 (1988): 5–37.

————. *Sacred Feathers: The Reverend Peter Jones (Kahkewaquonaby) and the Mississauga Indians.* Lincoln: University of Nebraska Press, 1987.

Smith, Paul. "Unified Capital and the Subject of Value." In *Mapping Multiculturalism,* ed. Avery F. Gordon and Christopher Newfield, 346–61. Minneapolis: University of Minnesota Press, 1996.

Stanton, William. *The Leopard's Spots: Scientific Attitudes toward Race in America, 1815–59.* Chicago: University of Chicago Press, 1960.

Stephens, John Lloyd. *Incidents of Travel in Central America, Chiapas, and Yucatan.* 2 vols. 1841. Reprint, New York: Dover, 1969.

————. *Incidents of Travel in Yucatan.* 2 vols. 1943. Reprint, New York: Dover, 1963.

Stern, Bernhard J. *Lewis Henry Morgan: Social Evolutionist.* 1931. Reprint, New York: Russell and Russell, 1967.

Stocking, George W. Jr. *Victorian Anthropology.* New York: Free Press, 1987.

Stowe, Harriet Beecher. *Uncle Tom's Cabin; or, Life among the Lowly.* Ed. Ann Douglas. Reprint, New York: Penguin, 1981.

Szwed, John F. *Space Is the Place: The Lives and Times of Sun Ra.* New York: Pantheon, 1997.

Taussig, Michael. *Mimesis and Alterity: A Particular History of the Senses.* New York: Routledge, 1993.

Taylor, Charles, and Amy Gutman, et al. *Multiculturalism: Examining the Politics of Recognition.* Princeton: Princeton University Press, 1994.

Tedlock, Dennis, and Barbara Tedlock, eds. *Teachings from the American Earth: Indian Religion and Philosophy.* New York: Liveright, 1975.

Terray, Emmanuel. *Marxism and "Primitive" Societies.* Trans. Mary Klopper. New York: Monthly Review, 1972.

Todorov, Tzvetan. *On Human Diversity: Nationalism, Racism, and Exoticism in French Thought.* Cambridge, Mass.: Harvard University Press, 1993.

———. " 'Race,' Writing, and Culture." In *"Race," Writing, and Difference,* ed. Henry Louis Gates Jr., 370–80. Chicago: University of Chicago Press, 1986.

Tomaszewski, Deidre Stevens. *The Johnstons of Sault Ste. Marie: An Informal History of the Northwest, as Portrayed through the Experience of One Pioneer Family.* Sault Sainte Marie, Mich.: Self-published, n.d.

Tompkins, Jane. *Sensational Designs: The Cultural Work of American Fiction, 1790–1860.* New York: Oxford University Press, 1985.

Tooker, Elisabeth. "Lewis H. Morgan: The Myth and the Man." *The University of Rochester Library Bulletin* 37 (1984): 23–47.

———. "The United States Constitution and the Iroquois League." *Ethnohistory* 35, no. 4 (fall 1988): 305–36.

Trautmann, Thomas R. *Lewis Henry Morgan and the Invention of Kinship.* Berkeley: University of California Press, 1987.

Treat, James. "Introduction: Native Christian Narrative Discourse." In *Native and Christian: Indigenous Voices on Religious Identity in the United States and Canada,* ed. James Treat, 1–26. New York: Routledge 1996.

———, ed. *Native and Christian: Indigenous Voices on Religious Identity in the United States and Canada.* New York: Routledge, 1996.

Trigger, Bruce G. "Foreword." In Georges E. Sioui, *For an AmerIndian Autohistory: An Essay on the Foundations of a Social Ethic,* trans. Sheila Fischman, ix–xv. Montreal: McGill-Queen's University Press, 1992.

Turner, Terence. "Anthropology and Multiculturalism: What Is Anthropology that Multiculturalists Should Be Mindful of It?" In *Multiculturalism: A Critical Reader,* ed. David Theo Goldberg, 406–25. Oxford: Blackwell, 1994.

Tyler, Steven A. "Post-Modern Ethnography: From Document of the Occult to Occult Document." In *Writing Culture: The Poetics and Politics of Ethnography,* ed. James

Clifford and George E. Marcus, 122–40. Berkeley: University of California Press, 1986.

———. *The Unspeakable: Discourse, Dialogue, and Rhetoric in the Postmodern World.* Madison: University of Wisconsin Press, 1987.

Volney, C. F. *The Ruins; or, Meditation on the Revolutions of Empires: And the Law of Nature.* 1890. Reprint, Baltimore: Black Classic Press, 1991.

Von Hagen, Victor Wolfgang. *Frederick Catherwood Archt.* Introduction by Aldous Huxley. New York: Oxford University Press, 1950.

———. *Maya Explorer: John Lloyd Stephens and the Lost Cities of Central America and Yucatán.* Norman: University of Oklahoma Press, 1947.

Wallace, Anthony F. C. *The Death and Rebirth of the Seneca.* 1969. Reprint, New York: Vintage–Random House, 1972.

Wallerstein, Immanuel. *Geopolitics and Geoculture: Essays on the Changing World-System.* Cambridge: Cambridge University Press, 1991.

Wesley, John. *The Works of John Wesley: Sermons.* Nashville, Ky.: Abingdon, 1984.

West, James L. "Indian Spirituality: Another Vision." In *Native and Christian: Indigenous Voices on Religious Identity in the United States and Canada,* ed. James Treat, 29–37. New York: Routledge 1996.

White, Hayden. *Metahistory: The Historical Imagination in Nineteenth-Century Europe.* Baltimore: Johns Hopkins University Press, 1973.

White, Richard. *The Middle Ground: Indians, Empires, and Republics in the Great Lakes Region, 1650–1815.* New York: Cambridge University Press, 1991.

Williams, Stephen. *Fantastic Archaeology: The Wild Side of North American Prehistory.* Philadelphia: University of Pennsylvania Press, 1991.

Wills, Garry. *Inventing America: Jefferson's Declaration of Independence.* New York: Vintage–Random House, 1979.

———. "A Tale of Three Leaders." *The New York Review of Books* 43, no. 14 (19 September 1996): 61–74.

Wilson, Edmund. *Apologies to the Iroquois.* New York: Farrar, Straus, and Cudahy, 1960.

Wolf, Eric R. *Europe and the People without History.* Berkeley: University of California Press, 1982.

Woodward, Ralph Lee Jr. "Changes in the Nineteenth-Century Guatemalan State and Its Indian Policies." In *Guatemalan Indians and the State: 1540 to 1988,* ed. Carol A. Smith, 52–71. Austin: University of Texas Press, 1990.

Young, Robert J. C. *Colonial Desire: Hybridity in Theory, Culture, and Race.* New York: Routledge, 1995.

Sᴄᴏᴛᴛ Mɪᴄʜᴀᴇʟsᴇɴ is assistant professor of English at Michigan State University. He is the coeditor, with David E. Johnson, of *Border Theory: The Limits of Cultural Politics* (Minnesota, 1997) and has published articles in the journals *American Literary History, Aztlán, The Centennial Review, The Canadian Journal of American Studies, Arizona Quarterly, Prospects, Early American Literature, College Literature,* and *The Minnesota Review.*